THE MAKING OF
SPANISH DEMOCRACY

THE MAKING OF SPANISH DEMOCRACY

Donald Share

Copublished with the Center for the
Study of Democratic Institutions
General Editor: Robert Wesson
Associate Editor: Jeffrey D. Wallin

PRAEGER

New York
Westport, Connecticut
London

Library of Congress Cataloging-in-Publication Data

Share, Donald.
  The making of Spanish democracy.

  "Copublished with the Center for the Study of
Democratic Institutions."
  Based on the author's thesis (Ph.D.)—Stanford
University.
  Bibliography: p.
  Includes index.
  1. Spain—Politics and government—1975–
2. Representative government and representation—Spain.
I. Title.
JN8209.S48 1986   946.083   86-515
ISBN: 0-275-92125-5 (alk. paper)

Library of Congress Catalog Card Number: 86-515
ISBN: 0-275-92125-5

First published in 1986

Praeger Publishers, 521 Fifth Avenue, New York, NY 10175
A division of Greenwood Press, Inc.

Printed in the United States of America

∞™

The paper used in this book complies with the Permanent Paper Standard issued
by the National Information Standards Organization (Z39.48-1984).

10 9 8 7 6 5 4 3 2 1

87-2688

A NOTE ON THE SERIES

This is the first book of a series entitled "Democracy in the World," sponsored by the Center for the Study of Democratic Institutions. The Center's mission is to help clarify basic issues confronting a democratic society, particularly issues involving justice and freedom in the interplay of twentieth-century institutions. The Center has worked mostly through interdisciplinary dialogues. However, the publication of books and monographs has been one of its oldest traditions, going back to a series of volumes on "Communism in American Life" under the editorship of Clinton Rossiter in the 1950s, and including works of many distinguished scholars.

This new series will treat a range of subjects, such as the failures and successes of democracy, studies of particular democratic institutions in one or various countries, relations of democracy to economic and social conditions, problems such as human rights that are closely related to democracy, questions of democracy and foreign policy, proposals for the improvement of democratic institutions, and interpretations and theories of democracy. It is hoped that the series will make information and ideas about democratic systems more widely available and also encourage study of their problems.

The general editor of the present series is Robert Wesson, Senior Research Fellow at the Hoover Institution in Stanford, California. Associate editor is Jeffrey D. Wallin, Program Director at the Center. The views and judgments expressed in these works are those of the authors only. The Center is responsible only for determining that their writing meets the highest standards of American scholarship.

Donald McDonald
Acting Director of the Center

FOREWORD

The Center for the Study of Democratic Institutions proudly presents herewith the opening volume of its series on "Democracy in the World."

The subject of this volume, the successful transition of Spain from an authoritarian regime to a well-functioning democracy, has not received as much attention as it has deserved precisely because it was so smooth and untroubled. Yet it is of great historical importance. It demonstrated the possibility of transition to democracy without revolution, breaking of political continuity, or even great pressure from below. It made possible a substantial enlargement of the Western democratic community, with the accession of Spain to the European Economic Community. It accompanied the democratization of Portugal and Greece. It has also been an important factor in the wave of democratization that has rolled over Latin America in the past half-dozen years; the Latin Americans still look to the Iberian motherland to some extent as a political model, and the success of democracy in the homeland of their dominant culture strongly suggests that it might succeed elsewhere. There have been important parallels between movement to democracy in Spain and in various Latin American countries, especially Brazil.

Professor Share's account of the maneuverings and pressures by which power holders after Franco were persuaded to relax their grip and permit the step-by-step implementation of responsible elected government is of itself a fascinating story. However, it also has considerable theoretical significance, and it should be instructive for all those who would like to see authoritarian regimes brought by peaceful process to legitimate democracy.

Robert Wesson
Series Editor

vii

PREFACE

> . . .the architect of social change can never have a reliable blue-
> print. Not only is each house built different from any other before
> it, but also necessarily uses new construction materials and even
> experiments with untested principles of stress and structure.
> Therefore, what can be most usefully conveyed by the builders of
> one house is an understanding of the experience that made it at
> all possible to build under these trying circumstances.[1]

This is a book about the birth of Spanish democracy. It is a study
of how democratic rule was restored through an extraordinary historical process. The story of Spain's democratization, while of great in-
trinsic value, is most important for what it reveals about the overall
process of democratic change. For centuries, the conditions for the
establishment of democratic rule have ranked among the great questions concerning students of comparative politics.[2] For those who
value democratic rule, the question must remain at the forefront of
scholarly pursuit for decades to come.

Spain's transition from authoritarian to democratic rule, between
July 1976 and December 1978, adds a new dimension to the study
of democratization. Before the Spanish transition, democratization had
taken two major forms.[3] Most democracies were born out of catas-
trophe: cataclysmic war, violent revolution, foreign intervention, and
political collapse were the most common preconditions for the establishment of democratic rule. In this universe of cases, which we
may call *democratization through rupture*, there was a clean and often
violent break with authoritarian rule. A far less common path, whose
importance was grossly exaggerated by scholars, involved an incremental, centuries-long process of democratization. This was the
"classical" route to democracy, or *incremental democratization* experienced in England and parts of Northern Europe.

The Spanish transition after Franco's death illustrates a novel
form of democratization. Leaders of the authoritarian regime initiated
a rapid transition to democracy. This new type of democratic transition will be called *transition through transaction*, to underscore the im-

portance of negotiation and compromise among political elites.[4] Unlike democratizations through rupture, there was no clean break between the authoritarian and democratic periods. Unlike the incremental route, Spain's democratization took only three years.

On the surface, transition through transaction appears to be a logical contradiction. *Why* would an authoritarian regime, especially a well-established one, initiate a transition to democratic rule? Moreover, *how* could an authoritarian regime give birth to a genuine democracy? Such a task appears to be tantamount to squaring a circle.[5] Nevertheless, as this study of the Spanish transition to democracy suggests, it is possible, albeit very difficult, to square such a circle.

Democratic regimes are the exception in an overwhelmingly authoritarian world.[6] In the context of powerful and sophisticated authoritarian regimes, the prospects for transition through rupture are not encouraging. Where such transitions do occur, they are likely to exact an exorbitant cost in human terms. Likewise, the incremental route to democracy appears to be historically closed.[7] For these reasons, students of democracy must look seriously at the Spanish case. Spain's transition through transaction was rapid and consensual and it involved very low levels of bloodshed. It has created a widely accepted and remarkably stable democratic system.

Chapter 1 describes how Spain's political and economic history were unfavorable for the development of parliamentary democracy. It serves to orient the general reader to some of the major themes and peculiarities of Spanish political development. Chapter 2 describes the changing environment of Spanish authoritarianism. It argues that political and economic conditions had weakened authoritarian rule by 1975, but had not dislodged the franquist regime. Chapter 3 surveys the political crisis within the franquist governing coalition, highlighting the contending plans to resolve the succession crisis surrounding Franco's imminent death. Chapter 4 describes the initiation and implementation of transition through transaction from the summer of 1976 through the spring of 1977. Chapter 5 discusses the consolidation of democratic rule from June 1977 to December 1978. Chapter 6 is dedicated to the democratic political system that has resulted from transition through transaction. Chapter 7 summarizes the general argument and specifies some of the conditions for transition through transaction in Spain.

This book highlights both the possibilities for and the constraints on transition through transaction. In its exploration of the feasibility of peaceful democratic change it offers some cause for optimism. At the same time, it points to an unusual set of conditions that facilitated transition through transaction in Spain, and that counsel caution to those who might hope for this type of democratization in other cases.

Notes

1. Albert Hirschman, "The Search for Paradigms," *World Politics* 22, no. 3 (April 1970): 343.

2. There has been a renaissance of scholarship on the question of democratization. Some of the recent works include Guillermo O'Donnell, Philippe Schmitter, and Laurence Whitehead, eds., *Transitions from Authoritarian Rule in Southern Europe and Latin America* (forthcoming); John Herz, ed., *From Dictatorship to Democracy: Coping with the Legacies of Authoritarianism and Totalitarianism* (Westport, Conn.: Greenwood Press, 1983); and Samuel Huntington, "Will More Countries Become Democratic?" *Political Science Quarterly* 99 (Summer 1984).

3. These forms of democratization are discussed in detail in my "Transition Through Transaction: The Politics of Democratization in Spain, 1975-1977" (Ph.D. dissertation, Stanford University, 1983), Chapter One. In addition, see Donald Share and Scott Mainwaring, "Transitions Through Transaction: Democratization in Spain and Brazil," in Wayne A. Selcher, ed., *Political Liberalization in Brazil: Dynamics, Dilemmas, and Future* (Boulder, Colo.: Westview Press, 1986).

4. This term was first employed by Giuseppe Di Palma in his "Founding Coalitions in Southern Europe: Legitimacy and Hegemony," *Government and Opposition* 2 (Spring 1980): 166.

5. Guillermo O'Donnell, "Tensions in the Bureaucratic-Authoritarian State and the Question of Democracy," in David Collier, ed., *The New Authoritarianism in Latin America* (Princeton, N.J.: Princeton University Press, 1979), p. 315.

6. In January 1984, about 36 percent of the world's population lived in democratic political systems. See Huntington, p. 197.

7. Robert A. Dahl, *Polyarchy* (New Haven, Conn.: Yale University Press, 1971), p. 39.

ACKNOWLEDGMENTS

On November 20, 1975, while I was an undergraduate student at the University of Madrid, Generalissimo Francisco Franco died. Directly or indirectly, this book is the result of a research project conducted in stages since that time. I was fortunate to witness a truly historic event: the end of the franquist authoritarianism and the struggle to craft a parliamentary democracy. I returned to Spain in 1977 to study the first democratic parliamentary elections in over 40 years, and again in 1981-82, as a doctoral student, to conduct a more thorough analysis of the transition to democracy. During those ten years I became increasingly fascinated with a perplexing question for students of political science: How can well-entrenched authoritarian regimes yield to democratic ones? The goal of this book is to shed some light on this question.

I have accumulated an awesome number of personal as well as intellectual debts during each stage of the project, too many to acknowledge fully. Nevertheless, I would like to mention some of the contributing individuals and collectives.

In Spain, Rafael Dezcallar, María del Carmen Hernica Vizuete, Julián Santamaría, Monica Threlfall, and the Department of Political Law at the University of Madrid (Autónoma) all contributed to the project. My dissertation advisor at Stanford, Gabriel A. Almond, was extremely instructive and insightful. Richard Fagen and Giuseppe Di Palma made major contributions to my work. Other collaborators at Stanford included Karen Bernstein, Arlee Ellis, Dennis Florig, Jule Kringel, Gary Meyers, Robert Packenham, and Kathy Teghtsoonian.

A number of scholars have helped me with the difficult transition from dissertation to book. I especially appreciated the careful comments of Scott Mainwaring and Stanley Payne. My colleagues at the University of Puget Sound, and the staff of the Center for the Study of Democratic Institutions, have been particularly supportive. A special thanks goes to Tim Amen, David

Balaam, Jama Lazerow, Katherine Petrinovich, and David Smith.

Marjorie Newman suffered the trials and tribulations of the research most directly, and she merits special credit. Finally, this book is dedicated to my parents, whose high esteem for education, foreign languages, and travel contributed to this endeavor long before I began to write.

CONTENTS

THE MAKING OF
SPANISH DEMOCRACY

1 THE INAUSPICIOUS LEGACY

> This struggle between different tendencies should be carefully noted as it appears in the different historical epochs, for it has consumed a great part of the historical energy of the Spanish people, but to the truce in the struggle, when the two opposite forces managed to unite in harmony, we owe the most fruitful moments of national life.[1]

This chapter will describe how Spain's economy, political history, political culture, and geopolitics have all formed an inauspicious environment for the emergence of democratic politics. While the inauspicious legacy of Spain's political environment did not prohibit the emergence or consolidation of democratic politics after Franco's death, it continues to pose a challenge to the long-term success of democracy.

Economic Underdevelopment

While there is no consensus among scholars concerning the relationship between economic development and political democracy, few would dispute that democratic polities do not fare well in conditions of economic stagnation and severe inequality. Yet these are the two conditions that have most characterized the Spanish economy for centuries.

Geographically, Spain is a poor country, plagued by harsh extremes in its climate and few natural endowments. It is among the most mountainous countries of Europe, a feature impeding national

1

integration and communication. Except for the northwest portion, the country receives little rain, as evidenced by the paucity of its rivers. But Spain's poor natural endowments cannot in themselves explain the delayed economic development of the country. Spanish economic underdevelopment has far more to do with political, social, and institutional rigidities, as well as intolerant and incompetent leadership.

It is ironic that by becoming the first great modern world power in the sixteenth century, Spain missed out on the economic, cultural, and political innovations of the next three centuries. The very nature of the Spanish Reconquest, a clear preliminary to subsequent imperial feats, marked Spain's political economic structure for centuries.[2] The Reconquest was first and foremost a political and religious crusade against Muslim Spain, but it had clear economic consequences. The Moors had rescued the Spanish economy from a crisis caused by years of mismanagement under the Visigoths. The Muslims introduced a number of technical innovations into the peninsula, notably efficient large-scale agriculture. The capture of Granada (1492) and the subsequent expulsion of the Jews and the Muslims deprived the Spanish economy of its most experienced financial sector and much of the artisan class, and weakened Spain's entrepreneurial stratum.

On the ruins of Muslim Spain, Ferdinand and Isabella consolidated a new social order, based on the *latifundia*, large estates. These frontier *latifundia* were granted by the crown in return for military service, and they were a fundamental part of the long-lived alliance between crown, landed aristocracy, and church. In fact, to this day landholding patterns reflect the heritage of the Reconquest, with *minifundia* agriculture predominant in the north and *latifundia* in the south. The presence of generally unproductive *latifundia* gave rise to a constant (yet frustrated) demand for land reform, and later contributed to the peculiar strength of Spanish anarchism.[3]

However, the fervor and fanaticism engendered by the crusade against the Moors propelled Spain into the position of Europe's first superpower. The monarchy marshaled the power of a more unified nation and projected it over much of the globe. The riches extracted from Spain's empire made the monarchy, church, and aristocracy wealthy, adding to Spain's status as a European hegemony. Out of this ephemeral prosperity arose Spain's Golden Age in the sixteenth century. But the limited socioeconomic system on which Spain's Golden Age was built precluded genuine economic development and instead created the foundation for three centuries of economic decay.

The very expanse of the empire led Spain into an almost endless series of costly wars against the Turks, the French, the British, the Protestants, and finally, its own American colonies. These wars partially explain the incessant drain on the resources of the crown, especially after extraction of precious metals in America slackened in the seventeenth century. As a consequence, Spanish monarchs resorted to excessive taxation and encouraged an export-oriented agriculture capable of earning foreign exchange. Through the monarchy's protection of the *Mesta*, the powerful sheep herders guild, Castille, Spain's geographic and political heartland, was depopulated, and its middle classes and manufacturing sectors were debilitated. This deformation later resulted in a peculiarly Spanish phenomenon in which an underpopulated, economically underdeveloped, agrarian center attempted to dominate a more populous and economically advanced periphery.[4] Against the backdrop of this economic imbalance arose another national characteristic, unique in its intensity: regionalism. The oft-noted relationship between economic and political regionalism in Spain differentiates the country from other cases of European regionalism:

> It is interesting to speculate on what would have happened had it been Ferdinand and not Isabella who put down the money for Columbus' voyage. It would then have fallen to the Catalans and Valencians to open up America, and Castille would have been excluded. One can hardly doubt that the whole course and character of Spanish history would have been different: the decline in the seventeenth century would not have occurred because the development of trade, industry and agriculture in Spain would have prevented it.[5]

The Spanish bourgeoisie, concentrated on the geographical periphery of the country and often opposed to the state, was weak. Spain had a "middle class enriched not by trade or industry but by ownership of land."[6] The Spanish bourgeoisie lacked political independence from the landed aristocracy and was all too willing to "thro[w] itself into the arms of the landed aristocracy and the royal bureaucracy, exchanging the right to rule for the right to make money."[7]

The weakness and dependency of the bourgeoisie was best witnessed during the Restoration Monarchy (1875-1931). During this regime the Catalan textile industry, damaged by the loss of American markets, was granted high protective tariffs by Madrid in return for tariffs on wheat, a Spanish version of the famous "iron and rye" coalition in Germany. With the rise of working-class opposition in the early twentieth century, the Catalan bourgeoisie proved unwilling to forge the type of bourgeois-proletarian alliance that in other European countries was able to challenge aristocratic control of the political system.

The Agrarian Question

The presence of a politically dependent and conservative bourgeoisie lies at the heart of the agrarian problem in Spanish history. The agrarian structure bestowed on Spain during the Reconquest was not fundamentally altered until the eighteenth century. Even under the reformist Bourbons, however, land reform served to change the *owners* of land, rather than alter its unequal distribution. Serious land reform aimed at benefitting the mass of landless peasants was not introduced until the Second Republic, but even this belated attempt to resolve the agrarian question was obstructed by political infighting and lack of resolve on the part of bourgeois politicians.[8]

With the advent of the franquist regime, the agrarian problem was tabled indefinitely. Franco's political coalition included Spain's largest landlords and his political economic program was aimed originally at preserving Spain's socioeconomic structures. The agrarian problem diminished in importance with the exodus of large sectors of the rural population into the cities, and the agricultural sector was rapidly overtaken in importance by the industrial and service sectors.

Industrial Growth

The two most significant features of Spain's industrialization are its belatedness and its unevenness. Only the Catalans, with more of a commercial tradition, were experienced in entrepreneurship, but they were confronted with a politically dominant Castillian state averse to such ignoble activity. Gerald Brenan goes so far as to suggest that "the principal cause of Spanish separatism has been the industrial and commercial apathy of the Castillians."[9] Catalan industry suffered from a perennial lack of capital, from Castillian agrarian policies, and from an artisan mentality in industry.

Only with an infusion of international capital did industrial production begin to grow rapidly, when from the 1850s through the early 1900s Spain adopted an "open door" policy toward foreign investments. Foreign capital played a major role in developing Spain's industrial infrastructure and controlled Spain's major export industries. Industrial growth, however, was concentrated in two regions, Catalonia and the Basque Country. Unlike Germany or Italy, industrialization did not accompany state-building. Instead, the rise of industrial capitalism rekindled Basque and Catalan regionalism and led many Spaniards to associate industrialization with national disintegration.

Shocked by the loss of protected colonial markets, in the pre-World War I period Spain's industries retreated behind some of the world's highest tariff barriers. Spain's neutrality during World War I was a needed catalyst for industry, but industrial growth was highly dependent on state economic policy and on an ephemeral period of economic prosperity. The world economic crisis in the interwar years demonstrated the difficulty of maintaining high levels of economic growth through state investment and industrial protectionism. Moreover, the boom in industrial production had the predictable consequence of spawning new forms of working-class opposition. The rise of a working-class challenge in the very centers of regional discontent overwhelmed Spain's constitutional monarchy, and created the explosive social situation that the dictatorship of General Miguel Primo de Rivera (1923-31) sought to defuse through greater state *dirigisme*.

By 1940, the Great Depression, the chaos of the Spanish Second Republic, the devastation of the Spanish civil war, and franquist economic policies all combined to weaken Spain's economy. In the aftermath of the civil war, the ostracized franquist regime was compelled to implement an autarchic political economic policy featuring slow, state-promoted economic recovery, and maintenance of low wages and levels of consumption. This policy was advocated by the Falange, Spain's small but active fascist party, and it helped Franco consolidate political control. In the late 1950s the autarchic policy had failed and Spain was on the verge of bankruptcy. Taking advantage of the new and favorable international political economic climate, Franco was able to reverse his economic strategy and embark on a policy aimed at attracting foreign capital through direct investments and exports.

The abandonment of autarchic economic policies led to a period of spectacular economic growth, often referred to as Spain's economic "miracle." However, with economic development came a whole host of related sociopolitical tensions that later served to complicate the Spanish democratization process after Franco's death in 1975.

Political Underdevelopment

This inauspicious economic legacy is closely linked to a political environment hostile to the emergence of parliamentary democracy. Spain had a legacy of religious and political intolerance, a unification of church and state, and a swollen and unproductive military aristocracy. To be sure, the blending of a militaristic frontier spirit with a crusading religious zeal provided much of the energy for Spain's subsequent centuries-long colonial expansion, but it may also have contributed to a political culture hardly conducive to democratic politics.

Although Spain's unification coincided with the Reconquest, this unification was in many ways incomplete. The confederation of the assorted realms of the Iberian Peninsula, spearheaded by the confederation of Castille and Aragon in 1469, was based largely on reasons of military expediency. A considerable amount of regional autonomy was preserved, embodied in the *fueros* (local political charters). Achieving temporary military unity and arriving at a durable political unity turned out to be very distinct matters, and the latter proved elusive for virtually every regime since the Catholic kings.

The persistence of regional resentment had dramatic consequences for economic development. The hegemony of Castille over Aragon and the other regions was also consequential since democratic political structures and traditions were least ingrained in Castillian society.[10] While political unity was always problematic for Spanish leaders, regional resentment of Castille's political domination gradually increased as Spain's power declined between the late seventeenth and early twentieth centuries. Regionalism occupied widely divergent positions on the political spectrum, ranging from Carlist clerical-authoritarianism, through bourgeois regionalism, all the way to regional working-class movements. Regionalism has been a thorn in the side of Spanish regimes of all political shades, and Brenan argues that "[t]he main political problem has therefore always been how to strike a balance between an effective central government and the needs of local autonomy."[11]

During the Golden Age of the sixteenth and early seventeenth centuries, Spain was a cultural leader and enjoyed an unequaled international status, but the development of political structures lagged behind. It was "a country whose evolution [was] arrested at the end of the seventeenth century, [and] which has since displayed an enormous amount of resistance to foreign intrusion, but no capacity for rejuvenation."[12] This isolation from Europe has been attributed to the political intransigence of its leaders and the rigidity of political structures. Political intolerance, in turn, was encouraged by delusions of political, economic, and religious grandeur:

> So great...was the old belief that Spain was the chosen people, set apart by God for the purpose of battling for the Catholic unity of Europe, so vast still was the power of the nation in both hemispheres, so brilliant also were the cultural activities that flourished during the centuries of expansion and growth...that there was no possibility for the dissenting party in Spain to make full use of its dissent and secure an entry into the new vital currents of Europe.[13]

With the War of Spanish Succession and the accession of the Bourbons to the Spanish throne, there was new hope for political and economic reform in Spain. The war was definitive proof of Spain's decline in world status, and peninsular politics (as well as those of its colonies) were increasingly overshadowed by the two ascending European powers, France and England. While the Bourbon kings modernized Spain's political structures, successfully challenging the power of the Catholic Church and the authority of regional *fueros*, they were firm believers in absolute monarchy. And while through the Bourbons some Enlightenment ideas filtered into the country, their suspicion of change, and their tolerance of repressive institutions such as the Inquisition, limited its impact. [14]

Instability in the Nineteenth Century

In the nineteenth century, following the heroic mass uprising against Napoleon (known as the Spanish War of Independence), only a minority of elites embraced the ideas of the French Revolution. Liberals attempted to implement their version of the English civil war and French Revolution in the famous Cortes de Cadiz of 1812. Most elites, however, remained hostile to liberal ideals and throughout the nineteenth century liberal political institutions were never successfully established against the resistance of clerical absolutism.

The nineteenth century was an epoch of unprecedented political failure and instability. Between 1814 and 1875 Spain experienced six different constitutions, one royal charter, 35 *pronunciamientos*, or coups (eleven of these successful), one republic, two periods of military regency, and two protracted civil wars![15] Throughout this turbulent century, there were a number of variations on the common theme of *las dos Españas,* the two Spains. One Spain remained staunchly religious and inflexibly absolutist, hostile to all ideas perceived as foreign. The other Spain, no less idealistic in its adherence to liberalism and anticlericalism, sought repeatedly and unsuccessfully to impose limitations on absolutist monarchs. As Ramón Menéndez Pidal lamented, both Spains shared an unwillingness to compromise with the other:

> It is not that the anti-catholics were numerous; they were in fact very few. But the intolerant anti-progressives looked upon anyone who proposed new-fangled notions as a downright enemy, even though those ideas were in no way a danger to religion. And vice versa, out-and-out modernizers pushed on their schemes without any regard for religious interests.[16]

Menéndez Pidal described this struggle as "the fated destiny of the two sons of Oedipus, who would not consent to reign together, and mortally wounded each other. Will this sinister craving to destroy the adversary ever cease?"[17]

There is no dearth of historical evidence supporting Menéndez Pidal's observation. The Cortes of Cadiz enacted Europe's first written constitution, calling for popular sovereignty, guaranteed human rights, a parliament elected by universal male suffrage, and elected local governments. Powerful social forces, including sectors of the Catholic Church and aristocracy, opposed the regime and helped to subvert it. Soon after his restoration, Ferdinand VII moved to revive the Inquisition, reimpose censorship, persecute liberals, and abrogate the constitution. Ferdinand's acceptance of the 1812 constitution might have prevented a century of violence and chaos, but he was averse to democratic ideals. By and large, elites "continued to venerate traditional norms, attitudes and values. The Spanish social elites persisted in viewing technological and organizational changes as possible threats to an almost divinely mandated social order."[18]

Traditionally, the military intervened in politics only when the established political order began to decay.[19] It is thus not surprising that this pattern of military intervention in the political sphere gained full force in nineteenth-century Spain. What is less well known is the fact that armed intervention in politics was often initiated in support of "liberal" regimes. In 1820 liberal officers forced Ferdinand VII to accept a constitution, beginning a tradition of military *pronunciamientos* that "became the customary way of changing government in the mid-nineteenth century."[20] This pattern of military intervention in politics continued into the twentieth century, although increasingly in support of political forces of the right and against the new, working-class forces of "disorder."

The short-lived and ill-fated First Republic (1873-74), proclaimed after General Prim's expulsion of Queen Isabella and an aborted attempt to find a more constitutionally oriented monarch, represented only a somewhat wider swing of the political pendulum. Unlike previous liberal experiments, the First Republic implemented a federal political structure and successfully opened up the country to foreign capital. It was, however, totally unable to manage the strains created by the traditional forces of reaction (the Carlists and the church), the new forces of opposition (especially anarchists), and the factional infighting among republican forces. The chaos of the First Republic soon convinced the military to restore the Bourbon monarchy in the person of Alfonso XII. The turbulence of the republic, but especially the rise in regional dissent and anarchist violence, reunited the army and church with each other and with the monarchy.

The Restoration Regime

The restoration of 1874 and the Constitution of 1876 marked the start of a regime that was remarkably stable. The stability of the Restoration monarchy, however, was based on a set of authoritarian political structures. Foremost among these was a powerful monarch, subject neither to the legislative control of France's Third Republic nor to the "conventions" of England's political system.

A second, innovative feature of the regime was the *turno pacífico* (peaceful alternation), an arrangement between the major political parties of the time guaranteeing alternating control of the government. This elite-level agreement between the conservative Cánovas and the liberal Sagasta was an attempt to "Anglicize" the Spanish system by establishing a precedent for peaceful political alternation. Initially at least, the system was also successful in distancing the military from politics and establishing a modicum of religious toleration.[21]

At best, the Restoration monarchy represented a tenuous compromise, a truce among oligarchical representatives of the "two Spains." It was a rapprochement induced by the widespread fatigue with political instability and the emergence of the new forces of regional unrest and mass organization. However, the entire system was based on a fundamental distrust of popular participation. The *turno pacífico* required an elaborate system of electoral manipulation and vote fraud, deeply ingrained in Spanish political folklore, and known as *caciquismo*. The *cacique*, or local political boss, was the linchpin of this system of corruption, and it was his responsibility to deliver the votes of his locality for the candidate designated from above. The system functioned best in rural areas, and was based on the *cacique's* dispensation of patronage, intimidation, and the *pucherazo* (ballot box stuffing). The presence and acceptance of *caciquismo* and *pucherazo* in Spanish politics of the time is well documented in studies of the politics and political folklore of the Restoration regime.

This systematized electoral manipulation stunted the development of a modern party system outside of large urban areas, and cultivated a basic distrust of electoral participation.[22] The most significant and directly consequential feature of the system, however, was its inability to incorporate the demands of the increasingly politicized working class and the frustrated peripheral regions. Mass and regional pressure, coupled with repeated foreign policy failures, further debilitated the political institutions of the Restoration regime. The working-class and regionalist uprisings of the early twentieth century were met with increasing repression on the part of an elite incapable of arriving at a political solution. The exaggerated strength of Spanish anarchism during the period was only one sign of the regime's inability to adapt to demands generated by a rapidly changing socioeconomic structure.

The Spanish American War and the loss of Cuba (1898), the last pearl of Spain's decaying empire, seriously eroded the Restoration regime's legitimacy. The embarrassing military defeat at the hands of Abd el Krim in Morocco (1921) added to the humiliation and insecurity of the regime and the armed forces. Political leaders called increasingly on the military to crush general strikes and regional protest movements, signaling a reassertion of the armed forces in politics and foreshadowing the military coup that eventually terminated the Restoration regime. After the architects of the Restoration party system disappeared from the political scene, Alfonso XIII (1902-31) became increasingly authoritarian and impulsive. The monarch's antidemocratic behavior culminated in his open collusion with the military and the formation of an authoritarian regime under General Primo de Rivera in 1923.

The end of the Restoration regime was mourned by very few within Spain. Its political isolation from the masses alienated potential sources of popular support. Its corruption and progressively authoritarian attributes deprived it of middle-class and intellectual support. Even the Spanish right, whose interests the Restoration regime had protected faithfully, turned away from the constitutional monarchy as the regime proved unable to contain mass unrest, regional dissent, and international crises.

The Dictablanda of Primo de Rivera

Primo's regime has often been referred to as a *dictablanda*, because it employed a relatively mild repression of its political opposition. While some have noted the fascistic trappings of Primo's system, it lacked the mass support, extensive mobilization, cult of violence, and expansionist zeal of Italian Fascism. Primo was a paternalistic, authoritarian modernizer, whose main accomplishment was to implement a vast public works program, improving Spain's backward infrastructure. His ability to stimulate the Spanish economy, as well as his successful resolution of the Moroccan conflict, initially gained him the support of a wide range of forces, including the Spanish Socialist Workers Party.

However, the general's early political success was largely a function of widespread exasperation with the chaos of the Restoration regime, and short-term policy results did not create a permanent reservoir of support for authoritarian rule. Furthermore, Primo's state-funded public works programs soon led to a serious economic crisis, exacerbated by the advent of the worldwide depression. In his inability to find political structures capable of integrating the most important social forces of interwar Spain, Primo shared a similar fate to his predecessors. His attachment to a strong central state and his unwillingness to acknowledge regional interests alienated the Catalans. The dictator's ultimate dependence on the armed forces and the church limited his ability to respond to mass pressure. His economic and political innovations directly threatened the middle classes. Spaniards deserted the dictator almost as quickly as they had come to support him.

The Second Republic

Spaniards accepted the advent of the Second Republic more because the authoritarian monarchy had thoroughly discredited itself than out of any inherent support for democratic political procedures or processes. In fact, a major flaw in the foundation of the Second Republic was that the regime was constructed by a coalition of forces advocating a specific political agenda instead of a neutral set of democratic "rules of the game." This agenda needlessly antagonized still-powerful sectors of the Spanish polity, especially the military and the church.[23]

The Second Republic was successful in eliminating the most blatant abuses of *caciquismo* and *pucherazo*, but was unable to contain an additional impediment to Spanish political development: political extremism. The Second Republic was Spain's first genuinely democratic regime, but it was plagued by the misfortune of being born within the context of the volatile and highly mobilized society of post-World War I Spain. It tried to graft parliamentary democracy onto a society experiencing rapid social change, but still characterized by elitism, class division, and semifeudal agrarian conditions. The result was a chaotic and fragmented party system, polarized from the start. Unfortunately, the very electoral laws that helped to weaken *caciquismo* were ill designed to prevent this fragmentation.[24]

The brief history of the Second Republic was thus characterized by the division of Spain into two hostile blocs, whose antagonism culminated in the anti-Republican uprising of July 1936. By that time the political center had been gutted in a fashion reminiscent of the German Weimar Republic. In the end, the Spanish polity was rather evenly divided between an antisystem right (composed of the rightist Catholic party, CEDA [confederación Española de Derechas Autónomas, or Spanish Confederation of the Autonomous Right], some conservatives, monarchists, and a few Falangists) and an increasingly antisystem left (the socialists, communists, anarchists, and some regional groupings). Spain's electoral law helped to convert small shifts in popular support for each bloc into parliamentary landslides for the victor.

The rightist and leftist political blocs were extremist both in word and in deed. Once in government, each bloc attempted to oveturn the policies of its predecessor in toto. For example, legislation enacted by the founding leftist coalition of 1931-33 (for example, autonomy for Catalonia, legalization of divorce, agrarian reform) was quickly reversed by the conservative government after 1934. Like a swinging pendulum, the Spanish electorate produced leftist and rightist governments consecutively in a period of only four years. By 1936, when the electoral pendulum swung back to the left, giving the Popular Front a narrow 236 to 210 majority in the Cortes (parliament), the Spanish right interpreted the results as a cause for war.

The electoral instability during the Second Republic had fundamentally structural roots. Regionalism, the urban-rural cleavage, and genuine class conflict provided the fuel for political polarization. In addition, parliamentary democracy was in retreat throughout Europe. However, even accepting these handicaps, the political culture of extremism, poor leadership, and irresponsible rhetoric on the part of political elites were equally to blame for the republic's demise.[25] The military was hostile to the Second Republic from the start. Nevertheless, a military coup in 1932 was foiled, and the military did not intervene again until drawn into the political struggle by civilian political forces.

With the advantage of hindsight, it is possible to understand how the leadership of the two major political forces engaged in a war of attrition involving irresponsible rhetoric, a dangerous syndrome that Giovanni Sartori has labeled "the politics of outbidding."[26] Over the course of the Second Republic, forces of moderation within each camp were marginalized and replaced by more maximalist leadership. The debate over which set of political actors sparked the political polarization appears trivial when compared to the general point that all major political forces succumbed to the centrifugal logic of fragmented, polarized party competition.

While the ultimate breakdown of parliamentary democracy was not foreordained, the particular virulence of the fratricide that characterized the Spanish civil war (1936-39) was somewhat more predictable. Despite the presence of important international forces in the civil war, the three years of armed conflict were the nadir of centuries of struggle between the two Spains. Once again, however, the collision of two halves of the Spanish polity failed to produce a political synthesis.

Franquism: The Regime of the Victors

The franquist regime attempted to end the problem of the two Spains by extinguishing the remains of democratic, republican Spain. In fact, the easiest way to describe franquism is to examine what the regime and its leader sought to eliminate. Perhaps most significant from the perspective of Spanish political development, franquism was overtly hostile to parliamentary democracy, a political form viewed as alien to Spanish political traditions. This objective was made crystal clear in Point Six of Franco's Programmatic Norms of the New State:

> All Spaniards will participate in the State within the family, municipality and the syndicate. No one shall participate by means of political parties. The party system shall be implacably abolished with all its consequences: inorganic suffrage, represen-

tation by groups fighting one another and parliament, as it has been known.[27]

In place of the parties, elections, and universal suffrage of *inorganic* democracy, the nation would now be represented by its "natural" constituent units: the family, the municipality, and the syndicate. In theory, this new form of political representation contrasted with the class- and ideology-based parties and trade unions of inorganic systems. In practice it entailed the elimination of previously existing political parties, except for the small political parties merged first into the Falangist FET y de las JONS (Falange Espanola Tradicionalista and Juntas Ofensivas Nacional Sindicalistas), and later into the Movimiento Nacional (MN, or National Movement).

In social terms, the suppression of all aspects of parliamentary democracy created what one historian called a "nation of suspects."[28] The suspicion extended to virtually every supporter of the democratic regime. Even citizens who voted for parties of the left were subject to repression. The punishment for having participated within a parliamentary political system would later pose a serious political cultural impediment to democratization in Spain.

The almost incomprehensible brutality toward all the *vencidos* (vanquished) on the part of the *vencedores* (conquerors) represented the culmination of Spanish political extremism. Paralleling the religious extremism of the Reconquest, franquism placed complete blame for the chaos of the Second Republic and the destruction of the civil war on the defeated side. The dictator summarized his version of forgiveness in late 1939:

> It is necessary to liquidate the hatred and the passions left us by our past war. But this liquidation must not be accomplished in the liberal manner, with enormous and disastrous amnesties and which are a deception rather than a gesture of forgiveness. It must be christian, achieved by means of redemption through work accompanied by repentance and penitence. The man who thinks otherwise is irresponsible or a traitor.[29]

There was no attempt to salvage the positive features of the republic and to correct some of its obvious defects. Instead, the franquist regime sought to erase all Spanish history between the Golden Age and the July 18 uprising. To this end, "[Franco] spoke in medie-

val cadence and resembled nothing so much as a man from the
Reconquest, ridding Spain not of the Moor and of the Jew, but of
the republican, the liberal, the capitalist, the communist, the Free-
mason, and the atheist."[30]

Religion was central to Franco's attempt to reconstitute Spain.
For the Catholic Church, franquism provided the means with
which to reverse the steady decline of religious influence over the
previous two centuries. In the nineteenth century the Catholic
Church had been abandoned by part of the Spanish middle classes.
In the twentieth century, some peasants and workers exchanged
their adherence to religious beliefs for the political doctrines of
anarchism, socialism, and communism. The church had shown itself to be the intractable defender of the upper classes, unable to
react to the changing social, economic, and political realities of
Spain with anything but bitterness. Thus, shortly after the conclusion of the civil war, Spain's cardinal primate blessed the franquist
uprising, dubbing it a "crusade." Franco ruled as "Caudillo of
Spain, by the Grace of God."

The church's uncompromising support for the dictator delivered direct benefits to the institution and to the regime. The church
regained state subsidies for clergy, won a repeal of all anticlerical
legislation, and obtained mandatory religious instruction in the
school, control over much of the educational system, the ability to
impose church censorship on all publications, and greater state
persecution of non-Catholics. The church was the only institution
to gain an explicit guarantee of institutional autonomy from the state,
a fact that became a thorn in the side of the franquist regime as the
church began to distance itself from the dictator in the 1960s. However, despite the granting of considerable autonomy to the church,
a series of accords between the Vatican and the franquist regime
gave the dictator permanent veto power in the papal appointment
of Spanish bishops.

A central target of the regime was the educational system. In
addition to reinserting religion into education, Franco sought to
purge all "liberal" instructors. One consequence was the expulsion
of the best university professors, and the creation of a serious short-
age of teachers. The instructors who had been killed or forced into
exile during the civil war were replaced by politically loyal, often
mediocre faculty. The regime's hostility to intellectuals was exem-
plified by the retort of a top nationalist general to Miguel de Un-

amuno's (a renowned philosopher and writer) appeal to reason: "Abajo la inteligencia! Viva la muerte! (Down with the intelligentsia! Long live death!)."

Regional movements were also fiercely repressed in the early years of Franco's dictatorship. Catalonia and the Basque Country were not only stripped of the political autonomy gained during the Second Republic, but were also deprived of a number of administrative and cultural freedoms enjoyed for centuries. Franco banned the use of regional languages in public places, and prohibited their instruction in schools. These two important regions, but especially the Basque Country, were treated as occupied territory and suffered from the excesses of franquist repression more than the rest of the country. The particular harshness with which franquism "punished" the Basques for defending the republic goes a long way toward explaining the continuing tragedy of Basque terrorism.

In order to fully understand the franquist regime it is necessary to briefly examine Franco himself. More than anything, he was a conservative, middle-class, professional soldier. Unlike Hitler or Mussolini, Franco was very much located in the mainstream of society, and he quickly rose through the ranks of the military hierarchy as a result of his exceptional astuteness and loyalty. He became Spain's youngest army general, distinguishing himself further in the brutal repression of the Asturian miners' revolt in 1934. Unlike like his German or Italian counterparts, Franco was not a charismatic leader or a skilled orator. Like much of the military establishment of the time, he despised "liberal" Spain and held it responsible for the decline of Spain, the loss of Cuba in 1898, and the chaos during the Second Republic. The military reforms enacted by a leftist republican government had the temporary effect of lowering Franco's rank, but he refused to collaborate in antirepublican activity until July 1936, after the victory of the Popular Front.

The rebels were originally led by a National Defense Council, formed by ten top military leaders, including Franco. This body governed territory occupied by the nationalist forces, and was viewed as a temporary government. In September 1936, the council made Franco caudillo, or supreme leader, concentrating all political powers in the hands of one man. In early 1938 Franco formed his first cabinet, which immediately confirmed the caudillo's ability to decree legislation. His accumulation of power within the nationalist camp was achieved through his skillful balancing of the disparate elements of the rebel coalition. While the dictator was supported by monarchists, Carlists, Falangists, Catholics, and the military, he was careful to prevent any one force from consolidating too much power. Neither a party boss nor a vicious tyrant, Franco was a "manipulator of men from a position of power."[31]

Franco's early speeches contained traces of totalitarian rhetoric and his regime sustained many trappings of Italian Fascism and German Nazism. However, his shallow emulation of totalitarianism and his apparent support of the fascist Falange obscured the essentially traditional nature of Franco and his regime. The Falange Española Tradicional (Traditional Spanish Falange, or FET) was established in 1934, and Franco initially adopted its 26-point platform. The "26 Points" included such "revolutionary" measures as substantial agrarian reform and nationalization of the banking system.[32] These characteristics conflicted directly with Franco's own conservatism as well as the political inclinations of his other, more powerful supporters. Having lost most of its key leaders in the Civil War, the Falange was soon fused together with a number of more conservative political forces under direct control of the dictator in the amorphous National Movement. While the hard-core Falangists struggled against this co-optation, they were unable to resist the power of Franco, the unfavorable turn of events in World War II, and, ultimately, the lure of government posts in the vast franquist bureaucracy.

The dictator's abandonment of totalitarian rhetoric and his distancing of the Falange were partially motivated by the defeat of the Axis powers and the postwar international hostility toward totalitarianism. Regardless of international outcomes, Franco was unwilling to implement a totalitarian regime.[33] The dictator's ties to the conservative, traditionalist church, the military, the middle classes, and the bureaucracy precluded his adherence to the revolutionary and totalitarian program of the Falange.

The franquist regime inspired Juan J. Linz's seminal work on authoritarianism, which he defined as

> political systems with limited, not responsible, political pluralism: without elaborate and guiding ideology (but with distinctive mentalities); without intensive nor extensive political mobilization (except some points in their development); and in which

a leader (or occasionally a small group) exercises power within formally ill-defined limits but actually quite predictable ones.[34]

The principal actors within the limited pluralism of Spanish authoritarianism were what sociologist Amando de Miguel termed political "families,"(*familias*).[35] The most important families during franquism were the Catholics, the military, the monarchists, and the Falange (later the National Movement). The boundaries separating these families were often blurred, and their membership overlapped to a considerable extent. In addition, there were important political divisions within each family, some of which became particularly pronounced in the twilight of the regime. The composition of Franco's cabinets demonstrated the eclecticism of the regime coalition, with cabinet posts distributed widely among the different families. A number of important cabinet "reshuffles" served to weaken families with too much power, and the prohibition of political organizations prevented any family from strengthening itself vis-à-vis the dictator.

The Political Structures of Franquism

The development of the political structures of Spanish authoritarianism reflected the pragmatism of the caudillo. No comprehensive constitutional plan was ever implemented, giving Franco tremendous leeway to respond to changing domestic and international situations.[36] The "Fundamental Laws," a term employed to describe the set of seven laws considered collectively as the franquist constitution, demonstrated the flexibility and ever-changing character of the regime. The establishment of Franco's dictatorship preceded any development of constitutional norms or political structures. The Fundamental Laws and the most important franquist political institutions were developed post-facto, mostly to add legitimacy to the existing distribution of power.

Despite the gradual institutionalization of the franquist regime, Franco's personal power remained virtually unlimited up until his death. In addition to his title as generalissimo of the armed forces and leader of the only legitimate political party, between 1938 and 1973 Franco was both head of state and head of government. Even in 1973, when Admiral Luis Carrero Blanco assumed the presidency (head of government), Franco continued to exercise supreme political power.

The first Fundamental Law, the Labor Charter (1938), was inspired by the Italian Fascist *Carta di Lavoro*. Its principal aim was to stifle working-class organization and to ensure labor compliance with the new regime. Together with legislation decreed in 1940, all working Spaniards were required to join vertical syndicates, in which owners and employees were (theoretically) to harmonize their interests for the good of the nation. The state-appointed syndical officials and labor magistrates were to direct this *cogestion*, and independent unions, strikes, or layoffs were forbidden. The vertical syndicate system was successful in keeping wages and working-class protest at extremely low levels until the mid-1950s.

The Constituent Law of the Cortes (1942) established the franquist legislature, but the Cortes had little in common with the parliaments of contemporary democracies. The use of the anachronistic terms *cortes* (parliament) and *procuradores* (deputies) was yet another sign of the regime's enduring traditionalism. Until 1967 the Cortes were indirectly elected by their "corporate" constituents (most importantly, the vertical syndicates and the National Movement), with a large number of the chamber appointed directly or indirectly by the dictator. Even after 1967, when 103 of its members were elected by heads of families and married women, the Cortes exercised virtually no power. While the legislature was asked to approve most legislation, Article 13 of the 1942 Law gave Franco the power to legislate by decree, without consultation of the Cortes. Between 1960 and 1972, for example, there were 203 such decree-laws.

With the Charter of Rights (1945), Franco again sought to present his regime as basically similar to the political systems of the victorious Allied powers. Again, however, this fundamental law was hardly democratic. The very use of the medieval term *fuero* (charter) suggested that to the extent basic rights existed they were a gift bestowed by a benevolent autocrat. Thus, while the charter provided a litany of basic rights, Article 12 noted that "any Spaniard may express his ideas as long as they do not interfere with basic principles of the State," and Article 33 warned that "the exercise of rights recognized by this charter must not in any case interfere with the spiritual, national and social unity of the country." Articles 13-18 gave the state wide powers to suspend the charter when necessary. The charter made no mention of rights of re-union and did nothing to limit a 1939 law giving military tribunals broad jurisdiction in civil matters.

The Law on Referenda (1945) was another part of Franco's attempt to demonstrate that his regime was not "totalitarian." Ironically, the law was decreed unilaterally by the dictator, without his having consulted the Cortes. Franco retained the sole right to hold referenda on any issue, but the caudillo was not obligated to call any referendum. Theoretically, after 1947 referenda were required to alter any Fundamental Law, but Franco preserved his right to decree additional Fundamental Laws, and he did so in 1958.

The first Fundamental Law to be submitted to a referendum was the Law of Succession for the Head of State (1947). This law represented the first serious attempt to give a comprehensive definition to the franquist regime, making Spain a "Catholic, social and representative" kingdom. In addition, Article 2 made Francisco Franco regent for life and the law gave him the right to name his successor at an unspecified future date. A Council of the Realm was established to advise the caudillo and to draw up a list of three candidates from which Franco could select future heads of government.

In 1958 Franco unilaterally decreed the sixth Fundamental Law, the Law on the Principles of the National Movement. The text of the law claimed that the principles were a "synthesis" of all previous Fundamental Laws and that their content was "immutable and permanent." All top governmental officials were required to swear allegiance to the principles, including any future successor to Franco. In general, the law gave the National Movement a permanent constitutional role in the Spanish political system, perhaps to counteract the Falange's decreasing power within the Spanish cabinet after 1956. The National Movement was reaffirmed as the sole arena for any future forms of political participation.

The Organic Law of the State (1966) marked the culmination of franquism's constitutional development. The law was clearly designed to modernize the Spanish system, ridding the constitution of its totalitarian trappings and endowing it with a pseudodemocratic façade. The law formally distinguished the offices of head of government and head of state, and spelled out the mechanisms for the selection of top government officials. It called for the future establishment of political "associations" (*not* parties) within the National Movement, but these were not authorized until 1974. While hailed as a move toward democratization of the franquist system, the Organic Law contained an unambiguous commitment to authoritarian rule. It clearly stated that Franco was to retain the dictatorial powers granted to him during the civil war.

In his defense of the law before the Cortes in 1966, Franco illustrated two essential characteristics of his regime. First, he demonstrated a pragmatic willingness to adopt a "democratic" vocabulary, more acceptable in the 1960s. Second, he held fast to the notion of authoritarian rule and to his unmitigated rejection of any form of liberal democracy.

> Democracy, which correctly understood is the most valued civilizing heritage of western culture appears in each period bound to concrete circumstances that result in political formulas that differ throughout the course of history.[37]

Franquism's legitimacy was based, first and foremost, on Franco's victory in the civil war and his ability to denigrate the previous democratic regime. Later, as the aura of the civil war dissipated, the dictator was able to point to his numerous successes in the international sphere, a period of spectacular economic growth, and an unprecedented epoch of social "peace." In the 1960s, Franco sold Spaniards (and the world) the impression that franquism represented a *democracia a la Española* (a Spanish version of democracy). In the final years of Franco's rule, when all of these sources of legitimacy were close to evaporating, Franco drew on a surprisingly large reservoir of personal loyalty from a population that, if nothing else, admired his and his regime's durability. In addition, even as the "charismatic" legitimacy of his regime eroded, the dictatorship was buffered by a politically demobilized population, rendered apathetic by 40 years of authoritarian rule.

Conclusion

This cursory overview of Spain's economic and political development portrays an extremely hostile environment for the establishment of parliamentary democracy. Even at the apogee of its imperial power, Spain's economy remained underdeveloped and distorted. With the decline of empire, its economy continued to lag behind its European neighbors and by the beginning of the nineteenth century it had become an impoverished European backwater.

Inextricably linked with economic decline was a steady political decay. Spanish leaders clung stubbornly to the political structures of reconquest and empire, rejecting the winds of change blowing across the Pyrenees. Like Cervantes' Don Quixote, they based their political visions on dreams of past greatness rather than on an acceptance of the realities of the country that surrounded them.

As in all European countries, the forces of political and economic modernity unleashed with the French Revolution emerged as a threat to the established order. Throughout most of the nineteenth century, however, traditionalism, absolutism, clericalism, and centralism could not be dislodged by liberals. While the Restoration regime signified a compromise between the stalemated ideologies of liberalism and conservatism, it took the form of an accommodation between political elites based on a disdain for democratic procedures. Unlike the experience in Northern Europe, the conservative and liberal rapprochement was too unstable and occurred too late to have incorporated the emerging working-class and regionalist movements. The Restoration compromise and the Second Republic both succumbed to the dual pressures of a still-powerful right and an increasingly mobilized left. Neither regime could draw on deeply rooted conventions or established political institutions.

Franquism temporarily resolved the problem of the "two Spains" by ignoring the significance of democratic, republican, liberal, and regionalist Spain. As the antithesis of democracy, franquism abandoned any attempt to reconcile *las dos Españas* and thus can be accused of having effectively frozen Spanish politics in a state of underdevelopment. By demobilizing the population, employing selective repression, and exercising an uncompromising authoritarian rule, Franco gave the average Spaniard 40 years of peace. As the future chapters will demonstrate, this peace facilitated an economic "miracle," but it left the perennial political problem of the two Spains without a permanent solution.

The root causes of this inauspicious political and economic legacy have long been a favorite topic of inquiry for Spanish intellectuals.[38] Some, like José Ortega y Gasset, point to the absence of a coherent, talented elite. Others have blamed specific leaders or dynasties for the decline. A number of scholars posit the existence of a Spanish "mentality" that was inherently antimodern.[39] The existence of an inhibitory political culture has been blamed on a whole host of factors, including the influence of the Catholic Church, the Moors, the imperial experience, or some combination of factors.

Was Spain really different, as the popular Spanish saying suggests, or, as more skeptical observers assert, do such differences form part of a Spanish myth that has conveniently justified political and economic underdevelopment? In many ways, this important question loomed large in the twilight of franquist authoritarianism.

Notes

1. Ramón Menéndez Pidal, *The Spaniards in Their History*, trans. Walter Starkie (New York: W.W. Norton, 1950), p. 105.

2. For an overview of the Reconquest, see Stanley G. Payne, *A History of Spain and Portugal*, Vol. 1 (Madison: University of Wisconsin Press, 1973), Chapter 4.

3. On Spanish agriculture, see Edward E. Malefakis, *Agrarian Reform and Peasant Revolution in Spain* (New Haven, Conn.: Yale University Press, 1970).

4. Richard Herr, *An Historical Essay on Modern Spain* (Berkeley: University of California Press, 1974), p. 47.

5. Gerald Brenan, *The Spanish Labyrinth* (Cambridge: Cambridge University Press, 1943), p. 41.

6. Ibid., p. 109.

7. Barrington Moore, Jr. *Social Origins of Dictatorship and Democracy* (Boston: Beacon, 1966), p. 436.

8. An excellent discussion of this problem is found in Franz Borkenau's classic *The Spanish Cockpit* (Ann Arbor, Mich.: Ann Arbor Paperbacks, 1963), p. 99.

9. Brenan, p. viii.

10. Herr, p. 41.

11. Brenan, p. viii.

12. Borkenau, pp. 297-98.

13. Menéndez Pidal, p. 125.

14. Ibid., 128.

15. E. Ramón Arango, *The Spanish Political System: Franco's Legacy* (Boulder, Colo.: Westview Press, 1978) p. 20.

16. Menéndez Pidal, p. 127.

17. Quoted in Walter Starkie's introduction to Menéndez Pidal, p. 11.

18. Karl Marx and F. Engels, *Revolution in Spain* (Westport, Conn.: Greenwood Press, 1975), p. 4.

19. See Stanley Payne, "The Political Transformation of Spain," *Current History*, No. 431 (1977), pp. 166-67.

20. Hugh Thomas, *The Spanish Civil War* (New York: Harper and Row, 1961), p. 13.

21. Raymond Carr, *Spain, 1805-1975*, 2d ed. (Oxford: Clarendon Press, 1982), p. 349.

22. M. Alcántara Saez, "Antología del Pucherazo," *Historia 16* April 1977, p. 144.

23. Juan J. Linz, "From Great Hopes to Civil War: The Breakdown of Democracy in Spain" in Juan J. Linz, ed. *The Breakdown of Democratic Regimes: Europe* (Baltimore: Johns Hopkins University Press, 1978).

24. Antonio Hernández Lafuente, "El Sufragio en la II República," *Historia 16*, April 1977, pp. 76-84.

25. This perspective is advanced persuasively by Linz; in addition see Malefakis. A number of writers place the blame for the democratic breakdown on political elites of the right or left. For example, Paul Preston, ed. *Spain in Crisis* (New York: Harper and Row, Harvester, 1978) provides evidence suggesting the right's culpability; and Richard Robinson, *The Origins of Franco's Spain: The Right, The Republic and Revolution, 1931-1936* (Devon, Eng.: David and Charles, 1970) points to the left's errors and provocations.

26. Giovanni Sartori, *Parties and Party Systems*, Vol 1 (Cambridge: Cambridge University Press, 1976), p. 139.

27. Quoted in Miguel A. Ruíz de Azua, "Las elecciones Franquistas (1942-1976)," *Historia 16*, April 1977, p. 85.

28. Max Gallo, *Spain Under Franco* (New York: E.P. Dutton, 1974), p. 66.

29. Ibid., p. 88.

30. Arango, p. 111.

31. Carr, p. 695.

32. Stanley G. Payne, *Falange: A History of Spanish Fascism* (Stanford, Calif.: Stanford University Press, 1961), p. 165.

33. Juan J. Linz, "From Falange to Movimiento-Organización: The Spanish Single Party and the Franco Regime, 1936-1968," in Samuel Huntington and Clement Moore, eds., *Authoritarian Politics in Modern Society* (New York: Basic Books, 1970), pp. 146-47.

34. Juan J. Linz, "An Authoritarian Regime: Spain," in Stanley G.

Payne, ed., *Politics and Society in Twentieth Century Spain* (New York: New Viewpoints, 1976), p. 165.

35. Amando de Miguel, *Sociología del Franquismo* (Barcelona: Planeta, 1975).

36. For an introduction to the franquist constitutional system, see Fernández Carvajal, *La Constitución española* (Madrid: Editorial Nacional, 1969).

37. Linz, "From Falange," p. 155.

38. See Herr, Chapter 2, for an excellent summary of this debate.

39. For example, Americo Castro, *The Spaniards*, trans. W. F. King and S. Margaretten (Berkeley: University of California Press, 1971), p. 46.

2 THE CHANGING ENVIRONMENT OF SPANISH AUTHORITARIANISM

Recent political changes in Spain do not fit properly into any of those grand theories of political change or development. Neither Marxist nor developmentalist theories of politics offer an acceptable explanation of the Spanish case[1].

While students of Spanish politics are unanimous in viewing Spain's democratization as historically unique, they emphasize a number of different factors contributing to such an unprecedented political transition. This chapter provides an overview of some of the factors that form part of an explanation for democratization in Spain after 1975. None of these factors alone constitutes a sufficient explanation for the Spanish transition, but together they form the general context within which political elites made crucial decisions. Each approach will be shown to have its strengths and weaknesses, since the commonly emphasized factors contributing to political change often did not exclusively favor democratic outcomes.

The focus of discussion will be on three highly interrelated approaches or emphases that help to explain Spain's exceptional democratic transition after 1975. The "economic" approach emphasizes the relationship between economic development and political democratization. A second approach focuses on "social pressure," especially the mass pressure from "below." A final approach emphasizes the international context within which democratization took place. In addition to reiterating the interrelatedness of these factors, it is worth stressing from the start that *all* three of these

factors contributed to Spain's democratic transition at least somewhat. At the same time, these environmental factors are by themselves insufficient to explain the initiation, the successful execution, and the subsequent consolidation of transition through
transaction. Only by considering the struggle among political forces
within the authoritarian coalition (see Chapter 3) in conjunction
with specific strategies pursued by the authoritarian elites (see
Chapter 4) can one gain a complete understanding of the Spanish
route to democracy.

Economic Development and Democratization

Few aspects of contemporary Spain have been examined as
thoroughly as its spectacular economic growth, especially during
the period of the economic "miracle" (1960-70). It is not surprising that the notion of a link between economic development and
democratization is widespread throughout the literature on Spain.
The idea that democracy was virtually inevitable, or at least very
probable, given Spain's level of economic development is expressed
by academics and political actors alike. Some suggest that Spain
offers unexpected confirmation of liberal developmentalist theory,
which posited a direct relationship between economic growth and
democratization. Others allege that Spain formed part of a wave
of democratization in the "late-late" industrializing countries of
Latin Europe and Latin America. Economic growth is central to
most explanations of political change in Spain. For example, one
historian asserts that

> what began as a program of economic reform that would be ac-
> companied by a modest degree of political liberalization ended
> by transforming Spain so completely that full democratization
> had become almost inevitable. The "cunning" of capitalism has
> brought about subtly and by peaceful means the destruction of
> the dictatorial regime that had sponsored it precisely to preserve
> itself and to avoid democracy.[2]

To what extent is this assertion accurate? Did economic development and its concomitants make democratization "almost inevita-

ble?'' A survey of the available evidence demonstrates both support for and important qualifications to the link between democratization and economic development.

Spain's spectacular economic growth began only after the franquist regime abandoned its autarchic policies in the late 1950s. Despite the fact that the international ostracism of Spain had come to an end by 1953, Franco stubbornly pursued autarchic policies until 1959, when he was forced to abandon this political economic model. Import restrictions had strangled economic activity; agrarian production lagged behind demand, fueling inflation; and Spain's balance of payments was running a serious deficit.

The definitive abandonment of autarchic economic policies took place in 1959 with a government shift that brought a number of Opus Dei technocrats to power.[3] The new government quickly implemented a stabilization plan, based on recommendations from the International Monetary Fund and the Organization for Economic Cooperation and Development (OECD). The change in economic policy wrought immediate results: By the end of 1959 a dramatic recession was in effect, but the balance of payments was positive for the first time in many years.

Between 1960 and 1970 Spain experienced unprecedented rates of economic growth. By 1971 the gross national product (GNP) was 85.4 percent higher than in 1963. Real per capita income grew at an average rate of 6.4 percent compared with 2.8 percent between 1940 and 1960.[4] Table 1 contains the average yearly growth rate of a number of economic indicators for the 1960-70 period. In addition, the rate of industrial productivity nearly doubled in the decade after 1960. Table 2 demonstrates the structural changes in the Spanish economy during the ''miracle.''

During the 1960s Spain experienced a veritable social revolution. Per capita income reached $650 in 1965, propelling Spain across what was then considered the ''threshold'' of the developed world. There can be little doubt that the average Spaniard's absolute standard of living improved considerably during this period, although there is less consensus regarding this improvement in relative terms. Between 1964 and 1972 the average hourly wage increase was 287.9 percent while the average cost of living increase for the same period was only 69.9 percent.[5] Enrique Uriel has argued that between 1955 and 1971 income inequality was reduced

**Table 1. Average Yearly Growth Rate
of Major Economic Indicators, 1960-70**

Indicators	Percent Average Yearly Growth Rate
Gross national product	8.5
Gross capital formation	11.4
Exports	12.2
Resources used	8.2
Imports	17.2
Public consumption	5.8
Private consumption	7.1

Source: Sima Lieberman, *The Contemporary Spanish Economy* (London: Allen and Unwin, 1982), p. 214.

Table 2. Sectorial Distribution of Spain's Work Force in 1960, 1965, and 1970

Sector	1960	1965	1970
Agriculture	41.3	33.2	29.2
Industry	31.4	34.7	38.1
Services	27.3	32.1	32.7

Source: José Amodia, *Franco's Political Legacy* (London: Allen Lane, 1977).

dramatically, but a number of economists have challenged this analysis. For example, one 1975 report concluded that the overall distribution of income in Spain had *worsened* during the 1960s.[6]

By 1975 Spain had clearly become an advanced capitalist industrial society. A number of writers from a wide range of ideological perspectives have viewed this growth as the major long-term cause for the emergence of democracy in Spain after 1975. Some argue that the entrepreneurial elite, seeking greater access to the European Economic Community (EEC), pushed for democratization. Others, from both a neo-Marxist and product-cycle perspective, make a fundamentally analogous argument.[7]

These attempts to relate economic development to democratization share in common a lack of concrete evidence to support the link, and there is strong evidence to at least question the relationship. The notion of widespread bourgeois disaffection with the franquist regime has been thoroughly attacked.[8] In addition, these analyses tend to overestimate the role of multinational capital in Spain. While Spain was increasingly penetrated by foreign capital after 1960, its dependency on foreign capital in no way approached the level of most Latin American countries. The Opus Dei technocrats were able to open the gates to a flood of foreign capital, but only for a short period. The state moved swiftly to reimpose limits on foreign investments. The period of autarchy was successful in establishing a relatively autonomous, if highly inefficient and outdated, industrial infrastructure that helped Spain to avoid a situation of extreme dependence.

Moreover, the major source of economic power in Spain, the financial aristocracy, had real reasons to fear democratization. The Spanish banking sector, alienated by the reforms of the republic and fearing widespread nationalizations, had unanimously supported Franco's rebellion in 1936. Their support was rewarded handsomely in the form of a grant of virtual monopoly over the Spanish banking system to the small number of existing banks. The Spanish banks used this monopoly to gain control over the majority of Spanish private capital. Spanish banks became some of the most profitable in the world and the Spanish financial sector came to dominate the industrial bourgeoisie, both economically and politically, through its control of investment capital.

Even without noting the political weakness and dependence of the industrial class in Spain, one could still question any attempt to view democratization as a response of the modern industrial elite. In comparative perspective Spain's industrial structure is highly fragmented and is dominated by a large number of very small firms. These small firms flourished during franquism and were not inclined toward pushing for political change. This makes it difficult to argue that big business exercised political hegemony or that industrialists represented a coherent political force. It is worth remembering that many large enterprises benefited from the autarchic policies of the pre-1959 period and/or subsequent policies of liberalization. There was widespread fear about potential future nationalization of industry on the eve of Franco's death.[9]

More sophisticated arguments have been advanced relating certain *factions* of the bourgeoisie to support for democratization.[10] In *The Crisis of the Dictatorships*, Nicos Poulantzas argues that transitions to parliamentary democracy in southern Europe resulted from internal struggles within the bourgeoisie. In the midst of an international economic crisis, the "domestic bourgeoisie" (favoring democracy and linked to the EEC) successfully wrestled hegemony away from the "comprador bourgeoisie" (composed of monopoly capitalists with ties to the United States).

As noted by Marxist and non-Marxist scholars alike, Poulantzas falls victim to a crude functionalism in which authoritarian regimes, unlike democracies, are unable to provide the "requisites" for sustained capital accumulation. Others observe that Poulantzas attempts to find an economic explanation for every change in the political structure. Moreover, the notion of a comprador bourgeoisie can be disputed. There is no evidence of a "hegemonic" faction of the bourgeoisie with links to international capital. To the extent that a hegemonic sector of the bourgeoisie under Franco could be identified, it would be the financial aristocracy, precisely the economic sector most supportive of the dictatorship.[11]

Finally, even had a coherent bourgeois opposition existed, the authoritarian regime likely would have been able to hinder its political articulation. The ability of the authoritarian regime to coopt political opposition and to avoid any form of organized political contestation remained intact throughout its history. Until the end of the regime, Franco remained independent from any pressure group, economic interests included.

It is often noted that the economic "miracle" created the middle class that had been lacking during the Second Republic. The presence of the new *clases medias* in the later years of the dictatorship is undeniable. Yet the immediate political consequences of changing class structure is more difficult to detect. Members of the new middle classes came to occupy positions of considerable political influence in the twilight of franquism. The less polarized class structure was a major factor in the consolidation of Spain's nascent parliamentary democracy. But these factors are still far from constituting evidence that the changing class structure somehow necessitated the initiation of a democratization from authoritarianism. Robert Moss, for example, argued in 1974 that "the remarkable rise in material prospects in Spain has transformed Spanish society but has had negligible impact on its political system."[12] M. Gómez Reino and his collaborators, writing on Spanish politics in 1975, noted:

> The facts show that...a country can grow economically and
> substantially transform its social structures without real changes
> in its political system, for long periods of time. Our case [Spain]
> is a clear example of the apparent lack of a causal synchronic rela-
> tionship between socioeconomic and political systems.[13]

Attempts to link economic factors to democratization appear
in a variety of forms throughout the literature on the Spanish transition. One approach is to suggest that the end of a period of rapid
growth with the advent of the recession in the early 1970s had a
relative deprivation effect, thus eroding support for authoritarian
rule. While economic crisis hardly favors any type of regime, there
is little evidence to support the relative deprivation theory. Survey
research supports the view that the franquist regime was not generally blamed for the recession of the early 1970s while it managed
to retain credit for the "miracle" of the 1960s. In the last years of
franquism, consumption rates, wages, and salaries continued to rise
above inflation, perhaps explaining why Spaniards by and large
perceived their positions as "better than average" throughout the
worst period of the recession.[14]

A related approach posits that economic development and
changing class structures had made authoritarian rule "unnecessary" given the new egalitarianism of Spanish society and the political apathy and demobilization nurtured by 40 years of
authoritarianism. Rather than highlighting economic crisis and relative deprivation, it focuses on economic success and a "disyn-
chronization" of political and economic structures.[15] However,
this approach overlooks the multiple political tensions exacerbated
by economic modernization. Perhaps most significant of these tensions was the regional question. The internationalization of capital in Spain, a key part of the economic "miracle," concentrated
capital and population in a few industrialized regions, principally
the Basque Country, Catalonia, and Madrid. The traditional Basque
and Catalan hostility toward Madrid, and especially toward franquism, combined with the regime's harsh repression of regional
opposition, made this economic concentration a potentially explosive political problem. Economic growth increased inequality
among regions, a factor that made any attempt to resolve the
regional problem especially tricky.

Attempts to link democratization with economic success must also contend with the important problem of the timing of the transition. It is not clear why democratization would have taken place during a period of severe economic crisis rather than in the late 1960s when economic development had not yet ground to a halt. The severity of the recession in Spain was particularly pronounced when compared with that of other OECD countries. Spain's economy was heavily dependent on the tourism industry and the escape valve of emigrant labor. Both were devastated by the worldwide recession and Spain experienced a much harsher, if somewhat delayed economic crisis. The crisis peaked in 1974 and 1975, the two years immediately preceding the transition to democracy in Spain; 1975 was the worst economic year since 1959 in terms of rising unemployment and declining industrial activity.[16] Table 3 compares the severity of the Spanish economic crisis with that of the OECD countries as a whole.

Spain's greater dependence on energy imports when compared with other OECD countries, its higher growth rate of energy consumption, its higher average yearly increase in hourly wages, and its larger percentage of its gross domestic product (GDP) consumed

Table 3. The Crisis of the 1970s in Spain and the OECD Countries

Economic Indicators	Spain	OECD
	(percentages)	
Periodic variation in growth rate of real GDP, 1965-73 & 1974-78	−62	−48
Periodic variation in growth rate of real domestic demand, 1965-73 & 1974-78	−79	−60
Periodic variation in growth rate of production, 1965-73 & 1974-78	−29	−65
Periodic variation in rate of inflation, 1965-73 & 1974-78:	+267	+80
Periodic variation in rate of unemployment, 1965-73 & 1974-78	+155	+113

Source: Sima Lieberman, The Contemporary Spanish Economy (London: Allen and Unwin, 1982), p. 273.

by public-sector spending all exacerbated the intensity of Spain's economic crisis.

It is thus problematic to argue that Spanish economic growth and its concomitants made democracy either probable or inevitable. A rapidly developing economic structure gave rise to numerous social forces in favor of democracy. However, economic development had earned the franquist regime a considerable amount of credit among Spanish elites and society. Moreover, the contradictions and strains within Spanish society, which franquist economic development often exacerbated, frightened many franquist elites.

Social Mobilization and Democratization

It is often alleged that growing levels of social mobilization, in conjunction with the activities of the organized democratic opposition, were the primary contributors to the crisis of franquism in the early 1970s. These forces of mass dissent are seen as having increased the costs associated with any continuation of authoritarian rule after Franco's death.

As with the emphasis on economic development, there is abundant evidence that can be marshaled in support of the social mobilization approach. Numerous works have been written documenting the struggles of workers, students, and the church against the franquist regime. José María Maravall has argued that pressure "from below" was one of the key factors behind Spain's transition to democracy.[17] He contends that strikes, terrorism, and university violence were a major source of concern for authoritarian elites, especially members of the *clases medias.* The combined effect of these pressures was to force moderate sectors of the regime to "escape from the crisis of the dictatorship with a strategy of pacts" with the left.[18]

Julio Rodríguez Aramberri, from a Marxist perspective, also begins his analysis of the Spanish transition by emphasizing the rise of mass opposition in the early 1970s. The result of this dissent, he suggests, was to split the ruling coalition of franquism between those favoring some form of political change and those rejecting any type of reform. The more "progressive" regime forces felt that "a solution had to be found to a political crisis that would, through inertia, develop into a crisis of bourgeois domination."[19]

Perhaps the major conceptual weakness of the social mobilization approach to the Spanish transition is the failure to explain why franquist elites eventually responded to increased mass pressures with *democratic reform* rather than with further repression or a more liberal form of authoritarianism. Franquist elites under the leadership of President Arias Navarro initially responded to the widely perceived "crisis" of the regime by initiating a half-hearted, limited democratic reform. Only when this conservative strategy failed was a more profound democratic reform initiated under Arias's succesor, Adolfo Suárez.

Increased social mobilization was *only one element* contributing to the regime's sense of political crisis in the twilight of franquism. The political maneuverings of franquist elites in response to the crisis of Spanish authoritarianism were much less a function of increased social mobilization than intraregime dynamics, pressure from hard-line authoritarian forces, and the strengths and weaknesses of various political strategies advanced by competing franquist elites.

The following sections examine some evidence regarding the most important sources of mass pressure: working-class opposition, student opposition, organized political opposition, the Catholic Church, and terrorism. While all of these types of social mobilization were on the increase in the years preceding the transition, the evidence suggests that mass pressure did not constitute a crucial challenge to authoritarian rule.

Working-Class Opposition

An important element of arguments emphasizing social mobilization is the contention that political opposition in the last years of franquism became extremely strong and that regime elites could no longer ignore mass dissent. There is certainly some evidence with which to build such an argument, but the tendency has been to overestimate the strength and significance of mass opposition.

Between 1960, when the first widespread strike activity was provoked by the government's harsh stabilization program, and Franco's death in 1975, there was a constant increase in the number of labor-related strikes. In 1966, 1.5 million hours were lost due to strikes, but by 1970 the figure had risen to 8.7 million lost hours, reaching 14.5 million by 1975.[20] Nevertheless, it is important to keep in mind that during the nearly 40 years of franquism, no key sector of the economy was ever completely paralyzed by an industrial conflict. For the most part, the regime was able to combine a policy of selective, often brutal repression of labor conflicts with a strategy of allowing strikes to exhaust themselves. Given the clandestine nature of trade unions and opposition organizations, strikers were not able to outlast the will of the employers (and the police repression) in most cases.

The weakness of labor opposition to the franquist regime, and, more importantly, the limited political impact of labor unrest, reflects one of the key strengths of authoritarian regimes. While inconsistent in its toleration of strikes per se, the regime was more consistent in obstructing any organized labor movement with links to the democratic opposition. Maravall, a partial advocate of the social mobilization thesis, admits this point when arguing that

> this [working class] pressure was always intense, but at a certain moment it largely divorced itself from organizational strategies and was not directed by any political or trade unionist goals. In addition, this pressure never went beyond the ability of the transitional government to react because, among other things, mobilization was supported by only a limited sector of the population.[21]

It is worth noting that strikes during franquism were concentrated in the Basque Country (especially in the province of Vizcaya), in Catalonia, and to a lesser extent in Asturias and Madrid. It was in the Basque Country where the dual nemeses of Basque nationalist terrorism and labor violence evoked the most brutal governmental repression, notably in the 1967-70 period when the region remained under a state of siege. The regional, as opposed to strictly class, nature of these foci of labor unrest worked against a truly national working-class opposition to the regime.

The Universities

The Spanish universities are often portrayed as a major hotbed of opposition to the franquist regime. Indeed, the universities provided vivid proof of Franco's failure to establish legitimacy among the Spanish youth and intelligentsia. At the same time, how-

ever, the universities were an example of the regime's ability to
fragment opposition and, when necessary, to meet political
challenges with sheer repression.

The antifranquist student movement emerged in the 1950s after
a period of harsh repression that had prevented significant campus
opposition activity. Franco had conducted a thorough purge of
republican sympathizers in the university, and the republican student organizations were effectively smashed. Between 1945 and
1955 there were a number of failed attempts to create a new
democratic student union to compete with the Falangist-led University Student Syndicate (Sindicato Estudantíl Universitario, SEU) in
which membership was compulsory. Between 1955 and 1960 a
struggle developed within Spain's universities between the Falangists and the democratic opposition. This competition was encouraged by the liberal atmosphere fostered during the tenure of
Joaquín Ruíz Giménez as education minister. The resulting chaos
and violence led to Ruíz Giménez's ouster, and marked the beginning of a more repressive university setting.

A number of factors contributed to increased democratic opposition activity on Spanish campuses after 1956. The economic
liberalization and political thaw advocated by the Opus Dei technocrats encouraged similar changes within the universities. The
Falangist SEU, attempting to respond to the opposition's success
and bitterly opposed to the Opus Dei's new influence in higher
education, began to undergo an internal renovation. These changes
coincided with the rise of the "generation of 1956," the first generation of university students who had not experienced the civil
war.[22] The Spanish Communist Party (Partido Comunista de España, PCE) and other opposition groups began to rebuild and
sought support on university campuses. Finally, the church, which
enjoyed considerable influence in the realm of Spanish higher education, was starting, albeit slowly and cautiously, to distance itself
from the franquist regime.

The regime was quick to respond to the resurgence of student
opposition. Military police encampments became a permanent feature of every Spanish university campus until the death of Franco
in 1975, as did the ubiquitous informers placed in university
classes. In 1965 the government abolished the increasingly politicized SEU and transformed it into an apolitical student service organization. A new clandestine student organization, the Democratic

Student Syndicate (Sindicato Demócratica Estudantíl, SDE) was formed in the same year. The SDE began as a semitolerated "association," but it became dominated increasingly by the leftist opposition. The SDE eventually failed to unify the Spanish student opposition and was disbanded in 1969 due to persistent government harassment, political divisions within the organization (especially the anger on the part of many members over the organization's drift toward the extreme left), and its inability to articulate a coherent political strategy.[23] The regime periodically purged the professional ranks of the democratic opposition, removing three of Spain's most prestigious tenured professors in 1965 and banishing them from the university system for life.

In the last years of the franquist regime, starting with the turbulence of 1968-69, the university became a constant battleground. As the regime reverted to harsh repression, the student movement became more radicalized and was infiltrated by a number of competing organizations of the extreme left. While the last years of franquism were characterized by a rise of student opposition to Spanish authoritarianism, it is possible to conclude in agreement with Fernández de Castro who writes: "In Spain, student subversion . . . never became more than another problem of public order for the regime, a problem which in its most acute moments—1968-1969—wasn't even barely in sync with the workers struggle."[24]

Organized Democratic Opposition

Any discussion of the role of social mobilization in Spain's democratic transition must consider the organized political opposition, that is, the structures through which mass dissent could have influenced political outcomes in authoritarian Spain.

If there is any point regarding politics during franquism on which almost all scholars agree, it is that the organized democratic opposition remained both weak and fragmented for the duration of the regime's history. One of the earliest signs of the opposition's weakness and disarray was the failed national strike planned by the PCE in 1958. Four years later the Munich Conference succeeded in gathering together a wide range of opposition leaders, but the meeting only highlighted the serious divisions within Spain's opposition. In 1966 Spanish police brutally repressed one of the first major syndical demonstrations, led by Marcelino

Camacho (head of the PCE-dominated Workers Commissions [Comisiones Obreras, CCOO], a clandestine workers organization), despite the fact that over 20,000 demonstrators were in attendance. In December 1969, thanks to a relaxation of press censorship, forces of the democratic opposition issued their first public manifesto calling for the restoration of civil liberties. In November 1971, Catalan opposition forces foreshadowed national trends by holding an assembly in a Barcelona church. The assembly, the first of its kind in Spain, called for a full amnesty for political prisoners, civil liberties, the restoration of the 1932 Statute of Catalan Autonomy, and the unification of all Spanish opposition forces. A harbinger of things to come, the government reacted severely, imposing stiff fines on those even suspected of having participated.

At the national level, political coordination of the plethora of clandestine and semitolerated opposition forces was more retarded. In fact, it was not until March 1976 that a single democratic opposition coalition could be said to have existed. The fusion of the two largest opposition organizations, the Platform of Democratic Coordination (Plataforma de Coordinación Democrática, CD) and the Democratic Junta (Junta Democrática, JD), ended almost 40 years of hostility between the two major forces of the Spanish left, the PCE and the PSOE (Partido Socialista Obrero Español, Spanish Socialist Workers Party).[25] It was not until late 1976 that some regional organizations were included in the unified opposition organization.

A constant problem facing the Spanish opposition was the large number of fragmented, feuding political organizations, a situation further complicated by the presence of a multitude of regional parties and groups. Even Spain's communists, by far the most unified of all opposition forces, were beset by splinter groups and political infighting. The Spanish socialists were a much weaker force under franquism, and were divided into even more competing factions. The incredible proliferation of democratic opposition parties toward the end of the franquist regime led some observers to speak of "taxi parties," parties whose members could easily fit into a taxi!

This inauspicious fragmentation and weakness was occasionally acknowledged by observers on the left. The editorial team of the leftist *Zona Abierta* concluded as late as 1977, after more than a year of relative political freedom for the opposition, that

1) The implantation and mobilizational capacity of the opposition is insufficient, 2) the possibility of convoking the people in the streets to topple the security forces of the state is practically null, and 3) to think that any party could put the common interest of the left before that of its own survival is simply idealistic. . . .[26]

According to another prominent leftist observer, "the democratic opposition lacked a clear political project or a unitary organization capable of imposing one."[27]

The weakness of the organized Spanish democratic opposition should not be taken as a sign that the population at large was unsupportive of the concept of democracy. Much to the contrary, there is strong evidence suggesting that Spaniards were quite amenable to democratic politics.[28] However, it is imperative to bear in mind that authoritarian regimes impose strict limits on political contestation. As Romero-Maura points out, "though they were free to act as they like in spheres which were politically inoffensive, even the friends of the regime found it impossible to mount any party organizations with an eye to the future."[29]

The Catholic Church

It might surprise some readers to find a discussion of the Catholic Church as part of a section on social mobilization and mass pressure from below. After all, Spain's cardinal primate had condemned the Spanish Republic and had blessed Franco's July 18 uprising as a "crusade." In fact, the Catholic Church constituted a loyal and powerful member of the franquist coalition until quite late in the regime's history.

The importance of the church as a franquist coalition partner was manifest in the 1953 Spain-Vatican Concordat, giving the church considerable control over Spanish education and granting Franco the right to nominate members for positions within the hierarchy of the church. According to a 1943 decree, Spanish universities were placed under the control of the church, whose role was to be "the theological army to fight heresy and the producer of the missionary phalanx that must affirm Catholic unity." The franquist regime furnished direct economic support to the church.

One especially important power granted to the church was the large degree of institutional autonomy guaranteed by the Concordat. Article 34, for example, guaranteed the autonomy of Catholic Action, one of the few truly autonomous social action organizations tolerated by the franquist regime. This explains why some of the earliest opposition to Spanish authoritarianism emerged at the grass-roots level of the church's organizational structure. In response to the harsh conditions resulting from the stabilization program in the early 1960s there was a rise in labor unrest, notably the bitter Asturian miners strike of 1962. Lay organizations like the Young Catholic Workers (JOC) and the Workers Brotherhood of Catholic Action (HOAC) began to support strikes by the working class.

In May 1960, almost 400 Basque priests published a letter denouncing police repression. In 1963, Aureli Escarré (abbot of Montserrat) supported human rights publicly and was exiled for his behavior. In 1966, 130 priests demonstrated in the streets of Barcelona against the regime's brutality. Publications linked to the JOC and HOAC began to support the democratic opposition. *Signo,* published by the JOC, affirmed in a 1965 issue that "to get involved in politics is a task for Christians," an assertion that could hardly have been more antithetical to Spanish authoritarianism.[30] *Signo* went even further one year later:

> This is our position: We support whatever the people freely decide upon. As far as the freedom for political parties is concerned, and following the teachings of John XXIII, when he speaks about freedom of association, we must oppose the single party regime, imposed from above.[31]

Despite these grass-roots actions, the Catholic hierarchy remained a staunch supporter of the franquist regime throughout the decade of the 1960s. In the mid-1960s the church leadership conducted major purges of the organizations linked with Catholic Action, pushing many church activists into clandestine leftist organizations. In 1967 the church hierarchy banned the journal *Signo.*

However, the radicalization of the church's base eventually affected the hierarchy and created a serious split among the leadership. The teachings of Vatican II had given a new legitimacy to the progressive minority within the hierarchy, although the Spanish Episcopal Council was still dominated by the conservatives.

Progressive positions were assumed increasingly by young clergy, and those working in the more turbulent regions of Catalonia and the Basque Country.

The gradual shift of the hierarchy toward more progressive positions appears to have had several causes. On a general level, while a clear beneficiary of its links with the franquist regime, the Catholic Church had fallen victim to a fundamental dynamic of authoritarian regimes. The church, as an organization requiring mass participation, was suffering the fate of most voluntary organizations under franquism. The depoliticizing, demobilizing, and antiparticipatory mentality of Spanish authoritarianism, in addition to the rapid pace of social change and secularization, weakened the links between the church and Spanish society. The church's slow distancing from the franquist regime can be understood partially as an attempt to reinforce its institutional autonomy and to find a new identity, autonomous from that of franquism.

A second cause of the shift in the attitude of the church hierarchy can be found in the state's repression of church members who became politically active. For example, as early as March 1966, a meeting of 400 students in a Capuchin friary in Sarriá (Barcelona) convened with the purpose of organizing a local sector of the SDE, was broken up by the police, who entered a church in violation of the provisions of the Concordat. The church hierarchy and the state came into open conflict in 1970 when two priests were among the 16 accused Basque terrorists in the infamous Burgos trial. By the end of 1970, 19 Basque priests were in prison, some for having denounced police torture in their sermons. Between 1971 and 1975, the church was subjected to a full-scale assault by the franquist regime. The attack included suspensions of church assemblies, fines for sermons preached against the regime, the unauthorized entry of police into churches, censorship of church materials, and attacks by the regime press, aimed at the "subversive activities" of the Spanish clergy. The loss of church immunity from state repression worried even the conservative clergy and favored the rise of a younger generation of church moderates. Cardinal Enrique y Tarancón's election as president of the Spanish Episcopal Conference in 1971 marked the rise to power of the progressive church hierarchy.

A third and crucial factor explaining the shift of the Spanish Catholic Church away from the franquist regime was the dramatic change in the politics of the Vatican after Vatican II, in 1962. The Vatican and the franquist regime gradually came into direct conflict over a wide range of issues relating to the increasingly outdated Concordat, and centering around Rome's open support for Spain's progressive clergy.

A first-ever assembly of Spanish priests and bishops was held in September 1971 and its conclusions became a national scandal. The 100 democratically elected members of the assembly pronounced themselves in favor of civil rights and they opposed church participation in the franquist regime. They also opted for a renegotiation of the 1953 Concordat. A survey of the delegates showed widespread opposition to the franquist regime, confirming the conclusions of previous studies on the Spanish clergy.[32]

On the whole, in the last years of franquism it is possible to characterize the Spanish Catholic Church as an institution with serious social and ideological divisions. These divisions could be witnessed both in the pastoral statements issued by church members and in the increasingly visible "camps" within the hierarchy. The consequences of such a rift were clear cut. First, and foremost, it signaled the definitive termination of the church's membership in the franquist authoritarian coalition. Divided as it was, it was highly unlikely that the church would be as supportive of any future authoritarian solution in any way similar to its role during the early franquist years. Second, and related to the first point, the church adopted a neutral stance vis-à-vis the transition to democracy initiated in late 1975. The presence of serious dissent within the church was also a major factor explaining the dramatic failure of the Christian democrats in the first democratic elections.

Terrorism

The most persistent direct challenge to authoritarianism came from terrorists, although it cannot be argued that this challenge in any way favored the transition to parliamentary democracy. From 1960 onward, terrorists stepped up their activity against the Spanish military, business executives, and other citizens. Terrorism was, however, the type of challenge for which the franquist regime was well equipped. The ability of the franquist-controlled media to portray terrorists as "savages," the regime's ability to confound terrorism with democratic opposition, and the population's abhorrence

of violence all explain why acts of terrorism were usually counterproductive.

It is often noted that the final crisis of franquism was ignited
by the terrorist killing of Admiral Carrero Blanco, generally considered to be Franco's own choice as the dictator's succesor. While
the audacious plot did cast considerable doubt on the viability of
franquism after Franco, it must also be pointed out that such acts
of terrorism had the immediate consequence of weakening reformist sectors within the regime. Terrorist attacks on police and
civilians touched off waves of brutal repression and provided the
regime with an excuse to persecute all political opponents, regardless of their links with terrorist violence.

The wave of terrorism that swept Spain in 1972, for example,
forced moderates in the cabinet to yield to *ultra* pressure and to
support a governmental crackdown on political opposition. The
period following Carrero's assassination, despite the rhetoric concerning *apertura*, involved fierce persecution of the Communist
Workers Commissions. This pattern was repeated as late as the
summer of 1975, when the government declared a state of siege
in the Basque Country and detained hundreds of opposition
members.

Terrorism arose precisely in those regions where franquist
repression was the harshest, especially in the Basque Country. In
this region, the state's use of coercion was so excessive, and the
ugly face of Spanish authoritarianism was so visible, that terrorist
actions, at least initially, were a widely supported reaction against
franquist repression. The franquist regime's subjugation of the
Basque Country, and its lack of sensitivity to Basque political traditions, were ultimately responsible for creating a subculture supportive of terrorism. The Basque problem outlived the dictator and
has continued to haunt Spain's new democracy.

Summary

These aspects of social mobilization—the increasing frequency
of labor conflict, the continuing violence within the universities,
the defection of the Catholic Church, and the persistent problem
of terrorism—were essential components of the Spanish transition
to democracy. They formed part of the context within which franquist elites eventually opted for a parliamentary democratic form

of political change. There can be little doubt that in the last years
of Franco's life, the perceived costs of containing this mobilization
through repression were rising rapidly. Insofar as these manifestations of mass discontent influenced elite political perceptions—by
filtering up the church hierarchy and distancing a key component
of the regime coalition, by convincing some entrepreneurial elite
of the need for a more democratic form of labor relations, by
alienating a whole generation of university students from whose
ranks future franquist bureaucrats would emerge—the continuist
option, advocated by hard-liners in the franquist coalition, became
less desirable and feasible. Social mobilization, in short, heightened
the sense of "crisis" that pervaded the last years of Spanish
authoritarianism.

However, as Linz noted in 1973:

> Despite the "opposition" of so many people and predictions of
> its impending doom since the end of World War II, the regime
> remains stable. Widespread opposition has not endangered it in
> recent years nor have massive force or terror been required to
> sustain it.[33]

The regime's ability to maintain control was all the more astound-
ing in a country like Spain, where over half the electorate had
voted for the leftist Popular Front only 30 years earlier. The explanation for this paradox lies in franquism's consistent ability to
keep the democratic opposition in a state of isolation and fragmentation. The use of selective repression for achieving this task was
a weapon employed by Franco without hesitation.

As Franco's death approached, leaders of the democratic opposition began to realize that the dictator's disappearance would
not involve a vacuum in state power and authority. It is in this context that the democratic opposition began its painful and glacial
move toward the acceptance of *democracia pactada* (a negotiated
democracy) and away from the notion of *ruptura democrática* (a
democratic break). It is clear that by 1975 much of the democratic
opposition, including most of the left, had abandoned the notion
of sweeping away the franquist system. In the words of Santiago
Carrillo, then secretary general of the PCE, violent change "doesn't
make sense where the security forces dispose of sophisticated
weapons and where the memory of the Civil War is a powerful dis-
incentive to political violence."[34]

Thus, on the eve of the dictator's death there were many social forces opposing authoritarian rule. However, as suggested by
the mysterious lack of mass mobilization in the months immediately preceding and following the death of Franco, these forces
lacked the type of coordination necessary to topple Spanish
authoritarianism.

International Pressure and
Domestic Political Change

It has also been argued that the Spanish transition to
democracy was part of a southern European wave of democratization, initiated by the Greek and Portuguese events of 1974. Moreover, it is common to encounter assertions that authoritarian rule
in democratic Western Europe was an anomaly whose end was
bound to come. To what extent can it be argued that pressures from
the international system were instrumental in Spain's regime
change? How did the international environment condition the Spanish transition?

In order to answer these questions it is necessary to review
briefly Spain's foreign relations since the end of World War II. This
overview will demonstrate that leaders in franquist and postfranquist Spain were well aware of the international context in
which they operated. At the same time, there is evidence that the
international environment provided Spanish elites with considerable room to maneuver.

The end of World War II and the defeat of the Axis powers
marked the beginning of an international ostracism few observers expected franquism to survive. In 1945 the representatives
of the United States, Great Britain, and the Soviet Union jointly
condemned Spain and called on the international community to
sever ties with what was perceived as the only remaining bastion
of European fascism. In 1946 France, the United States, and Great
Britain called for an economic boycott of Spain, enacted by the
United Nations in December of that year.

Attempts by the international community to crush franquism
through external pressure initiated a pattern, repeated frequently
over the next 40 years, in which foreign pressure was converted
into political capital by the authoritarian regime. The boycott initiated by the United Nations united the Spanish people and the

chief of state and prompted the first series of massive rallies in the Plaza de Oriente, featuring a classic franquist display of xenophobia. From that point forward, Spanish responsiveness to foreign pressure can best be understood by Carrero Blanco's dictum that Spain "must not do anything which might appear directly or indirectly dictated by the exterior."[35]

Franco survived the years of ostracism in the 1940s by following an autarchic economic policy (favored by the Falange) that, while increasingly draining Spain of its foreign reserves and slowing its economic recovery, provided the dictator the space within which to consolidate his control over the country. The isolation that Franco successfully portrayed as "imposed" on Spain by an unsympathetic West was therefore not totally unwelcome by his regime.

With the onset of the cold war, Spain's status as a fascist holdout began to wane, in comparison to its value as an anticommunist ally. When the General Assembly of the United Nations voted to admit franquist Spain in December 1955, the regime experienced its "decisive moment of consolidation."[36] The UN reversal was of tremendous symbolic importance for the regime, and it caused disarray and shock among Spain's exiled opposition, which had counted on international pressure to topple franquism.

The 1950s witnessed one victory after another for the regime in the international arena. In the context of the cold war, the United States took the lead in reintroducing Spain into the international community. In 1953 Spain signed an economic and military pact with the United States and a Concordat with the Vatican, gaining the seal of approval from, respectively, the leading political economic and religious forces in the world. In 1955 Spain officially entered the United Nations and in 1958, the International Monetary Fund and the World Bank. In that same year U.S. Secretary of State John Foster Dulles visited the major U.S. Air Force base outside of Madrid and told the Spanish people: "This [base] is the symbol of the close relations between our two countries and proof of our resolve to defend jointly our independence and western civilization against the threat of materialistic despotism and atheism."[37] By 1960 Spain's isolation was virtually ended. In 1962 Spanish Foreign Minister Castiella felt confident enough to solicit Spain's entry into the European Economic Community. While the effort failed, Castiella found considerable support for franquist Spain from European conservatives and liberals.

U.S. aid to Spain represented a modest financial sum, and mostly took the form of loans and credits for agricultural imports. However, this infusion of capital was crucial for an economy that by the late 1950s was on the verge of bankruptcy. The change from autarchy to liberal capitalist development would have been much less likely without the U.S. initiative.

More important was the inflow of foreign investment capital in the decade of the economic "miracle." Between 1960 and 1970 the amount of foreign captial rose from 9 billion to 66 billion pesetas, or about 10 percent of Spain's gross investment in fixed capital.[38] However, despite the increasing dependence of Spain's economy on Western capitalist investment, Franco often appeared to conduct his domestic policies with impunity. Franco confirmed the death sentence of Communist leader Julián Grimau García in 1963, after massive protests from European governments. The sentence, carried out by the particularly repulsive method of the *garrote vil* (a form of slow strangulation), lost Spain a great deal of its hard-won international respectability. Nevertheless, the political impact was minimal: Only two weeks after a pair of suspected communists were executed, the United States and Spain renewed an important five-year military and economic pact.

Franco refused to curtail these acts of repression despite the fact that they obstructed efforts by his foreign minister to gain Spain's entry into the EEC. In 1964 the EEC's Birkelbach Report on Spain made it clear that democratization was a requisite for EEC entry. It was not until March 1970 that Spain was able to sign a preferential trade agreement with the EEC. The agreement lowered EEC industrial and agricultural tariffs and reduced Spain's import barriers.

By 1970 it was clear that Spain enjoyed a wide range of foreign relations. Spain's relations with the United States, by far the most important country in economic and military terms, were excellent. On August 6, 1970, Spain and the United States renewed their military and economic accord, giving the authoritarian regime $20 million in rent for military bases and $125 million in weapons credits. President Nixon's trip to Spain in October of that year underscored the solidity of U.S.-Spanish relations.

In general, Spanish-European relations were worse than Spanish-U.S. relations. However, even traditionally hostile France increased its economic and military coordination with franquist Spain. De Gaulle courted franquist Spain as part of his plan for a

neutral and independent Mediterranean, and this interest culminated in a visit to Madrid. West Germany remained more hostile
to Spanish authoritarianism, but in 1970 Foreign Minister Walter
Scheel visited Spain. A rather surpising fact is that Spain maintained relations with a number of East European countries. In January 1970, Spain's foreign minister met with his Soviet counterpart
for the first time since the civil war.

To some extent, this thaw in Spain's relations with the exterior
reflected the undeniable fact, circa 1970, that Spanish authoritarianism was an entrenched political system that could not be toppled through international pressure. After the United States broke
the ice in the 1950s, most other nations followed suit with vary-
ing speed. An additional reason for the numerous policy successes
in 1970 was the hope that the naming of Juan Carlos as Franco's
successor and the cabinet shift of 1969 had paved the way for a
slow democratic evolution of franquism. While informed observers
interpreted these events with much greater skepticism, the international community seemed willing to bank on democratic transition after Franco's death.

Nevertheless, in late 1970 the Burgos trial once again demonstrated that while Franco knew how to take advantage of international relations, he had no intention of allowing international opinion to impinge on his domestic political behavior. The nine death
sentences and over 500 years of imprisonment handed down by
a military tribunal to 16 youths accused of being Basque terrorists
outraged international public opinion. Anti-Spanish violence in
many European capitals, and the symbolic decision by six European countries to ban the annual live transmission of the Christmas
Mass from Avila, Spain, only served to convince rightist Spanish
leaders that they were again victims of an international conspiracy.
On December 16 the regime reverted to the use of a proven
weapon: Huge rallies were staged in every major city to denounce
foreign intervention in Spanish affairs.

A similar cycle of events occurred as late as Septemeber 1975.
In response to a wave of terrorist atacks, the government cracked
down and decreed a harsh law on terrorism, giving police virtually unlimited powers. As a result of this law, five suspected terrorists were arrested and executed and six more were sentenced
to life imprisonment. The European reaction was immediate: All
EEC ambassadors were withdrawn from Spain, the Council of Europe and the EEC Commission issued statements demanding am-

nesty, and trade talks were broken off. Again, the aging dictator was able to rally an enormous crowd in the Plaza de Oriente, just as he had almost 40 years earlier, and the end result was a strengthening of the hardliners within the government.

To summarize, it is hard to conclude that franquist politicians were seriously constrained by foreign policy concerns. In fact, the history of franquist foreign relations shows a series of unexpected victories that overshadow the periodic setbacks. In the context of the cold war, an authoritarian regime, which might otherwise have been more isolated, enjoyed considerable autonomy. The United States under Truman, Eisenhower, and Kennedy, Germany under Adenauer, and France under de Gaulle all came to accept the presence of a strong, stable, anticommunist authoritarian regime. By the time East-West relations began to thaw, and in the context of détente, Spain was already fully integrated into the capitalist West and enjoyed normal diplomatic relations with a wide range of nations. If the EEC continued to prevent Spain's entry into the Common Market for what were, ostensibly, political reasons, EEC citizens nevertheless flocked to Spain's beaches in droves and consumed Spanish exports with fervor.

As a final consideration, it is important to turn away from an analysis of "direct pressure" in order to look at the international context from a more symbolic perspective. It can be argued that the international system was of greater importance for the Spanish transition, culturally and intellectually, for a younger generation of Spaniards. The flip side of Spanish xenophobia and ultranationalism was a deeply rooted resentment over being excluded from a more developed Europe. The famous tourist slogan of the 1960s, "Spain is Different," had a distinct pejorative undercurrent to it that reflected a national inferiority complex. The desire for integration into Europe, the essence of which was captured by the widely used term *homologación,* increasingly permeated Spain's ruling elite. This *Europeismo* became an almost mythical aspiration for large sectors of the Spanish political elite. In interviews with franquist elites, *Europeismo* was often mentioned. In the words of one top-ranking official in Adolfo Suárez's first government:

> International factors were influential, not at all in terms of external pressures, but rather in terms of the faith in "Europe" shared by the political class. People, rather naively, came to believe that once democracy was achieved we would immediately

become a member of "Europe." The myth of Europe was an indirect but undeniable influence in the transition.[39]

International events in the years preceding the transition were also important to the extent that they served as lessons or reminders to Spanish political elites, both within and in opposition to the franquist regime. Throughout the franquist regime, international political events received more extensive coverage than domestic affairs. For the Spanish transition, the events in Greece and Portugal in 1974 were of primary symbolic importance. In the latter case, the coup of April 25, 1974, and the subsequent and chaotic dismantling of Portuguese authoritarianism, could not help but leave its mark on Spanish politics. In the months following the Portuguese coup, there was a counterattack by right-wing hardliners within the franquist regime (known as the *Gironazo*) that effectively sunk President Arias's "Spirit of February 12 Reform" (discussed in Chapter 3). At the same time, the democratic left opted for a more intransigent and confrontational strategy, temporarily confident that it could replicate the events of nearby Portugal.

The events in Greece were also the cause of great concern for a majority of franquists and opposition members, especially those favoring a monarchical solution to the Spanish regime crisis. It will be recalled that the Spanish monarchy, in the person of Juan Carlos, was seen by a wide range of regime forces as the ultimate "guarantor" of the franquist system. His elimination from the political scene after Franco's death would have meant the disappearance of a key source of security for the great majority of franquists, and the Greek events could not help but evoke such fears.

Conclusion

Each of the three approaches in this chapter highlights a challenge to authoritarian rule in the twilight of franquism. The social changes and expectations resulting from rapid economic growth; the rising levels of mass opposition manifest in the Spanish universities, the working class, and the church; and the widespread desire for Spain's integration into Europe all contributed to the erosion of the legitimacy of Spanish authoritarianism.

However, while these factors helped to erode the franquist regime's popular support and create a situation of political crisis, they did not directly work in favor of any one solution to the crisis. Each of these factors discussed in this chapter was a double-edged sword. In the discussion of economic development, it became clear that the political consequences of the "economic miracle" and of the subsequent recession were extremely complex. If the "miracle" had increased expectations, it had also earned the franquist regime a great deal of passive allegiance and had made many Spaniards wary of appeals for political change. Moreover, if economic growth and the internationalizaton of capital in Spain had created new interests favoring European integration, it had simultaneously exacerbated other problems (for example, regionalism) and had fostered interests for whom democratization might prove extremely threatening.

When discussing mass pressure, it was acknowledged that the regime was subject to increasing pressure from below. The working-class struggle, student dissent, and the opposition from the Catholic Church were all arenas for such challenges. But franquism was always able to maintain order and control the streets, even if such control was often costly in human terms. The ability of Spanish authoritarianism to obstruct the development of links between these various centers of democratic pressure, the exceptionally difficult conditions within with Spanish opposition leaders were forced to operate, and the sheer repression they faced best explain the inability of mass pressure to determine the course of politics in the last years of the franquist regime.

Lastly, it has been argued that the international environment did not significantly constrain franquist leaders in the latter years of the dictator's life. When keeping the overall success of franquist foreign policy in perspective, the occasional international ostracism and pressure become fairly insignificant. Symbolically, however, the lure of unification with Western Europe, and the encouraging (as well as frightening) events in other southern European countries, had a considerable impact on political elites.

After 1973, the franquist regime experienced a serious crisis. The factors examined in this chapter all contributed to the *intensity* of this crisis, but they were not responsible for its genesis, nor its eventual resolution. The crisis was, by and large, *internal and political.* It revolved around the inability of the regime's leadership to encounter a political solution to the succession problem. This inability can only be understood in the context of the political struggles taking place between the franquist coalition forces. It was the struggle among these regime *familias* that eventually gave rise to a succession of attempted resolutions to the crisis. Chapter 3 presents an overview of these forces and the power struggle between them. To understand why some attempted solutions failed, and why parliamentary democracy was successful, it is necessary to focus the analysis on the internal politics of franquism and, ultimately, leadership and political strategy. These factors are discussed in detail in the next two chapters.

Notes

1. Jorge de Esteban and Luis López Guerra, *La crisis del estado franquista* (Barcelona: Labor, 1977), p. 2.

2. Edward Malefakis, "Spain and its Francoist Heritage," in John H. Herz, ed., *From Dictatorship to Democracy: Coping with the Legacies of Authoritarianism and Totalitarianism* (Westport, Conn.: Greenwood Press, 1983), p. 217.

3. The Sociedad Sacerdotal de la Santa Cruz (Opus Dei) is a secular institute of the Roman Catholic Church. This worldwide lay organization is centered in Rome, with branches in over 70 countries. In Spain, Opus Dei was associated with a politically conservative and economically liberal group of technocrats who became especially prominent in the spheres of government, education (especially the universities), and business.

4. Sima Lieberman, *The Contemporary Spanish Economy: An Historical Perspective* (London: Allen and Unwin, 1982), pp. 212 and 214.

5. Ibid., p. 258.

6. The GINI index, a measure of income distribution in which 0 equals perfect equality and 1 perfect inequality, was .3778 in 1964; .4461 in 1967; and .487 in 1974. The trend for salaries showed a similar increase in inequality. In addition, some economists have argued that the working classes as a whole lost ground during the 1960s. See Roberto Carballo, "Salarios," in Roberto Carballo et al, *Crecimiento económico y crisis estructural en España, 1959-1980* (Madrid: Akal, 1981), pp. 269-70. Alison Wright concludes that "between 1960 and 1970 there was hardly any change in the distribution of income." See Alison Wright, *Economía Española (1959-1976)* (Zaragoza: Ediciones Heraldo de Aragón, 1980), p. 142. Yet another view is Enrique Uriel, "La teoría de la información y mediación de la distribución de la renta," *Anales de Economía,* July-September 1974, p. 54.

7. For an example of each approach, see Malefakis, p. 220; Nicos Poulantzas, *The Crisis of the Dictatorships* (New York: Verso Editions, 1976); and James R. Kurth, "The Political Consequences of the Product Cycle: Industrial History and Political Outcomes," *International Organization* 3, no.1 (Winter 1979):30.

8. See, for example, Julio Rodríguez Aramberri, "The Political Transformation in Spain: An Interpretation," in Ralph Miliband and John Saville, eds., *The Socialist Register, 1979* (London: Merlin Press, 1979), p. 76.

9. Pedro Schwartz, "Politics First—The Economy After Franco," *Government and Opposition* 1, no.11 (Winter 1976), pp. 96-97.

10. In addition to Poulantzas, see José Acosta Sánchez, *Crísis del franquismo y crísis del imperialismo* (Barcelona: Anagrama, 1976), pp. 56 ff.

11. See José María Maravall, "Transición a la democracia, alineamientos políticos y elecciones en España," *Sistema,* No.36 (May 1980), p. 69, and Aramberri.

12. Robert Moss, "The Blocked Society," *European Review* 24, no.1 (Winter 1973-74):4.

13. M. Gómez Reino et al, "Sociológia Política," in Fundación FOESSA, *Estudios sociólogicos sobres la situación social de España, 1975* (Madrid: Euramérica, 1975), p. 1146.

14. Rafael López Pintor, "Transition Toward Democracy in Spain: Opinion Mood and Elite Behavior," presented at a conference on "Prospects for Democracy: Transitions from Authoritarian Rule in Latin America and Latin Europe," October 12-14, 1980 (Washington, D.C.: Woodrow Wilson International Center for Scholars, 1980), p. 12.

15. For example, see de Esteban and López Guerra, p. 67; and Guy Hermet, "Spain Under Franco: The Changing Nature of an Authoritarian Regime," *European Journal of Political Research* 4 (1976): 324-25.

16. John Cloverdale, *The Political Transformation of Spain After Franco* (New York: Praeger, 1979), p. 4.

17. José María Maravall, *La política de la transición, 1975-1980* (Madrid: Taurus, 1981), pp. 17-31.

18. Maravall, "Transición a la democracia...," pp.76-77.

19. Aramberri, p. 178.

20. Maravall, "Transición a la democracia," p. 271.

21. José María Maravall, "Transitions to Democracy, Political Alignments and Elections in Spain," presented at a conference on "Prospects for Democracy: Transitions from Authoritarian Rule in Latin America and Latin Europe," October 12-14, 1980 (Washington, D.C.: Woodrow Wilson Center for International Scholars, 1980), p. 14.

22. On the significance of this generation, see the provacative work by Pablo Lizcano, *La generación del 56: La universidad contra Franco* (Barcelona: Grijalbo, 1981).

23. José María Maravall, "Students and Politics in Contemporary Spain," *Government and Opposition* 2 (Spring 1976):161-62.

24. Ignacio Fernández de Castro, *De las Cortes de Cádiz al Posfranquismo, 1957-1980* Vol. 2 (Barcelona: El Viejo Topo, 1981), p. 400.

25. The JD had been formed in the summer of 1974 by a number of political groups, largely under the aegis of the PCE. The PSOE and a number of other groups opposed to the PCE's role in the JD refused to participate and instead formed the CD in the spring of 1975. Thus there were two principal opposition organizations revolving around the PSOE and the PCE. However, even these two organizations excluded a considerable number of (especially regionalist) political groups. A good discussion of these organizations is found in Aramberri, p. 181.

26. "Análisis de coyuntura: Dos projectos del gobierno, dos tácticas de la izquierda," *Zona Abierta* 11 (1977):5.

27. Aramberri, p. 177.

28. López Pintor, p. 15.

29. Joaquín Romero Maura, "The Spanish Political System on the Eve of Spain's Probable Entry Into the EEC," unpublished manuscript, 1979.

30. *Signos,* June 12, 1965, cited in José Antonio Biescas and Manuel Tuñón de Lara, *España bajo la dictadura franquista (1969-1975)* (Barcelona: Labor, 1980).

31. *Signos,* May 14, 1966, cited in ibid.

32. A 1970 survey of 15,156 Spanish priests, conducted by the Episcopal de Clero, showed a marked preference for moderate left political ideologies, although it also documented the presence of compounding generational and ideological cleavages. See de Esteban and López Guerra, p. 62.

33. Juan J. Linz, "Opposition in and Under an Authoritarian Regime: The Case of Spain," in Robert A. Dahl, ed., *Regimes and Oppositions* (New Haven, Conn.: Yale University Press, 1973), p. 174.

34. Moss, p. 6.

35. Laureano López Rodó, *La larga marcha hacia la monarquía,* 7th ed. (Barcelona: Plaza and Janes, 1979), p. 91. The *integralista* movement, which saw Spain as the last stronghold of Catholicism in an increasingly heretical Europe, has a long tradition dating back at least as far as the Inquisition.

36. Ibid., p. 142.

37. Quoted in Fernández de Castro, p. 315.

38. Lieberman, p. 245.

39. Interview on March 30, 1982.

3 THE POLITICAL CRISIS OF THE FRANQUIST REGIME

The succession, the transition, the agreements and disputes, appear to be a family affair, an extensive family of "electives" and of representatives by birthright, leaders of groups and heads of tendencies within the National Movement.

The Franquist Families

There is surprisingly little published research on the politics of the franquist regime. This neglect goes hand in hand with a tendency to view Spanish authoritarianism as a monolithic dictatorship dominating society, or, as Dionisio Ridruejo put it, a political desert. The common interests that unite the participants in authoritarian coalitions have usually been the focus of scholarly studies, to the virtual exclusion of the strains that pit one regime group against another.

Juan Linz's seminal research on franquism was instrumental in calling attention to the "limited pluralistic" characteristics of authoritarian regimes.[2] He stressed the intraregime struggles between the *familias* of franquism and noted Franco's success in maintaining a balance among them. Authoritarian coalitions are sustained by what Edward Feit has called "cohesion without consensus." "It is a cohesion that rests on the fear among influentials in the different groups, that if they break the uneasy coalition, they will not share in the resources that are distributed, such as wealth, power and status."[3] Regime *familias* remain weak vis-à-vis the dictator (or junta, as the case may be). In franquist Spain, *familias* finding themselves at the pinnacle of their influence were suddenly purged from power. The ability of the dictator to subjugate them was based on his success in preventing the formation of organizational links (of a political nature) among members, or between members and masses.

The resulting diffuseness of regime groups constitutes a nightmare for scholars interested in assessing the relative strength of various *familias* and their influence on political outcomes. Whereas in most parliamentary democracies one can study concrete organizations and activities by their members (as well as patterns of support for these groups—through campaign donations, and so on), in franquist Spain observers study the behavior of individuals (*personalidades*) and cliques (*grupúsculos*). Rather than benefiting from more or less coherent ideologies, expressed via published party programs, the researcher must be satisfied with vague statements and political intrigues. Most seriously, it is especially difficult to determine which families represent specific political and economic interests.

Despite these obstacles, this chapter attempts to outline the major *familias* of the regime with the focus of discussion on the last period of franquism (approximately 1969-75), after the succession of Juan Carlos had been decided.

The National Movement

The history of the National Movement (MN) begins with the Falange's failure to achieve hegemony within the franquist coalition.[4] The MN was created after Franco's 1937 Decree of Unification fused a number of disparate political groups into what Linz has appropriately called "an anti-party party."[5] Within the MN, the Falangists (especially the original members, known as *camisas viejas*, or old shirts) waged a protracted but ultimately unsuccessful struggle to gain control of the organization, and to channel the course of politics in a Falangist direction. By the end of the franquist regime, the MN had become a bureaucratic albatross, and its most prominent members were considered to comprise one of a number of regime *familias*. However, despite the fact that the MN was never allowed to dominate Spanish politics, it was nevertheless granted a special role within the system. The MN is somewhat hard to describe in cut and dried terms since it was "a shapeless, controversial, politically promiscuous institution—the one that offers the best insight into the regime created by Franco."[6]

The MN was officially defined in Article Five of the Organic Law of State as a doctrine, a "consensus" of all Spaniards concerning that doctrine, and an organization. At the heart of the MN were the Fundamental Principles, whose 12 principles and three additional articles were deemed "immutable," and whose permanence was to be guaranteed by the MN's National Council. The National Council became one of the true centers of political power during franquism, both because its 100 members were automatically members of the Cortes (forming a type of upper chamber) and because 40 of its members were directly appointed by Franco and were thus considered to be *the* elite of the regime. The head of the MN was also the head of state and government (Franco, for all practical purposes), although a separate secretary-general (with cabinet status for much of the regime's history) existed.

The MN performed several important functions. Most importantly, its National Council oversaw the constitutional changes and controlled all forms of political participation. Through its Press, Radio, and Propaganda Office, the MN controlled an enormous chain of media enterprises. In addition, the MN ran the vast syndical structure (the Organización Sindical, OS). These powers translated into a formidable bureaucratic organization and a not inconsiderable patronage network.

The MN bureaucracy became an important career path for those interested in becoming administrators or politicians. It attracted a large number of young Spaniards, from a variety of social backgrounds, and with a considerable range of political inclinations. By and large, the MN provided opportunities for the new *clases medias* to tap into the regime's vast patronage network. In the 1950s and 1960s the MN (together with the church) constituted the major legal arena of political participation for the increasing number of youths with university training.

The University Student Syndicate was an exemplary microcosm of the MN. Until the mid-1940s, the SEU, as the student wing of the Falange, was a militant organization that called for the nationalization of industry, agrarian reform, and the separation of church and state. The SEU was occasionally involved in violent confrontations with the franquist regime, opposing the increasing traditionalism and clericalism of the government. Eventually, however, the SEU (like the Falange as a whole), was coopted by the regime, becoming a compulsory student syndicate whose leaders were selected by the government. In the turbulent atmosphere of the university system, the SEU was controlled, and occasionally repressed, by the government. The organization did, however, enjoy some degree of autonomy. Challenged by the growing illegal democratic opposition, and not completely detached from its Falangist heritage, the SEU became a forum for discussion and exchange of a surprisingly wide range of political views. It was the *generación del 1956*, a term used to describe the first generation of university students that had not experienced the civil war, that attempted to breathe life into the SEU. Under the leadership of Ortí Bordas (1962-63) and Martín Villa (1963-64), both future collaborators with Adolfo Suárez during the democratic transition, the SEU underwent a partial internal liberalization. Eventually, however, the government disbanded the organization, fearing its increased politicization.

The history of the National Movement is also a history of a bureaucratic organization struggling for its autonomy and for access to political power. Beginning with the rise of the Opus Dei technocrats in the late 1950s, the MN came to covet jealously its privileged position within the regime. As the Opus Deistas began to consolidate their positions within the cabinet, as well as their role in Spain's universities and business elite, the MN, especially (but by no means exclusively) the *camisas viejas* of the organization, became the Opus Dei's fiercest rival for power and its most bitter enemy. The struggle against the Opus Dei exacerbated the generational gap within the MN and led to the formation of at least two major camps within the organization.

On the one hand, the hard-liners within the MN sought to counter the Opus Dei by steering franquism away from the "deviations" of the liberal-technocratic Opus Deistas. Fervent nationalists and ardent franquists, this group of aging war veterans became known as the "bunker" because of their intransigent and entrenched political positions. Girón, head of the Spanish Civil War Veterans, and Piñar, head of Fuerza Nueva, were the two most prominent leaders of the bunker. In the later years of franquism, this group became increasingly isolated but remained remarkably powerful due to their presence in such institutions as the Council of the Realm, the National Council, and the Syndical Organization hierarchy. On the other hand, there emerged a tendency among younger generations within the MN, which was articulated in a number of concrete political orientations, including populism, quasi-social democracy, Gaullism, and Mexican-style democracy. These political orientations blurred into one another, and the membership of such political groups often overlapped. It is from these overlapping currents within the MN that a number of key regime reforms emerged in the 1960s. For example, in 1964 a plan to allow poliltical associations within the MN was proposed by some of the more progressive members, with the goal of containing all political activity within the MN. Likewise, the greater press freedom in the late 1960s came from within the MN.[7]

The common denominator of these tendencies was a recognition of the need to revive the MN, if only to counter the influence of the Opus Dei. The naming of Juan Carlos as Franco's successor was viewed initially as a victory for the Opus Dei and a setback for the MN, traditionally more hostile to the monarchy. However, many younger MN members, especially those belonging to the prince's generation, saw a need to secure a place for the MN in the monarchy of the future. These reformists saw their efforts as a way to wage battle with the Opus Dei and Carrero Blanco. Many of the younger members of the MN, particularly those who had risen through the bureaucracy into positions of importance (but who were too young to have experienced the war), were more concerned about the future ability of franquism (and the MN) to adapt to the imminent regime crisis than about the concrete nature of that adaptation. For many MN bureaucrats, the organization was less of a political party and more of a career path. Thus the MN was a peculiar beast: It contained within it the staunchest franquists as well as the least politically compromised (and therefore most flexible) group of regime bureaucrats.

The Opus Dei

The Opus Dei was a second important *familia* within the franquist regime. If the MN was largely a bureaucratic stronghold, the Opus Dei cultivated its support among the financial aristocracy, the industrial elite, the intellectuals, and the professional classes.

While shrouded in utmost secrecy, in the late 1950s the organization consciously sought to infiltrate the Spanish government, university system, and business elite.

Although there was considerable diversity among politicians linked to the Opus Dei, there were a number of characteristics common to the membership. Perhaps the most important of these was the faith in *desarrollismo* (developmentalism), very much in harmony with the widespread appeal of liberal economic theory in the 1960s. In order to achieve this rapid development, Opus Dei technocrats sought to modernize the Spanish State. Modernization, viewed as a requisite for sustained capitalist economic development, was perceived as a largely technical problem. A related characteristic of the Opus Dei mentality was a confidence in the ability of new technology to solve developmental problems. This *cientifismo* meshed well with the demobilizational and apolitical emphases of Spanish authoritarianism.

The Opus Dei technocrats were loyal franquists. Their liberal economic strategies went hand in hand with a highly authoritarian and elitist view of politics. Carrero Blanco, a key member of Opus Dei and a close collaborator with López Rodó, called himself "a man totally identified with the political work of the *Caudillo*, grounded in the Principles of the MN and the Fundamental Laws of the Realm."[8] Carrero's first government in 1973 launched a fierce attack against political reformers within the regime. The Opus Dei became one of the most active forces opposing the radicalization of the Spanish Catholic Church in the late 1960s and early 1970s. Opus Dei cabinet officials were generally unwilling to tolerate increased levels of political participation or press freedom.

In addition to being the architects of Spain's economic "miracle," the Opus Dei politicians were instrumental in assuring that Juan Carlos would be named as Franco's successor, instead of the legitimate heir to the throne, Don Juan de Borbón (Juan Carlos's father, exiled in Portugal). A major concern of the Opus Deistas was to ensure a smooth and orderly transfer of power after Franco's death.[9] The *operación principe*, whose main architects were López Rodó and Carrero Blanco (both Opus Deistas), was viewed as a way of guaranteeing a reformed but fundamentally authoritarian monarchy after Franco. With Carrero Blanco a certain successor to Franco as head of government (and therefore the "protector" of the franquist legacy), the transition to a monarchy under young Juan Carlos was seen as the safest hedge against any abrupt return to parliamentary democracy.

To summarize, the rise of the Opus Dei technocrats entailed a shift away from Falangism and an an endorsement of bureaucratic-authoritarian capitalism. The Opus Dei's initial rise to power was in part a reaction against certain anachronistic features of Falangist political-economic policy. Most importantly, Opus Dei politicians sought to reverse the autarchic economic policies that were slowly strangling the Spanish economy. In addition, the Opus Deistas rejected many of the "restrictive" social policies advocated by the Falange, namely the regulated wage system and the bulky labor relations edifice. In the economic sphere, at least, the Opus Deistas sought to bring franquist Spain more in line with the advanced capitalist economies of Western Europe.

The Military

It might be expected that in an authoritarian regime resulting from a successful military rebellion, and led by a powerful military general, the armed forces would be the most powerful *familia* in the emerging authoritarian regime. Indeed, if one counts the number of cabinet posts held by members of each *familia*, it is clear that the military enjoyed the greatest presence in franquist governments.

However, rather than emphasizing the military's direct political influence, it is more accurate to stress the military's considerable *autonomy* during franquism. In terms of economic and material wealth, the franquist armed forces clearly suffered under authoritarianism. By 1973 Spain's per capita defense expenditures were only about 20 percent of those in the average NATO country.[10] Compared with other European countries, even Spain's southern European neighbors, Spain dedicated a minuscule portion of its GNP to the armed forces.[11] Franco kept the military poorly equipped and, with few exceptions, he restricted the influence of military leaders to matters of military importance.

Given the history of the Spanish military, Franco's grant of autonomy to the armed forces was prudent. Much of the literature on the Spanish armed forces stresses that Spain's military is best studied as an essentially bureaucratic (rather than political) institution.[12] The Spanish military has traditionally behaved like most bureaucracies: It has cherished its autonomy and has fought to defend its control over rank, promotion, and internal organization. The armed forces were "prepared to repress, even to oppress, if they believe themselves to be in a situation of self-defense—like most other social groups when given half a chance."[13]

The preservation of the military's autonomy has taken on special significance in a country like Spain where the middle classes have traditionally sought employment in the armed forces, rather than in the stagnant private sector. Given the poor pay and absence of prestige associated with the military career, the armed forces placed exaggerated emphasis on security, autonomy, and "order." Contrary to what is commonly assumed, the Spanish armed forces have not viewed their role in society in predominantly political terms. Rather, as Stanley Payne persuasively argues, the military has intervened in politics only when its interests, defined more in terms of societal "order" than in terms of a concrete political orientation, are challenged: "Throughout modern Spanish history, elements of the military have intervened in politics only during periods of uncertain legitimacy or incipient breakdown when the established government seemed unable to govern."[14]

This portrayal of the Spanish armed forces helps to explain the military's peculiar, even counterintuitive, role during the franquist regime. The army's granting of a virtual *carte blanche* to Franco is explainable on two levels. First, the armed forces were more than willing to return to their barracks and hand power to a trustworthy general after "order" had been restored. Second, Franco understood the army and protected its autonomy throughout his regime, never touching the overinflated officers corps. By avoiding any modernization of the Spanish armed forces, Franco avoided a costly drain on Spanish budgets as well as any unpopular reform of the archaic bureaucratic military structures. The sacrosanct (but highly inefficient) principle of seniority promotion was never challenged.

From the very start of his long tenure in power, Franco kept the military apart from politics to the best of his ability. There were instances when he used the military to resolve internal political problems, but Franco took precautions against overinvolving the armed forces. Periodic changes of regional commands, removal of any potential political challengers, the use of promotions and retirements to isolate dissenters, and cooptation of dissident military figures into the government were all employed to this end. Finally, Franco was careful not to entangle the armed forces in any foreign adventure that, like the Portuguese, Greek, or Argentine cases, could have upset the military equilibrium. The dictator's diplomatic handling of the potentially explosive Spanish Sahara crisis is a good example of Franco's desire to avoid international military conflicts. Franco's precipitate withdrawal from its northwest African colony removed Spain from the tricky regional struggle for control of the Sahara.

By 1975 the Spanish armed forces were a largely apolitical bureaucracy, despite the very visible political presence of reactionary *ultras* within the military institution. Many of the rightist generals had been retired, although political change among the younger generation of officers came much slower than in the MN or the church. The inbreeding resulting from the armed forces' self-recruitment system, and the military's general isolation from society, tended to limit the presence of democratizing elements. The key to the military's willingness to tolerate political change (of a democratic or nondemocratic nature) after Franco's death revolved around the abruptness of the change. The military, regardless of the presence of a powerful right wing, would be "unwilling to put the cohesion of the military at risk by involving it in a political adventure," unless the death of Franco was followed by political chaos, mass uprisings, economic disaster, or a visible power vacuum.[15]

The Church

The loss of the church as a loyal authoritarian coalition partner dealt a blow to any hopes for the continuation of authoritarian rule after Franco's death. The result of the church's evolution, from legitimator of franquism to a position of open conflict with the regime, caused a serious polarization within the institution. The increasingly isolated integralist right was typified by the Brotherhood of Spanish Priests, whose members opposed any form of democratic change and whose hierarchy published consistently threatening documents aimed at regime and church reformers. In addition, the Warriors of Christ the King, a rightist Catholic terrorist organization, made its presence known throughout Spain in the last years of Franco's life.

At the same time, many of the church's members, frustrated by the slow pace of change within the institution, opted for participation in a number of leftist organizations. Even among less radical Catholic progressives, there was considerable support for center-leftist parties in the democratic opposition. The two best examples of Catholics who defected from the regime are José María Gil Robles and Joaquín Ruíz Giménez. Gil Robles had led the anti-Republican Catholic right during the Second Republic, and had initially supported Franco's rebellion. Ruíz Giménez was a younger, more progressive Catholic who became a liberal-minded minister of education under Franco. By the 1970s, both had joined the democratic opposition and Ruíz Giménez had founded the influential opposition weekly *Cuadernos Para el Diálogo*.

Within the regime there remained a small but influential group of reformist Catholics who rallied around the study group TACITO. Sharing in common their youth and background in Catholic organizations, the TACITOs favored a gradual transition to a democratic monarchy. Through frequent articles published in the Catholic daily *YA*, TACITO espoused a democratic solution to the regime crisis and argued that a Christian democratic Spain was the best way to avoid the reemergence of the historic problem of the "two Spains." Later, TACITO played an important role in Suárez's Unión de Centro Democrático (UCD).

In summary, the church, like the MN, was an extremely divided *familia*. At the grass-roots level, Spanish Catholics increasingly participated in the democratic opposition. The hierarchy was slower to adopt progressive positions and on the eve of Franco's death remained painfully split on political issues. It is this political division that best explains what some observers have called the "spectator" role played by the church in the years of the democratic transition. Given its internal division and the overall uncertainty regarding Spain's political future, the Catholic Church adopted a wait and see attitude. Together with the military's low profile, the church's abstention from active political activity in the early phases of the transition was a key factor in the emergence of parliamentary democracy in Spain.

The Struggle to Control the Transition

Spain's democratic transition was controlled by members of the authoritarian regime, but Spanish authoritarianism was *not* a monolithic edifice. Only by studying the constant tension between franquist *familias*, as well as the intra-*familia* political struggles, is it possible to understand how a strategy for democratization triumphed after Franco's death.

All franquist governments contained members from each of the *familias*, consistent with Franco's desire to reward all members of the authoritarian coalition with cabinet posts. Shifts in the relative political influence of the *familias* were largely a function of small increases in the number of cabinet posts (or acquisition of more prestigious posts) held by *familia* members. Major policy changes during the franquist regime were generally associated with major cabinet shuffles, such as those of 1957, 1969, and 1973. For example, the 1957 cabinet shift was the first major victory for the Opus Dei technocrats at the expense of the hard-line Falangists and liberal Catholics. This change spelled the end of plans to institutionalize the regime according to Falangist doctrine. Franco retained some MN members in his cabinet, but favored less politicized (that is, less Falangist) members. The Opus Dei's rise to power began a fierce political rivalry between the Opus Dei technocrats and the bureaucrats of the National Movement, centering around a number of ideological, political, and personal disputes, but especially the succession question. In the 1960s the MN suffered a series of political defeats at the hands of the Opus Dei technocrats, giving rise to an internal renovation within the National Movement and creating a split between Falangists and more politically promiscuous bureaucrats.

In the 1960s the various regime groups jockeyed for influence over Franco's choice for his successor. Since 1947 Spain had been a monarchy without a monarch. In addition to those favoring one of at least three possible candidates for the throne, there were groups supporting presidentialist solutions. As far as the major regime *familias* were concerned, the most important struggle took place between the MN and the Opus Dei. Many MN members, notably hard-line Falangists, were opposed to the restoration of the monarchy, especially in the person of the legitimate heir, Don Juan de Borbón. In its opposition to the liberal Don Juan, the MN had support from many hard-liners in the military and the church, as well as conservatives within the Opus Dei. A number of Opus Deistas advocated a restoration, but in the person of Juan Carlos. Juan Carlos, it was widely (but mistakenly) believed, would lack the experience and confidence to adopt an antifranquist political stance similar to his father's. Having been raised in Spain under the watchful eye of Franco and the dictator's most trusted supporters, Juan Carlos was considered to be an ideal figurehead for a future Spanish authoritarian regime.

The Opus Dei had visions of a conservative monarchy, in which Juan Carlos would be bound by the Fundamental Principles of the MN and in which a strong president, Carrero Blanco, would protect the franquist legacy. It was also hoped that by deciding on the tandem of Juan Carlos and Carrero, and thereby definitively ruling out other options, Franco would finally end his uncertain balancing act among *familias* and cast his lot definitively with the Opus Deistas. However, until 1969 the Opus Dei plan gained little support from the dicator. In 1962 Franco dealt a temporary blow to the Opus Dei, evidently fearing it had become too powerful. A militant Falangist and ardent antimonarchist was appointed vice-president. The cabinet shuffle of 1965 weakened the Opus Dei and cast further doubt upon the viability of the Opus Dei plan. Nevertheless, Franco's decision in 1969 to designate Juan Carlos as his successor marked a significant defeat for the Falangist sector of the MN. In retrospect, the dictator's selection of Juan Carlos turned out to be the choice that could satisfy most members of the franquist coalition. Despite the inevitable doubts surrounding Juan Carlos's experience and skill, all but the hard-liners of the MN came to accept Franco's choice. Had Don Juan or any other conceivable contender been selected, a serious division among regime ranks would likely have resulted.

Juan Carlos's appointment turned attention away from the succession issue and toward the problem of the exact nature of the monarchy after Franco's death. Unlike his father, Juan Carlos's political proclivities were unknown. In retrospect, this lack of political definition greatly facilitated the prince's ability to gain support from a wide range of regime (and even antifranquist) forces. His rearing in Spain under the thumb of Franco (who treated Juan Carlos as family), his unquestioning participation in franquist fanfare (especially his taking of an oath of loyalty to uphold the franquist Fundamental Principles), his constant proximity to regime conservatives, and the evident support he received from the Opus Dei—all seemed to indicate the prince might chart a conservative course after Franco's death. On the other hand, his youth, his peculiar family history (the inauspicious record of his Bourbon ancestors and those of his Greek wife), as well as the obvious need for Juan Carlos to establish new sources of legitimacy for a post-Franco crown seemed to provide some hope for reformists within and outside of the regime. In short, the successor had been chosen and was widely supported by the franquist *familias*. "Succession to what?" remained an open question, however, and was still a bone of contention for franquist coalition partners.

In the summer of 1969 franquism's most shocking financial scandal, the MATESA affair, exploded, implicating a number of top Opus Dei politicians.[16] The MN bureaucrats exploited the scandal with zeal, denouncing it as evidence of the corruption of the Opus Dei technocrats. Fraga Iribarne, minister of information and tourism, saw to it that the details of the affair were leaked to the press and widely disseminated. In true franquist form, the resulting cabinet shift of October 1969 punished the MN and removed only the most flagrant Opus Dei offenders. Five of the six economics ministries went to the Opus, as well as the Ministry of Tourism and Information (traditionally an MN stronghold) and the Ministry of Foreign Affairs. The cabinet shift was one of the most dramatic in the history of the franquist regime, and it resulted in what many observers called the most homogeneous technocratic cabinet in history. The outcome was a government of younger, more technocratic, conservative Opus Deistas, with Carrero as vice-president of the government. Indeed, it appeared that Franco had finally decided to put his eggs in the basket of the Opus Dei and the *operación príncipe*.

A wave of terrorism in 1970-72 led to the first in a series of attacks by the hard-liners within the army and the MN. The Burgos trial of December 1970 revealed a serious division within the regime between the hard-liners in the MN and military and the government, which, ironically, was assailed for being "soft" on terrorism. The shameful military trial in which nine accused Basque terrorists were summarily sentenced to death pleased the hard-liners. Franco's decision to commute the death sentences shortly before Christmas of 1970 was a sign of his continued support for Carrero Blanco, who preferred life terms. The scars created by Burgos ran deep, however, and the hard-liners gained momentum as reformists within the regime became increasingly uneasy.

In 1971 and 1972, terrorism and labor-related strikes, concentrated in the Basque Country, fueled further attacks by the regime right against the Opus Dei-dominated government. Hardliners within the armed forces urged Franco to appoint a strongman as president of the government, since they began to doubt the ability of the aging dictator to rule for much longer.

Franco's decision to step down as president and to appoint Carrero Blanco in his place (June 8, 1973) was viewed as a concession to the hard-liners. Carrero Blanco was on the extreme right of the Opus Dei and was regarded as a proponent of law and order and, due to his career in the Navy, a friend of the armed forces. His first government, aimed at pleasing hard-liners and demonstrating to the democratic opposition the government's resolve to meet all challenges with force, was a strict law and order team. The presence of hard-liners in the cabinet was a signal that the *mano dura* (iron-fisted) approach to opposition and mass pressure would be employed. A curious feature of the government was the apparent demotion of top Opus Deistas. Carrero began to surround himself with politicans who were first and foremost, loyal to Franco, distancing himself from the more "liberal" Opus Deistas.

Whether Carrero Blanco could have consolidated his power after Franco's death is an open question. More than likely, he would have attempted to. The evidence suggests that Carrero Blanco saw himself as the guardian of franquism.[17] It is safe to venture that Carrero never would have tolerated a political transformation as profound as that which took place after Franco's death. Juan Carlos would have had a much more difficult time replacing Carrero, a powerful and respected Navy admiral, than was the case when he fired Arias in 1976.

Carrero Blanco's assassination in downtown Madrid on December 20, 1973, caused disarray among the franquist political class. As a result, during the two remaining years of Franco's life, hard-liners were especially sensitive to and suspicious of attempts to reform the franquist system. In addition, regime supporters who might have had faith in the ability of Juan Carlos to create a franquist monarchy now began to accept the inevitability of a more significant form of political change. In a word, if Carrero's presence had added an element of certainty to Spanish politics (even if that sense of certainty was partially illusory), his death provoked an atmosphere of confusion and crisis.

Arias and the February 12 Spirit

On December 29, 1973, Franco appointed Carlos Arias Navarro to replace Carrero Blanco as head of government. Arias occupied the presidency until Franco' death in November 1975, and was subsequently reappointed by Spain's new head of state, King Juan Carlos. Arias was a conservative franquist, belonging to none of the *familias* of the regime, and consequently resented by all of them. His appointment by the bereaved Franco is probably best explained in terms of Arias's personal friendship with the caudillo as well as his proven loyalty. It is also likely that Franco intentionally selected a politician removed from the inter-*familia* struggles and intrigues of the late franquist regime. After a career as Spain's top police official, Arias had become mayor of Madrid and minister of the interior. He was despised by the democratic opposition, who referred to him as "the butcher of Malaga" for his alleged behavior in that Andalusian city during the civil war. In the words of a top cabinet minister:

> [He] conserved, during his entire mandate, a gigantic oil painting of Franco, which hung in front of him, while at his back hung a small photographic portrait of the King. He had been Governor, Director General, Mayor, Minister and President of the Government, all with Franco. He doubted whether it was correct to oversee the reform even then. He was a man of the age when audacious decisions are always hard to take. . . .[18]

Arias, like many regime elites, felt that the franquist system must be adapted to accommodate the future head of state, Juan Carlos. In this sense, he was often described as a somewhat "liberal" franquist politician, insofar as he rejected the bunker's opposition to any mention of political change. In fact, his first government embarked on a timid program of political reform,

presented to the Cortes on February 12, 1974. The program, hence-
forth dubbed "the Spirit of February 12," consisted of three major reforms. First, Arias sought to create a new pseudodemocratic
legitimacy by increasing participation for those who accepted the
franquist regime. This took the form of the so-called *asociaciones*
(an intentional semantic differentiation from the term "parties"),
which could only operate within and under the supervision of the
MN. Falling far short of any acknowledgement of open party competition, this reform was a reiteration of Franco's "organic" view
of politics in which "contrasts of opinions" could be aired within
a single, regime-dominated, movement. While some liberal franquists chose to view this reform as the first genuine step toward
democratization, it is probably more accurate to understand this
measure as another attempt at cosmetic democracy, similar in
many respects to the regime's earlier façade "democratization" of
the Cortes.

Second, Arias proposed to further democratize the Cortes by
enacting a law on political incompatibilities. One of the chief
characteristics of the franquist political system was the exaggerated
political overlap between the Cortes, the government, the
bureaucracy, and local governments. The Cortes, of course, was
designed to be corporatist in composition, and reforms of the late
1960s signified only a slight modification. Adding to this problem
was the traditional acquisition of multiple political positions by
franquist politicians, a tradition that Arias sought to reform. Finally,
the "spirit" reforms attempted to democratize local government.

These timorous proposals, drawn up by the two most liberal
members of Arias's cabinet, were quickly assailed by hard-liners.
In the course of the next six months, Arias showed himself to be
unable and unwilling to confront the regime right and defend the
"spirit." Ironically, Arias's reform attempt was combined with an
increase in the level of repression against all types of political opposition. In part to convince the hard-liners of his franquist colors,
and in part because of his own reluctance about the reform, Arias
lashed out against the left, punishing the Basque country particularly harshly.

Arias's "spirit" reforms failed for a number of reasons. They
provoked a successful counterattack by the bunker, spearheaded
by the flamboyant head of Spain's Civil War Veterans Brotherhood.
Girón's offensive against Arias's "spirit" came only three days after

the fall of the dictatorship in neighboring Portugal, and may have reflected genuine fear among the franquist hard-liners that any attempts to emulate Caetano's reform of Salazarism could bring similar results. The timidity of the reforms failed to rally much support from regime liberals and led the democratic opposition to adopt a more uncompromising stance. More seriously, it was obvious that Arias was personally unwilling and unable to sell his own wares. Incapable of dominating the hard-liners, as Carrero plausibly could have, Arias invariably diluted his reforms so as to render them ineffectual, and he capitulated in response to the most minimal protest. This vacillation was the product of Arias's own personal reticence. Torn between his belief that franquism must be revived if Juan Carlos were to assume Franco's role as chief of state, but fearful that these reforms could spiral out of control, Arias was ultimately responsible for the shipwreck of his own proposals. A final reason for the failure of Arias's "spirit" reforms can be found in Franco's own behavior after he recovered from a serious illness in the fall of 1974. Franco quickly became convinced by the bunker that Arias had been too zealous in his reformism, and too lenient with political opposition. The dictator then pressured Arias into firing his most liberal cabinet member, causing a wave of resignations by liberals throughout the regime elite and the first serious wave of "secession" of regime liberals from the authoritarian regime.[19]

The Spanish press described the politics of the period as a simultaneous braking and acceleration of the reform. Arias was unable to present a reform that could appeal to either the bunker or regime reformists, and the result was a failed reform that only served to exacerbate the crisis of franquism. The contradictions of Arias's attempt to respond to the imminent regime crisis were manifest in the realm of public order, where his government's apparent political impotence provided the rationale for regime opposition to take to the streets. That Arias should have responded to this opposition from below with increasing brutality made it obvious to all that he was unable to encounter a viable political solution to the regime crisis. In the months before Franco's death, the Arias government employed a level of coercion seldom witnessed during the franquist regime.

To summarize, in the late history of the franquist regime, a number of political *familias* existed: a conservative but fundamentally bureaucratic military, with a vocal and visible sector opposing democratization; a group of Opus Dei technocrats favoring an authoritarian monarchy under Juan Carlos and Carrero Blanco; the divided Catholics, split between the democratic opposition, regime reformists, and the regime right; and the amorphous MN, divided between a younger generation of opportunistic reformist bureaucrats and an older generation of Falangist hard-liners.

As Franco's death neared, two major tensions were eroding the coherence of the franquist coalition. First was the inability of any *familia* to gain political hegemony, and the regime's increasing difficulty in maintaining a balance among them. Second, the internal chaos within the franquist political class and the concomitant uncertainty vis-à-vis the near future led to a polarization of regime forces and a higher level of infighting between groups than normally witnessed during franquism. On the one hand, the fearful hard-liners, egged on by the radicalization of the democratic opposition and the rise in terrorist violence, lobbied the government to use its repressive capabilities against these perceived threats. The opposition of the bunker was largely responsible for the failure of President Arias's attempts to implement a mild reform. On the other hand, moderate franquists within the regime, the great mass of franquist *políticos* from a variety of *familias* who were loyal to the dictator (but whose loyalty to him after Franco's death was hardly certain), became increasingly doubtful about the ability of Arias's government to adapt to the crisis.

The Failure of Limited Democratic Reform

The long-awaited death of Francisco Franco evoked surprisingly little opposition activity. The huge crowds waiting hours to bid a final farewell to the deceased dictator were a clear sign that Franco's regime enjoyed considerable support and would not easily collapse with the death of the head of state. The presence of Juan Carlos at the burial of Franco, one day after the young monarch's coronation, symbolized that he was very much part of the franquist regime and could not be expected to liquidate Spanish authoritarianism overnight.

Franco's death occurred at a time of great domestic speculation and worry over the course of politics after Franco. Only weeks before the dictator's death, a prominent liberal cabinet member commented that "the problem with democratization will be to carry it off while avoiding the threat of a totalitarianism of the left or the right, both of which presently loom large on the horizon."[20]

King Juan Carlos's initial declarations and actions as head of state contained a mixture of caution and optimism. In his coronation address, the young monarch stated:

> Our future will be based on a national consensus and accord. . . . A free and modern society requires the participation of all in the decision making forum, in the media, in education, and in the control of the national wealth. To make this project each day more certain and effective should be the task of government and society.[21]

Immediately after Franco's funeral, the king met with José Antonio Girón, head of the rightist Spanish Civil War Veterans Brotherhood, and reportedly assured the aging franquist of his continuing loyalty to the dictator.[22] One day later, Juan Carlos granted a limited pardon, freeing the nine labor leaders jailed in the infamous "process 1001" trial.[23]

One positive sign was Cardinal Enrique y Tarancón's speech during the coronation ceremony. The cardinal argued that "patriotism is compatible with all sincere political systems, however different they may be, always if the common spiritual and material good is the goal of those proposing the system."[24]

Early Obstacles to Crisis Resolution

There were also serious obstacles to the resolution of the crisis. In early December 1975, with many Spaniards sighing relief over the apparent smoothness of the transition from Franco to Juan Carlos, the extent of elite polarization over the future of Spanish politics became more evident and the actions of Juan Carlos more contradictory and ambiguous.

Immediately after the transfer of power, hard-line franquists publicly reiterated their unwillingness to tolerate anything other than a mild reform of the system. This hostility was manifest in their coolness toward the new monarch, and in the incessant pressure placed on President Arias to limit any reform plans.

In the months of January, February, and March 1976, the contradictions of the Arias government were manifested on three levels.
First, the *policies* of the government were a peculiar mixture of reform and immobilism. They reflected the contradictory pressures
from the right and from the expectations raised by the king, which
were widely supported by the population and intelligentsia. On the
one hand, Arias committed himself to the gradual legalization of
several political parties, and the convocation of local elections and
general elections to a new bicameral legislature. On the other hand,
Arias was conspicuously vague with reference to the proposed
legalization of parties. The appointed upper house, which would
represent the bastions of franquist authoritarianism, was to have
powers equal to the elected lower house. The National Movement
would continue to play a dominant role in the proposed system,
and its leader would become president of the government. The
government's behavior often seemed to contradict its democratic
promises. In March 1976 the government arrested many of the opposition's leaders, and in May the government imposed punitive
measures against Spanish periodicals that had become overly
critical.

Second, the *internal division* within Arias's cabinet, between
those advocating such mild reforms and those desiring more profound democratic changes, became increasingly virulent, undermining the cohesiveness of the government. The reformers, often
while abroad, made statements to foreign periodicals that seemed
to contradict the cautious behavior of the government. The president's speeches harped on the achievements of the deceased dictator and vilified the democratic opposition. Arias even censored
the television appearances of his own cabinet members! Encouraged by the rise of Basque terrorism, press criticism, opposition activity, and increasing pressure from his right, the president
moved right and dug in against the demands of liberal cabinet
members. He was aided in this intransigence by an unexpected
ally, Minister of the Interior Fraga Iribarne, who for complex personal reasons, was determined to limit the reform. By early spring,
the split in the Arias government between reformers (including
Areilza, Suárez, and Calvo Sotelo) and hard-liners (including Arias
and Fraga Iribarne) was increasingly apparent. By April, with Arias
refusing to negotiate with the democratic opposition, reform-
minded ministers were talking more or less openly about possible
replacements for Arias.

Third, the most significant resurgence of *mass-level opposition*
since the civil war, during January, February, and March, was met
with intermittent tolerance and brutal police repression, contributing to a spiral of violence and social tension. A tremendous rise in
labor unrest, political demonstrations in favor of amnesty for political prisoners, and cultural acts aimed at criticizing the regime
all contributed to the climate of fear. The political activity reached
its peak in the Basque Country, where it became violent. During
most of the transition period, terrorism enjoyed considerable support from the Basque population, especially as the cycle of violence
between suspected terrorists and security forces spilled over to the
Basque population at large. A steady increase in Basque terrorism,
culminating in early March, turned the region into a virtual war
zone. By March 9, an estimated two-thirds of the Basque population was on strike in protest over police repression in the region.[25]

Despite this increase in civil disorder, it cannot be argued that
this increase threatened the survival of the regime per se, at least
in the short term. The opposition remained weak, divided, and
timid. It had little control over labor unrest and even less control
over events in the Basque Country. Moverover, the prospect of es-
calating violence and repression frightened opposition leaders and
even served to close the gap between frustrated regime reformers
and the moderate democratic opposition. Nevertheless, if the opposition was unable to capitalize on this rise in civil unrest, the increased popular activity did form the context within which an intraregime struggle for leadership of the reform occurred.

The increasing restlessness of the leadership of the armed
forces was an ominous sign. Military leaders warned publicly that
the armed forces would defend the "institutional order," and
warned against toleration of the "enemies of Spain."

The Intervention of Juan Carlos

As the reform dragged on, Juan Carlos began to make his political presence more evident. On May 2, 1976, the monarch made
a speech in which he declared that syndical freedoms "must par-
allel the principles of freedom and representation in the political
sphere." On May 22, Juan Carlos met at the Zarzuela Palace with
his father, Don Juan de Borbón, the legitimate Bourbon heir to the
throne and an avowed antifranquist. There were widespread
rumors that father and son were discussing conditions under which

Juan de Borbón might renounce in favor of his son, thus enhancing the monarchy's legitimacy.

The most startling event was *Newsweek's* April 26 publication of an interview in which Juan Carlos was quoted as describing President Arias as "an absolute disaster." Moreover, the king's office made no denial of the validity of the comment. The impact of the monarch's statement appears to have been twofold. First, it increased demands for a more direct, rapid reform approach. Juan Carlos was urged by many prominent observers to use his wide-ranging powers to bypass the franquist Cortes and impose a reform. Second, the king's statement prompted the bunker to rally its forces against such calls for reform from above. Basque terrorism continued to frighten the franquist right and Cortes President Fernández Miranda's attempt to speed a piece of the reform legislation through the legislature caused widespread resentment among the procuradores. The Cortes president was able to get the measure passed eventually, but only at the price of provoking considerable hostility from the usually passive franquist legislature. There was much talk about a massive boycott during future sessions and the general sense was that a confrontation was near. On May 12 the rightist counterattack gained steam as 126 *procuradores* (members of the Cortes, or parliamentarians) published a document warning the government "to follow most scrupulously the rules of the current legal system."[26]

During the month of May, the major parts of the Arias reform project began to move slowly through the maze of the Spanish legislative system. The month of June 1976 began with a victory for the Arias reform in the Cortes. The Law for Political Associations, a key component of the Arias reform, passed the Cortes with 338 votes in favor, 91 votes against, and 24 abstentions. Before the vote, Adolfo Suárez (secretary-general/minister of the National Movement) gave a well-publicized speech in support of the law, thus gaining his first serious national press coverage. However the atmosphere in the chamber was extremely hostile to the government. References to Franco drew great applause while defenders of the law were often met with mild approval and, at times, total silence.

On June 10 and 11 the Arias reform was suddenly buried. On June 10 the Cortes shocked the nation by sending the Penal Code Reform (a key piece of the Arias reform legislation) back to committee for a "technical study." The Penal Code Reform had already been approved by a Cortes committee loaded with reformers by

Fernández Miranda, but the plenum was skeptical. Facing heavy opposition, and the likelihood of between 150 and 200 votes against the measure, the government decided to postpone a potentially embarrassing confrontation. The setback for the Penal Code Reform was especially serious, because it effectively invalidated the recently approved Law for Political Association. It is hard to determine the precise reasons for the unanticipated defeat, but the Basque Homeland and Liberty Party's (Euzkadi Ta Askatasuna, ETA) assassination of a local MN leader in Vizcaya on the same day of the vote surely contributed to the rejection. Reformers had clearly underestimated the strength and will of the bunker when threatened with extinction. For the opposition, the fiasco in the Cortes and the National Council confirmed the thesis that there could be no negotiation with the Arias government.

Eventually, a new Cortes committee watered down the Penal Code Reform by explicitly (so it seemed at the time) banning the political activity of the Spanish Communist Party. The National Council, for its part, produced its own version of political reform that was far more conservative than the original Arias legislation. According to the National Council, the reform of the Cortes "can only be understood as an evolution of the actual institutions, in order to make them more representative, efficient and effective in the new Spanish monarchy." The councilors demanded assurances that the reform would be carried out according to the franquist Principles of the National Movement although, perhaps paradoxically, the idea of constitutional reform was not opposed. The National Council report called for the use of the term "The July 18 State" (the franquist term) rather than "The Spanish State." Finally, the National Council insisted that the Principles of the National Movement "continue to be the ideological basis of the national political order." Even with these antidemocratic modifications, the report passed only after much opposition from rightist sectors within the National Council.

The Metamorphosis of the Democratic Opposition

While the franquist right was dealing a series of defeats to the reform program of the Arias government, the democratic opposition was slowly moderating its political stance. This change was quite apparent on May 29, when Felipe Gónzalez, the PSOE secretary-general, stated that the Spanish situation was different from postwar Italy or Germany. He stated a willingness to negotiate with bourgeois forces supporting authentic democracy. While González attempted to argue that the PSOE still supported the strategy of a democratic break with authoritarianism, his public statements cast increasing doubt on this contention. The seemingly contradictory or ambiguous statements made by a number of opposition leaders during this period are easily explained. First, the opposition was badly fragmented. There were literally hundreds of political groups, and it was impossible to know the real strength of any of them. Even among the political organizations with serious hopes of surviving the transition period there was logically a great deal of competition and back stabbing. For if it made sense for all democratic forces to be allied in order to achieve a common short-term objective (a democratic transition), all were equally aware that in any future elections there would be a bitter struggle for survival in which allies would quickly become enemies.

The issue of the Communist Party, for example, bitterly divided opposition groups, and often split parties themselves. Personal rivalries, like that between Enrique Tierno Galván of the Popular Socialist Party (Partido Socialista Popular, PSP) and González of the PSOE, also damaged opposition cohesiveness. Some, like the communists, were less willing to accept the idea of political compromise if that compromise involved their exclusion from political life. Others, like the PSOE were willing to bargain with the government, as their leaders' statements increasingly revealed, but only after the government guaranteed basic democratic liberties. Most groups in the opposition continued to demand the legalization of *all* political parties and the formation of a provisional government to oversee the transition. However, the opposition revealed a willingness to negotiate on almost all issues, frustrated only by the intractable behavior of the Arias government. In short, the democratic opposition was making an effort to demonstrate its willingness to negotiate and its ability to abandon maximalist positions. This effort was partially obstructed by the opposition's internal discord, and by the stubbornness of President Arias.

Spain, the Monarchy, and the World

It is important to pay some attention to the international environment in the period following Franco's death. Juan Carlos enjoyed substantial international support after the dictator's death. While no head of state attended Franco's funeral on November 23, 1975, four days later the heads of state of West Germany, France, the United Kingdom, and the vice-president of the United States were in attendance at Juan Carlos's public coronation ceremony. This was a clear sign that the major Western powers were solidly behind the young monarch.

Perhaps the most important element of the international environment was the situation in neighboring Portugal. The Portuguese revolution was entering one of its most radical phases during the delicate transition between Franco and Juan Carlos. Peregrine Worsthorne of the London *Sunday Telegraph* wrote on November 13, 1975, that "the conservative forces from all over Europe will support the Spain of Juan Carlos even more since the lesson of Portugal."[27]

International reactions to Arias's cautious reform plans were generally negative, especially on the part of West European governments. Sweden pressured its travel agents to cancel Spanish tourism bookings in protest over the speech, but Spain felt little direct pressure to democratize more quickly. The United States was especially conciliatory toward the Arias government. Foreign Minister Areilza met Henry Kissinger on January 24 and the U.S. position was spelled out clearly. The U.S. secretary of state advised his Spanish counterpart to resist European pressure, and to implement reform gradually and cautiously. Moreover, Kissinger reportedly warned the Spanish not to call elections until the regime possessed an electoral vehicle with which to retain power.[28]

In early June 1976, Juan Carlos traveled to the United States on an official state visit. Speaking to the U.S. Senate, the king promised to oversee the transition to a democratic monarchy. "The monarchy," in the king's words, "will uphold the principles of democracy, social peace and political stability while at the same time assuring the orderly access to power by the different governmental alternatives, according to the freely expressed wishes of the people."[29] The timing of the king's visit was especially significant. President Arias had proven incapable of implementing a genuine democratic reform, and the monarch had become frustrated with him. By receiving the unconditional backing from the United States, Spain's most trusted and powerful political and economic patron, the king had strengthened himself in preparation for the replacement of Arias and the execution of a far more thorough democratization strategy.

Conclusion

Arias's tenure as president after Franco's death presented a number of paradoxes. Hard-liners successfully employed the regime's institutions to block measures promoted by the head of state, a rare occurrence in authoritarian regimes. The franquist Cortes had approved, by a wide margin, a law legalizing political parties, but had rejected a Penal Code reform that would make the party reform effective.

President Arias's leadership was also contradictory. Arias was caught between the regime reformists and the hard-liners, and when faced with this cross fire the president lacked the resolve to carry through with the reform. In retrospect, it is easy to see that Arias, in addition to lacking the skill and charisma to guide the reform through the Cortes, also lacked the independence from his own past that would have been necessary to make the reform successful. Although confirmed by the king as president after Franco's death, Arias remained Franco's president. Relations between Arias and Juan Carlos were never good but had become especially strained after the *Newsweek* incident. Long periods transpired without contact between the two leaders. Arias infuriated the king by refusing to show him the content of his speeches beforehand.[30] The president was suspicious of all those who enjoyed close relationships with the king, especially Torcuato Fernández Miranda and Areilza. Arias's personal and political links with hard-liners deprived him of the necessary independence. His personal vacillations, his open affection for Franco, his deep hate and distrust of the opposition, his leadership style, and even his language were all characteristic of the old franquist politics. As Areilza noted in his diary in early February 1976, well before the Arias reform had encountered serious difficulties, "the Monarchy cannot be consolidated with an honest and patriotic but vacillating and fearful man who continues to believe that Franco is alive and directing the country from his tomb."[31]

A final paradox of the Arias presidency was that despite the slow moderation of the democratic opposition, there had been virtually no dialogue between government and opposition. If the opposition's demands for a clean democratic break from authoritarian rule had been unrealistic, their new call for a *ruptura pactada* (a negotiated break with authoritarianism) deserved serious consideration from the government. The democratic opposition could not be expected to moderate its position further until the government expressed its willingness to bargain in good faith.

Arias's inability to push his own reform program, his unwillingness to open a dialogue with the opposition, and his government's dependence on repression to quiet mass unrest all placed King Juan Carlos in an uncomfortable situation. After interviewing the Spanish monarch in April 1976, Arnaud de Borchgrave reported that "what worries the King the most is the fact that Arias's policies—or non policies—are polarizing Spanish politics by turning both the right and left against the government."[32] Thus, few were surprised when King Juan Carlos asked for and received Arias's resignation on July 1, 1976.

Notes

1. Ignacio Fernández de Castro, *De las Cortes de Cádiz al Posfranquismo 1957-80* Vol. 2 (Barcelona: El Viejo Topo, 1981). p. 474.

2. Juan J. Linz, "Opposition in and under an Authoritarian Regime: The Case of Spain," in Robert A. Dahl, ed., *Regimes and Oppositions*, (New Haven, Conn. Yale University Press, 1973); and "Spain: An Authoritarian Regime," in Stanley Payne, ed., *Politics and Society in Twentieth Century Spain* (New York: New Viewpoints, 1979).

3. Edward Feit, "The Rule of the Iron Surgeons: Military Government in Spain and Ghana," *Comparative Politics* 1, no. 4 (July 1969): 490.

4. The Falange was a small fascist party during the Second Republic that supported Franco's July 18 uprising. It aspired to become the single party of Spain after the civil war and hoped to bring about a national syndicalist revolution. Franco, a traditional military Catholic, was highly distrustful of the Falange and eventually absorbed it into the National Movement. For two fascinating studies of the Falange, consult Stanley Payne, *Falange: A History of Spanish Fascism* (Stanford, Calif.: Stanford University Press, 1961); and Juan J. Linz, "From Falange to Movimiento-Organización: The Spanish Single Party and the Franco Regime, 1936-1968," in Samuel Huntington and Clement Moore, eds., *Authoritarian Politics in Modern Society* (New York: Basic Books, 1970).

5. Linz, "From Falange to Movimiento-Organización, p. 132.

6. José Amodia, *Franco's Political Legacy From Dictatorship to Façade Democracy* (London: Allen Lane, 1977).

7. See Raymond Carr and Juan Pablo Fusi, *Spain, Dictatorship to Democracy,* 2d ed. (London: Allen and Unwin, 1981), pp. 190-91; and Amodia, p. 150.

8. Fernández de Castro, p. 481.

9. An excellent piece of support for this assertion is Carrero's appeal to Franco to name Juan Carlos as his successor. Carrero is reported to have said to Franco: "I must point out to His Excellency that a heavy weight, that of concern about the future, begins to fall on the immense majority of Spaniards who have complete faith in the Caudillo. They know that while you are alive nothing will happen, but they fear, with reason, what might happen when you are gone. I share that fear." Laureano López Rodó, *La larqa marcha hacia la monarquía,* 7th ed. (Barcelona: Plaza and Janes, 1979), p. 419.

10. Edouard de Blaye, *Franco and the Politics of Spain* (New York: Penguin, 1976), p. 397. Spain spent 1.8 percent of its GNP on defense in 1976, compared with 2.8 percent in West Germany and The Netherlands, 3.1 percent in France, and 7.3 percent in Greece.

11. World Bank, *World Development Report, 1983* (New York: Oxford University Press, 1983), p. 199.

12. Kenneth Medhurst, "The Military and the Prospects for Spanish Democracy," *West European Politics* 1, no. 1 (February 1978): 43; Joaquín Romero Maura, "After Franco, Franquismo? The Armed Forces, The Crown and Democracy," *Government and Opposition III,* no. 1 (Winter 1976): 39-43; Feit, p. 486.

13. Romero Maura, p. 48.

14. Stanley Payne, "The Political Transformation of Spain," *Current History,* No. 431 (1977), p. 166-67.

15. Romero Maura, p. 45; and Robert Moss, "The Blocked Society," *European Review* 24, no. 1 (Winter 1973-74) p. 8.

16. MATESA, a textile conglomerate, was found to have banked a huge sum of government financial aid, allocated for the purpose of export credits and foreign investment. The scandal led to the arrest of top MATESA officials, and three Opus Dei ministers were directly implicated.

17. Rafael Borrás Betriu, *El día en que mataron a Carrero Blanco* (Barcelona: Planeta, 1974), p. 194.

18. Alfonso Osorio, *Trayectoria política de un ministro de la corona,* 2d ed. (Barcelona: Planeta, 1980), p. 50.

19. Giuseppi Di Palma, "Party Government and Democratic Reproducibility: The Dilemma of New Democracies," address delivered at a workshop on "The Future of Party Government" (Florence, Euro-

pean University Institute: June 9-17, 1982), p. 29. In addition to Cabanillas, Marcelino Oreja (under secretary of information and tourism), Juan José Rosón (director of Spanish Television and Radio), Barrera de Irimo (minister of finance), and Fernández Ordoñez (president of Instituto Nacional de Industria) all left the government.

20. *ABC*, November 7, 1975. (*ABC* is a prominent Spanish daily newspaper.)

21. *Informaciones*, November 27, 1975.

22. *ABC*, January 24, 1976.

23. The "process 1001 trial," named for its case number, resulted in the sentencing of nine communist Comisiones Obreras (Workers Commisions) labor organizers to sentences of 12 to 20 years.

24. *YA*, November 27, 1975.

25. *ABC*, March 9, 1976.

26. *Informaciones*, May 13, 1976.

27. Quoted in *ABC*, November 13, 1975.

28. José María de Areilza, *Diário de un ministro de la monarquía* (Barcelona: Planeta, 1977), p. 66.

29. *Informaciones*, June 3, 1976.

30. See Samuel D. Eaton, *The Forces of Freedom in Spain 1974-1979, A Personal Account* (Stanford, Calif.: Hoover Institution Press, 1981), p. 37, regarding Arias's January 28 speech, and Areilza, p. 152, regarding the April 28 speech.

31. Areilza, p. 84.

32. *Newsweek*, April 26, 1976.

4 TRANSITION THROUGH TRANSACTION UNDER SUAREZ

The Appointment of Adolfo Suárez

Arias's leadership satisfied few people within the regime and even fewer outside it. The franquist hard-liners considered his reforms scandalous and vetoed them at every opportunity. Reformers within the regime were convinced that Arias could never sell his plan. The democratic opposition lost confidence in the government and was firmly convinced that a "negotiated break" with authoritarianism was possible only with a new president. Arias was incapable of, and disinterested in, either imposing a rightist solution, which would have satisfied the bunker, or a democratic solution, which would have gained the support of the opposition and many reformers within the regime.

Thus, few were disappointed when King Juan Carlos asked for and received Arias's resignation on July 1, 1976. Arias's removal, and the monarch's choice of Adolfo Suárez two days later, suggest that the king, together with his friend and collaborator Torcuato Fernández Miranda (president of the Cortes and Council of the Realm), were taking swift action to bring about a more genuine democratic change. It is likely that Juan Carlos was implementing a plan, or *operación*, designed to place liberals and confidants in the three most crucial positions in the franquist political structure. From these positions, the franquist apparatus could be manipulated to produce the desired results.[1] The first such position was the presidency of the Cortes, which was held simultaneously by the president of the influential Council of the Realm. The post of Cortes president would be of vital importance only if the reform should take the "legal route," in which case the president would have tremendous leeway in structuring the path of legislation, controlling the composition of committees, guiding the debates in the plenum, and modifying the voting procedure. The Council of the Realm presidency was, potentially, of greater importance. In the franquist system, the head of government was selected by the head of state from a *terna* (a list of three names), proposed by the Council of the Realm.[2] Traditionally, the Council president wielded great influence over Council members. A second key position in the regime was the presidency of the government. The president, in consultation with the head of state, named his cabinet and was generally in charge of governing the country. A third position of importance was the vice-presidency for defense affairs, which, in addition to constituting the second ranking post in the cabinet, was customarily given to Spain's most senior military officer.

After Franco's death, Juan Carlos was initially able to place his supporters in just one of these three positions, and then only by good fortune. Rodríguez de Valcarcel, the staunchly franquist president of the Cortes, retired after his term expired in late 1975. This gave Juan Carlos the opportunity to appoint his tutor and close personal friend, Torcuato Fernández Miranda, a prestigious law professor who held a number of important posts during the franquist regime.

Like so many of the important actors in the democratization process, Fernández Miranda had a contradictory political trajectory. He entered politics through the university during the wave of liberalization associated with Education Minister Joaquín Ruíz Giménez. When Ruíz Giménez and other liberals were purged in the mid 1960s, Fernández Miranda clung to the career of Admiral Carrero Blanco, a loyal franquist hard-liner. Under Carrero's presidency, Fernández Miranda became minister-secretary general of the National Movement and vice-president of the government. When Carrero was assassinated in 1973, Fernández Miranda was considered the logical choice to be named president, but Franco evidently distrusted his independence and ambition and the dictator appointed his close personal friend, Carlos Arias Navarro. Feeling deceived, Fernández Miranda began to distance himself from the leading figures of the franquist regime and approach the politicians of the

future, especially King Juan Carlos. Fernández Miranda clearly supported a transition to a conservative monarchy, but it would be
mistaken to consider him a life-long democrat.

Juan Carlos's decision to appoint Fernández Miranda met stiff
resistance within the regime. The young king was still extremely
weak vis-à-vis the hard-liners, many of whom distrusted Fernández Miranda's fickle character and his access to and influence over
Juan Carlos. Ironically, regime reformers were also opposed to the
appointment, since Fernández Miranda had been the close collaborator of Carrero Blanco, the fiercely repressive and staunchly franquist admiral who occupied the presidency between 1969 and
1973, and who was widely considered to be Franco's "real" successor. Even more ironic was the fact that Arias was instrumental in gaining the acceptance of Fernández Miranda's appointment
and that Juan Carlos therefore felt incapable of sacking Arias at the
start of his reign.[3] The vacillation of the young and inexperienced
king, the political strength and entrenchment of the bunker, and
the absence of a clear and acceptable replacement all contributed
to this delay.

Nevertheless, very early on in the second Arias presidency,
Fernández Miranda and the king began to search for a suitable
replacement, a politician who could appeal to the major factions
of the regime without being too strongly identified with any one
of them. The choice had to be a close friend of the king, or one
enjoying his confidence. In the last months of the Arias government, Fernández Miranda came to the conclusion that Adolfo Suárez was the best choice.

Why Suárez?

Adolfo Suárez, minister of the National Movement in Arias's
government, was only 43 years old at the time. Suárez came from
a relatively modest middle-class family but rose quickly through
the franquist bureaucracy, using the National Movement as his
vechicle. In the MN, particularly the University Student Syndicate
(SEU), it was not necessary to be endowed with vast quantities of
wealth or education. Personal contacts were the way to rise quickly
and obtaining a political patron was the *sine qua non* of political
advancement and survival. Suárez found his mentor in Fernando
Herrero Tejedor, civil governor in Suárez's native Avila and min-

ister of the MN under Carrero Blanco. Herrero Tejedor, along with other MN conservatives, had formed the Union of the Spanish People (Unión del Pueblo Español, UDPE) in 1975. Herrero, as minister of the MN, made his protegé, Adolfo Suárez, UDPE president.

UDPE was typical of many of the franquist "associations" that developed in the last year before the dictator's death. It was ambiguous in ideology and more centered around personalities than political programs. The association was formed by 130 notables of the regime, including both extreme conservatives and Falangist populists. The UDPE has been described variously as "a clearly continuist effort by the regime. . . which tried to emulate the Mexican P.R.I." and as a party aspiring to become the Gaullist party of Spain's future.[4] UDPE leaders expressed interest in leading a "reform from within," which, while preserving most of the institutions and personalities of the regime, could co-opt some of the moderate democratic opposition.

For Suárez, the UDPE presidency provided an opportunity to refine his skill at playing the politics of patronage. He quickly surrounded himself with a number of young MN members, many of them his best friends from the days in the SEU. Many of these same individuals later followed Suárez into UCD. Suárez's personal attributes suited him well for his meteoric rise through the franquist bureaucracy. He was a nonintellectual who related more to people than to concrete ideas. His links with the *familias* of the regime were well balanced, though he was considered a Movement politician. Juan Luis Cebrián, the young editor of *El País*, described Suárez as a

> Falangist type, obsessed with the efficiency of the state apparatus, as well as social justice according to his own conception of it. In him, one finds, as in few other members of the political class, the conditions of a declassé. He suffers, or enjoys (depending on one's views) the populist sentiments which can be found in this country, which separate him even more from the ruling classes of finance and the economy.[5]

A socialist leader who first met Suárez in the autumn of 1976 was attracted to his open personality, and recalled that "he demonstrated a personality ideal for democracy. Democracy doesn't require rigid and blunt politicians, but rather flexible and malleable ones."[6]

After Herrero Tejedor was killed in an automobile accident in 1975, Suárez found a new political patron in Torcuato Fernández Miranda. Through Fernández Miranda, Suárez quickly became friends with Prince Juan Carlos, a member of Suárez's generation, and during 1975 and 1976 the two met regularly. While Franco was still alive, the young prince asked Suárez to write a report on political options after the caudillo's death. Suárez's suggestions contained a plan slightly more conservative than the one finally selected in 1976, but far more progressive than Arias's.[7] Suárez remained a relative political unknown until his brilliant defense of the Law for Political Association, as minister of the National Movement in June 1976, gave him his first real public exposure. His good looks, youth, personal charisma, and excellent oratorical skills were widely noted during that period. Suárez also distinguished himself within the cabinet. With Fraga out of the country, Suárez took charge of the government's response to the wave of popular and terrorist violence that shook the Basque country during March 1976. He received considerable praise for his moderation and serenity during the crisis, and Juan Carlos was reportedly quite impressed with Suárez's ability.[8]

While Juan Carlos remained unsure of who should replace Arias, the monarch began to cultivate his own support base among young members of the various *familias* of the regime. In mid-May, a series of "political" dinners was organized by a prominent journalist and close supporter of Juan Carlos. The dinners were attended by liberal Opus Dei technocrats, Christian democrats, monarchists, and MN members. The participants in these dinners shared three main features: their identification with the regime (in which, typically, they held second-string positions), their youth, and their loyalty to Juan Carlos. In this group, future President Suárez would find his most loyal base of support.[9]

The President by Surprise

As Arias proved incapable of implementing serious democratic reform, Juan Carlos became more convinced that Suárez was an ideal replacement. However, getting Suárez included in the presidential *terna* (the Council of the Realm's list of three candidates) was no easy task and involved an intense operation for which Torcuato Fernández Miranda proved invaluable.[10] Fernández

Miranda's strategy involved convincing several of the younger members of the Council of the Realm to vote for the young National Movement bureaucrat with impeccable franquist credentials. Even with this effort, Suárez was third in the voting and was nearly excluded from the list. Fernández Miranda, upon leaving the Council of the Realm vote, announced that he was "ready to give the king what he requested," a comment subsequently interpreted as a sign that Suárez had been included in the *terna* at the king's behest.

The fact that Suárez could be sold to the Council of the Realm as a man of the regime explains the virtually unanimous shock and sense of deception among regime reformers and the opposition created by his appointment. The conservative historian, Ricardo de la Cierva, entitled his reaction to the appointment, "¡Que Error! ¡Que Inmenso Error!" (What a Mistake! What an Immense Mistake!), published in *El País.*[11] De la Cierva called the appointment "a big mistake that only a miracle can correct," and predicted that "things will be papered over for several weeks...but will heat up in the autumn and then explode." One scholar noted that "Suárez began as President amidst the lack of confidence and credit of almost the entire political class."[12] Only on the extreme right was there temporary satisfaction, and some military officials seemed to be satisfied with the choice.

Suárez's First Government

Suárez's attempt to form a new government immediately encountered difficulties. All of the big names of the regime, and most of the members of the Arias government, refused to join what was expected to be another ill-fated cabinet. Anxious to put together a government quickly, and eager to head off speculation that Suárez was in political trouble, the president chose a government of young, inexperienced, second-string ministers. The president selected a set of ministers fairly similar to himself, with the obvious exception of the military ministers, who remained unchanged. In retrospect, it is apparent that Suárez's success in bringing about a transition to democracy was greatly facilitated by his selection of a team of young, loyal, political unknowns who were far less likely to challenge him (at least immediately), as Areilza and Fraga had challenged Arias.

The new government drew its membership from a number of

franquist political associations, including the amorphous Union of
the Spanish People, Silva Muñoz's conservative christian
democratic Spanish Democratic Union, the reformist study group
FEDISA, and the Independent Parliamentary Group. The most visible component of Suárez's new government was the christian
democratic group known as TACITO.* TACITO represented the
most progressive group of regime Christian democrats and published frequent articles in the Catholic daily, *YA*. While Suárez was
not a member of the group, his closest political associate and second vice-president of the government, Alfonso Osorio, was a member. In addition, three of Suárez's cabinet members were affiliated
with TACITO.

Another important feature of the Suárez government was its
youth, a factor that led some observers to dub it "the government
of undersecretaries." Considering that the four military ministers
remained unchanged, the average cabinet age of 50 years, compared with 55.5 and 54 during the two Arias governments, is
remarkable.[13] Moreover, Suárez's appointments to secondary posts
in the ministries and at the local and regional governmental levels
led to a significant rejuvenation of the franquist leadership.

The Suárez Reform

With his own team in place, Suárez began execution of a carefully conceived political operation. The term *operación politica* (political operation) was commonly employed by the press to describe
Suárez's plan. This term is significant because "it describes a decisive element in the character of the transition: that it was preconceived, structured and planned like a type of military operation,
with set goals and support groups."[14] Nevertheless, politics, like
a military operation, often involves considerable improvisation, and
the Spanish transition was no exception.

With the help of Suárez's closest collaborators, and under the
guidance of Fernández Miranda, it was decided that the operation
would consist of three parts. First, the government would have to
seek confidence from three major political forces. On the right, the
military would be the key actor, since only with their support could

---

*See Chapter 3, section entitled "The Church."

the predictable hostility from hard-liners be offset. To this end, no military minister in the cabinet was replaced with the change of presidents. The second political force, the democratic opposition, would have to be convinced to drop its skepticism vis-à-vis the Suárez government. Some degree of support and confidence would have to be garnered if the Suárez reform were to be successful. At the same time, however—and directly related to obtaining military support—the communist left would have to be ostracized and the opposition kept weak and divided. The prospect of a strong, united, Marxist left would surely force the military into the hard-liners' camp. Finally, and most important, the reform-oriented regime members would have to be rallied behind the plan.

The second prong of the operation involved the elaboration of a new reform law that could be passed by the Cortes. According to Osorio, one of its chief architects, this law was to be more "flexible" and comprehensive than the Arias measures.[15] Third, the reform, once approved by the legislature, would be approved directly by the people in a referendum, marking the first instance of direct popular participation in the reform process. All three parts of the operation were difficult and each required a high level of political skill.

Most observers doubted that Suárez's plan could be successful, and many felt that the "legal route" of reform had already been exhausted. Suárez was attempting to hold a referendum from above, ignoring the opposition's demands for a provisional government. But his reform sought to create a more democratic legislature that might subsequently write a new constitution. In addition to controlling the transition, the regime would exact conditions and limits to democratization. For franquist reformists this type of reform was attractive, but there were a number of dangers in Suárez's strategy. The regime right had already undermined Arias's more conservative reform and could easily repeat this performance. Even if the regime right could be convinced, the skeptical opposition was unlikely to support the ex-secretary-general of the National Movement in his attempt to democratize from above. Suárez's gamble that the opposition would eventually adhere to his strategy was based on the hope that, once the reform was approved by the regime, the democratic opposition would refrain from attacking the plan. Suárez reasoned that the opposition would fear a rightist coup and would be forced to support his democratization strategy. The president figured that the opposition was too weak and divided to risk any type of mobilization against his reform.[16]

Both Juan Carlos and Suárez were careful to cultivate an image in line with their reform plan. The two young leaders made very conciliatory speeches in the summer of 1976, promising democratic reform, but guaranteeing respect for the franquist regime. One good example took place during Juan Carlos's trip to Galicia in July 1976. Summer trips by Franco to his native El Ferrol (Galicia) had become an institution during franquism and Juan Carlos's visit there was no coincidence. However, the king quickly broke with tradition when he took the audacious step of addressing a Galician crowd in Galician, the long-banned language of the region. During the same trip, the king paid an equally symbolic visit to Franco's widow in El Ferrol.[17] On August 7, the government made the conciliatory gesture of reinstating three prominent professors to their university chairs, from which they were purged in 1965. On November 7, Juan Carlos repealed a 1937 statute forbidding economic and administrative autonomy in the Basque Country.

Both types of symbols were present in Suárez's initial programmatic statement, anxiously awaited by a skeptical opposition and doubtful regime reformists. The speech was "deliberately ambiguous and shrewdly elastic."[18] For the opposition, Suárez's July statement contained some important promises. The constitutional reform would be submitted to the people, and general elections were to take place in the spring of 1977. Legal reforms would attempt to bring Spanish laws into conformity with "social realities," especially in the area of political pluralism. Where Suárez's initial declarations broke with Arias's reform was in his mention of the government's willingness to negotiate with "all political forces," and the recognition of the "diversity of regions within the confines of the unity of Spain." Finally, an amnesty was to be granted to about 400 political prisoners. For the right, Suárez was careful to stress that the maintenance of public order would remain a high priority.[19]

Reactions to Suárez's statement were dramatic and prompt. On July 2, 32 prominent democratic opposition leaders representing a wide range of groups had sent a document to King Juan Carlos, complaining that the reform process, to date, had completely excluded the opposition. On July 27, a week after Suárez's programmatic statement, the opposition issued a revised document applauding "the new language of Suárez. . . which for the first time does not exclude the opposition, and in fact publicly recognizes the need to dialogue with it."[20] The document suggested that while negotiation had been impossible under Arias, there were new prospects for compromise, and new possibilities for avoiding a dangerous *ruptura*. The concept of democratic rupture, affirmed the document, might now be replaced by the term "democratic change."

In contrast with the initial skepticism of the liberal daily *El País* after Suárez's appointment, its August 3 editorial argued that Suárez's impressive first actions were a reminder of the "range of options open to public leaders at all times." It suggested that differences in both leadership style and skill were clearly in evidence. In examining why Suárez had obtained so much confidence in so short a time, in stark contrast to Arias's government, *El País* asserted that, unlike Arias, the new president did not operate according to "Franco time."[21]

Suárez was ecstatic over these subtle changes in the opposition's statements and with his obvious eradication of some of the most serious skepticism surrounding his appointment. He told Osorio in late August that he felt his reform strategy was working better than expected. "We are going to win and govern for twenty years," said an elated president, already thinking ahead to democratic elections.[22] But elections remained a long way off in every sense.

According to the government's Institute of Public Opinion, the public continued to be largely indifferent to the whole political process. Despite the evidence of considerable apathy, the Institute's polls showed a clear rise in support for the government since Suárez had become president. The Suárez govenment viewed the results as another positive sign for the reform.

Negotiations with Two Oppositions

The Suárez government immediately initiated a series of contacts with a wide range of opposition political leaders. In early September, Suárez met with representatives of every major political association of the regime. These contacts were designed to sound out the extent of support for and opposition to Suárez's reform plan, soon to be announced to the public. The president found support for his plan from his own UDPE and from the Independent Parliamentary Group, a group of liberal *procuradores*. However, most other groups expressed hostility toward the reform. It is interesting to note that the most common concern was the nature of the future electoral law. A second worry of regime groups was the Suárez might legalize the Spanish Communist Party. The president assured these representatives that the electoral law would benefit regime groups and that the Communists would never be included in the reform.[23]

The Right

From the start it was clear that the PCE was the *bête noire* of the franquist right. In fact, it was commonly felt among the franquist elite, especially the military, that the Communists should remain off limits in any political reform. Since Suárez did not choose to replace any military ministers, the approval of the reform by the military seemed problematic. On July 16, the cabinet discussed the programmatic statement drawn up by Suárez. Lieutenant General Fernando de Santiago, military vice-president, and an extremely prestigious figure in military circles, walked out of the meeting in protest. De Santiago told Osorio that he could accept Suárez's call for amnesty and national reconciliation, but as a Catholic he felt that sovereignty resided in God alone, not in the people, as Suárez's statement had boldly asserted.[24] Nevertheless, Suárez was confident that he could convince the armed forces to accept the reform. Fernández Miranda suggested that Suárez convene the top military leadership to explain his objectives. A meeting between Suárez and the 29 highest ranking military officials took place on September 8, 1976, under tight security and secrecy. During the meeting Suárez promised that the PCE would never be legalized, citing Article 271 of the newly reformed Penal Code. In addition, Suárez assured the military that it would be exempt from military reform if the armed forces would support the reform plan.

> [Suárez] appeared to be one of them. He anticipated their worries and uneasiness and was inflexible regarding basic principles. He never treated the military with so much deference. Nobody could doubt his fidelity and closeness to the regime. Change was necessary and if it were not initiated now the country would en-

ter a process whose end point was unknown. All was to be taken care of and carefully planned. All political parties would be legalized, and he could guarantee that there would be no risk of losing the elections, because his technicians had studied it carefully. It would be done slowly, without haste, step by step. . . . The legalizations would have a limit: the Communist Party.[25]

According to one top-ranking military official present at the meeting, the military leadership was "obviously horrified by what it heard, but was fascinated by Suárez and did not immediately complain."[26] At any rate, Suárez considered the meeting a victory. The president felt "his exposition had been brilliant, and although some had asked him pointed questions, he had been able to answer with clarity—the approval had been absolute."[27] This assessment seemed to be corroborated when, at the September 10 cabinet meeting, none of the military ministers raised objections to Suárez's Political Reform Law.

The honeymoon with the armed forces was short lived, however. On September 15 the minister of syndical relations admitted to having met with Workers Commissions (the influential PCE-directed clandestine labor union) representatives as part of his efforts to draw up a syndical reform law. Vice-President General de Santiago was outraged, and on September 22 he resigned from the government. On the same day, in a letter to top military officers, de Santiago explained that he could not agree with any reform that might include the Communist left.

Despite warnings from his closest aides that the resignation could snowball, endangering the entire reform, Suárez took advantage of the resignation to replace the reactionary general with Manuel Gutiérrez Mellado, a well-known supporter of Juan Carlos and the reform project. Gutiérrez Mellado had been a close disciple of Manuel Diez Alegría, the lieutenant general and army chief of staff who was fired by Franco for his excessive liberalism. Suárez thus took advantage of the resignation to fill the last of the three key regime posts with a supporter of the reform.

Gutiérrez Mellado's appointment provoked further hostility from within the military leadership. In the short term, the president's gamble paid off since it bolstered his prestige and proved he could stand up to the military when necessary. Under the surface, however, this was the first of a series of incidents underscoring a basic contradiction between the Suárez reform and the military. On the one hand, Suárez continued to assure the military that he would not deal with or legalize the Communists, and some of Suárez's actions seemed aimed at conveying that message. For example, in August 1976 the president fired the Spanish ambassador in France for simply meeting with Carrillo when the latter solicited the return of his passport. On the other hand, Suárez was increasing his contacts with the Democratic Coordinator, the opposition coalition whose main driving force was the PCE.

The Democratic Opposition

At the same time that Suárez attempted to rally the support of the right, he began to negotiate with the democratic opposition. Initially, the president had more to prove to this skeptical sector than to his fellow franquists. Vice-President Osorio initiated contacts with Christian democratic leaders while Suárez dealt with the socialist and regional opposition leaders. In addition, Suárez initiated contacts with the PCE, always through intermediaries and always under a cloak of secrecy. Suárez wanted to know whether the PCE would accept the monarchy and the "rules of the game" in a new democracy. Had the military been aware of these contacts, the entire Suárez plan would have been in jeopardy.

On September 11, Suárez appeared on national television to explain his Political Reform Law. In the speech, he argued that "we have to get the people to speak as soon as possible. . .and in so doing we are fulfilling the King's wish, conveyed to the govenment, to 'take the pulse of, and become more familar with, the aspirations of the people'. . ." Suárez, in marked contrast with Arias, stated that "democracy should be the work of all citizens and never the obsequious concession or imposition, regardless of its origin." However, at the same time he cautioned that "in the project I am presenting to you there is no attempt to create a clean slate." Initial reactions to the speech were guarded and somewhat negative. However, when the actual text of the Political Reform Law was published, it was clear that the reform went well beyond that proposed by Arias. Table 4 (which appears in the next section of this chapter) compares some of the key features of the two reform laws.

The opposition was clearly caught off guard by the profundity of the Political Reform Law and refrained from rejecting it outright. The Democratic Coordinator officially rejected the plan because it failed to establish a provisional government and didn't satisfy other of its demands. But individually, opposition leaders were more optimistic about the Suárez reform. Ruíz Giménez (Izquierda Democrática) argued that the Political Reform Law could easily form the basis for democratization. Tierno Galván (Popular Socialist Party) noted the ambiguity in the law and criticized the absence of any provisions for a responsible government, but he also admitted that it was a far cry from Arias's reform project. Felipe González (Socialist Workers Party) argued that the reform "could be a way to liquidate franquism." In the eyes of the government, these statements were sufficient proof of support for the reform. Vice-President Osorio recorded in his diary that "the truth is, despite all the [opposition] statements, that the opposition is seriously convinced that the selected route is an adequate one."[28] In retrospect, Tierno Galván corroborates this view from an opposition perspective, recalling that the Political Reform Law "left the opposition satisfied in principle."[29]

Suárez's unexpected initiative and audacity exacerbated the state of confusion within the Spanish opposition. Opposition leaders seemed to oscillate between periods of unity and incredible divisiveness, between fits of radical rhetoric and admirable moderation, and between states of confidence and paranoia. The Political Reform Law was an important impetus for a change taking place under the surface of the opposition's often aggressive statements. This change was reflected in the gradual shift in meaning of the term *ruptura,* or democratic break. Taken to its most radical extreme, *ruptura* meant an abrupt end to the franquist regime, either through its collapse or overthrow, and an assumption of power by the democratic opposition. A more realistic version came to signify the formation of a provisional government of regime reformists and democratic opposition leaders. In its final version, *ruptura* (now often appearing as *ruptura pactada,* negotiated democratic break) was employed to describe democratization, regardless of the formation of a provisional government to oversee the transition. While franquist elites might control the democratic transition, negotiation with opposition leaders might at least exact guarantees (fair elections, civil liberties, equal access to the media, and so on). By altering the content of the terms, opposition leaders were making it easier to accept Suárez's idea of democratization ushered in by franquists and through the franquist legal structures.

The realization that the regime could not be toppled by force, coupled with the impossibility of negotiation under the Arias presidency, had created a paradoxical position for the opposition. It was forced into pushing for *ruptura* even though many opposition leaders dreaded its consequences and would have preferred a more gradual transition. The rhetoric of *ruptura,* ingrained in the opposition for many years, was hard to shed, and it continued to plague the democratic opposition up until the 1977 parliamentary electoral campaign. Thus, maintaining the rhetoric of *ruptura* publicly, while slowly gutting the term of its original meaning, was a way of acquiescing to the Suárez reform while saving face. The Suárez plan, and the president's early overtures to the opposition, unblocked the dilemma of the opposition.

In summary, while refusing to admit it publicly, the opposition gradually accepted the fact that under Suárez's leadership "the change from franquism to democracy was possible without exceeding the legal confines of and control by the regime." It was extremely difficult for the opposition to swallow the Suárez reform without receiving any guarantees from the government. The opposition's abstention from the Suárez reform ran the risk of turning the first democratic elections into a sham, at which point either a rightist coup or a regime collapse might occur. Deep down, either prospect was perceived as undesirable by opposition leaders. Moreover, the opposition was divided over the question of the Suárez reform. Failure to participate in the first elections might mean ceding the advantage to competitors.

The approval of the Penal Code Reform early in Suárez's presidency meant that political parties could become legal by registering with the Ministry of the Interior. Until October, only franquist organizations, such as UDPE and UNE (Unión Nacional Española, or Spanish National Union), took advantage of this system. The opposition was divided over this provision. Some opposition forces saw the registration process as an opportunity to force open the door of reform and a way to work within the franquist system. Most of the opposition believed that registration would only legitimate the franquist system. Political parties were fearful of being branded as collaborators with franquism, but at the same time they were eager to gain legal recognition so they could begin to prepare for elections. In early October, the Spanish Social Democratic Party (Partido Social Demócrata Español, PSDE) registered, along with the PSOE *histórico* (a social democratic splinter group). Both parties attempted to get a jump on the PSOE of Felipe González. The short-term effect of these registrations was to divide the democratic opposition, since the PSOE resented what it viewed as the opportunism of the social democrats.

Other issues continued to divide the democratic opposition, despite the progress made toward unification. *Le Monde* reported on October 10 that "the opposition is too divided. . .and too worried about being left out of the liberalization, to make a head-on assault against the government."[30] A major source of division was the distrust and competition between the two largest socialist parties, the PSOE and the PSP. A second bone of contention concerned the poor working relationship between the PSOE and the PCE. Finally, the national democratic opposition was unsuccessful in fully integrating the regional opposition, especially Basque and Catalan groups.

The inability of the democratic opposition to present a unified political platform until late in the autumn of 1976 facilitated Suárez's maneuverability. In late October and early November, the president turned his attention away from the squabbling opposition to the approval of his reform law in the Cortes. Suárez postponed authorization of the PSOE's 27th Congress until December, after the scheduled Cortes vote on the political reform. The Socialists were bitterly disappointed, but were careful not to stir up too much Cortes opposition to the reform. The democratic opposition took action that made very clear its support for the Suárez reform. On November 6, shortly before the reform was to go before the Cortes, democratic opposition leaders published their most conciliatory platform to date. There was no longer any mention of a provisional government or regional autonomy. The opposition agreed to participate in the Suárez reform if a number of concrete civil liberties were restored, and if equal access to the media was guaranteed. Thus, as Suárez approached his confrontation with the right, he was quite confident that the democratic opposition was behind his strategy for democratization.

Preparing for Confrontation

The most serious danger facing the Suárez reform came from the franquist right. In July the Cortes had rejected a second draft of the Penal Code Reform. This was only narrowly approved after a provision was added outlawing "all parties subject to international discipline or whose goal is to install a totalitarian regime," a clear attempt to ban the PCE. Only one military *procurador* voted in favor of the measure. Vice-President Osorio noted that "analyzing the vote, I arrive at the conclusion that the issue of the PCE will be used as the battle horse in the debate over the Political Reform Law."[31] The 175 *procuradores* who voted against the Penal Code Reform feared that Suárez might legalize the PCE.

The franquist right had reacted with anger and dismay when the Political Reform Law was published. For example, in early September, José Antonio Girón, national councilor and councilor of the realm, affirmed in Malaga: "We look with anger at those who have proposed, from a position of power they didn't conquer, the systematic destruction of our institutions. We are not going to facilitate the work of traitors."[32] On the more moderate franquist right, the formation of the Popular Alliance (Alianza Popular, AP), led by Fraga Iribarne, clearly signified the acceptance of elections by much of the regime. At the same time, AP saw itself as a way to limit the democratic reform. AP's platform warned that "the feeling of insecurity is growing," and criticized "the breakdown of public order, the unnecessary acceptance of *rupturista* ideas, and the presence of permissive attitudes."

Most observers predicted that Suárez faced difficult odds with his reform project, and most expected the president to experience a defeat similar to Arias's. The *Financial Times* of London asserted that "Suárez's government, which evidently felt strong enough to announce the early retirement of two ultra-right generals, isn't presently strong enough to confront the establishment." The New York *Times* was even more skeptical, stating that "a genuine democracy cannot emerge out of non-democratic institutions such as the Cortes or the National Council."[33]

The Political Reform Law

"Democracy, the result of the effort and work of the Spanish people, cannot be improvised." So began the preamble to Suárez's

Political Reform Law, and it could almost be considered the president's watchword. This was a peculiar law, very concise and occasionally straightforward, but vague on those points where ambiguity was essential.

Immediately after his appointment, Suárez drew up a plan that was much closer to Arias's reform. It called for a Senate composed of 102 elected members: 2 per province, 40 representatives of universities and cultural organizations, 50 representatives of "professional guilds," 40 royally designated senators, and 18 senators selected by an elite ex-officio electoral college. However, after deliberating with his cabinet, a more progressive version of the reform was approved on September 10, 1976. Table 4 compares the Arias and Suárez reform measures. It is likely that Suárez, bolstered by his initial contacts with the military, felt that the more progressive version could be approved, and would facilitate subsequent negotiations with the opposition. It is also likely that King Juan Carlos urged his president to implement the more genuinely democratic reform.

The revised version called for a Senate composed of representatives from "territorial entities" and directly elected by universal suffrage. In place of corporate representatives were 40 royally designated senators, which, while appearing to safeguard the franquist legacy, was more accurately a mechanism giving the king the right to determine the majority of the upper house as he saw fit. In fact, one of the most important features of the final version of the law was the increased power given to the monarch. The king could convoke referenda on his own initiative and could decree an electoral law. The power of the monarch was also enhanced in the process of constitutional amendments. Article 3 of the Reform left the door open for the writing of a new constitution, which the king could submit directly to people for approval. The Arias reform, in contrast, had granted the power to amend the constitution to a franquist senate, subject to the approval of two-thirds of both houses and a referendum.

Unlike the Arias reform, Suárez's Political Reform Law explicitly accepted the notion of popular sovereignty. Article 1 states that "democracy . . . is based on the rule of law, [the] expression of the sovereign will of the people." Another important difference was that the Suárez reform made no mention of the National Movement, or the National Council. Like the Arias reform, however, there was no provision for government responsible to the legisla-

Table 4. The Arias Reform and Suárez Reform Compared on Selected Points

Issue	Arias Reform	Suárez Reform
Composition of lower house	300 deputies of the "family," elected by majoritarian system	350 deputies directly elected through proportional representation
Composition of upper house	265 senators, 200 directly elected by majoritarian system, 40 lifetime National Council members, 20 representatives of local government and legal institutions, 5 appointed by King	240 senators, 200 directly elected by majoritarian system, 40 royal appointees
Duration of terms of houses	Upper house: 6 years Lower house: 4 years	Both houses: 4 years
Selection of presidents of legislature and Council of Realm	President of upper house is president of legislature; Senate chooses him/her from a *terna* of the Council of Realm	King selects the president of each body
Role of the National Movement	A "surveillance committee" of the Senate is the heir to National Council of National Movement	No mention of National Movement or National Council
Initiator of constitutional reform legislation	Senate	Congress of Deputies, government or monarch
Provisions for royal convocation of referenda	None	Monarch may convoke referenda at any time

Source: Compiled by the author.

ture. Moreover, in the absence of any statement to the contrary, it was simply assumed that the king would continue to select the president from a *terna* presented by the Council of the Realm. The Council of the Realm was to be more democratically constituted, but it still contained five lifetime members and a president, all appointed by the monarch. For the democratic opposition, the Suárez reform was a great step forward but hardly a guarantee of parliamentary democracy.

Officially, the Suárez reform was to be the eighth Fundamental Law, and was therefore an amendment to the entire constitution. However, despite the fact that the Political Reform Law clearly contradicted many of the other Fundamental Laws, there was no clause derogating any other parts of the constitution. Suárez avoided confronting the franquist regime by simply adding another Fundamental Law that contravened much of the existing constitution! By presenting it as an additional Fundamental Law, Suárez did more than simply avoid direct confrontation with the existing constitution. His very willingness to pursue the established route of constitutional reform legitimated the Fundamental Laws, as well as the regime that had produced them. The Political Reform Law attempted to do so without ever mentioning democracy or a new constitution. By giving birth to a democratic constitutional reform, the franquist regime could be "retroactively legitimated."[34] While Suárez's reform did not appear so at the time, it was really far more than a constitutional amendment. As one legal scholar noted at the time, "the new project does not so much reform the Fundamental Laws as it creates new procedures for decision making."[35]

The Process of Approval

Suárez and Fernández Miranda had no doubts that there would be problems getting the law passed. Nevertheless, it was hoped that it would be possible to wield what one observer called "a mixture of suaveness, calls for patriotism, and veiled threats—including the dissolution of the hardly representative Cortes," to steer the law through the franquist legal process."[36] The contours of this strategy were illustrated on October 21, when, during a press conference, Fernández Miranda used both implicit threats and suasion. The Cortes president did not directly threaten to dissolve the legislature should it reject the reform, but did point out that the Tenth

Legislature's term had already been extended, and that new elections could be called at any time. More directly, Fernández Miranda exhorted the press to treat the Cortes with respect since they were about to perform "a work of exemplary patriotism."

There was initial hostility to the Political Reform Law from within the Cortes. One of the most ominous reactions came from the Popular Alliance, the largest group within the chamber. On November 2, its spokesperson stated that he was against the law because it had been presented in a "take it or leave it fashion."[37] Numerous objections were raised by other *procuradores.* These included the electoral system (*procuradores* wanted a guaranteed majoritarian system for both houses), the National Movement (explicit protection was sought), the Senate (deemed too weak), the absence of "organic representatives," the power of the king (viewed as excessive or too limited), and the overall unconstitutionality of the law.

The first stop in the franquist legislative process was the National Council of the National Movement. The National Council, by law, was to issue a report on all constitutional amendments. While nonbinding, these reports were usually an accurate barometer of an amendment's prospects. The less ambitious Arias reform had been rejected by the National Council. By the time the stronghold of hard-line franquism finished its deliberations, it had recommended a series of changes in the law that would have seriously undermined the Suárez reform. The National Council's report proposed co-equal chambers of the Cortes (rather than a more powerful lower house), a senate representing "economic, social, and professional interests," and the Council of the Realm's approval of all referendums called by the monarch.

El País lamented that "the loneliness of the government was graphically apparent during the National Council plenum." While applauding Suárez for his willingness to appear before the Council, *Cambio 16* interpreted his reception as a sign that the legal route to democratization was exhausted.

> A government which has to negotiate democracy with the ghostly institutions of the dictatorship immediately loses credibility with the opposition. It loses all authority, and is unable to control the situation. The means—consulting authoritarians on the issue of democracy—are contrary to the ends desired. The

rebellion of the National Council is proof of the crisis of the reform.[38]

Others suggested that the king must now act to call immediate elections and must be careful to avoid "succumbing to the legalism of Arias and Suárez."[39]

On October 21, after exercising its right to ignore the nonbinding report of the Council, the government published the law, along with the National Council's report, and the period for presentation of amendments to the Law began. A subcommittee of the Cortes Committee on Fundamental Laws, packed with liberals by Fernández Miranda, formally rejected most of the amendments.

The Law in the Cortes

On November 3, Suárez met with key members in his government and the Cortes to discuss strategy for getting the Political Reform Law approved. One part of his strategy was to use the electoral law as a bargaining chip, but to refuse to negotiate on all other issues. If a substantial number of *procuradores* could be satisfied with the electoral law, they might support the reform, feeling that they had at least come away with something in return.[40] The basic strategy was to divide and conquer: If the hard-liners could be isolated, and a solid core of regime supporters united, then the large mass of undecided *procuradores* might be convinced to jump on the reformist bandwagon. The decision to negotiate on the electoral law was aimed at those *procuradores* who were more fearful of an opposition victory in the first elections than of the concept of elections per se.

The plenum of the Cortes took place on November 16, 17, and 18, amidst great doubts concerning the passage of the law. On the first day, Miguel Primo de Rivera, despite his earlier opposition to the Arias reform, gave a very influential speech in support of the Law. His address was typical of the defense used by supporters of the Suárez reform and is worth quoting at length:

[This law has been assailed] by those who don't want to understand that what is being aimed at is the making of a new constitution based on the legality of the current constitution, for the first time in Spanish history, and who label any proposed solu-

tion *rupturista* and treasonous; or others, opposed to this position, who try to deny the legitimacy of the present system and
demand a rupture. But thank God, between these two positions
are the majority of reasonable politicians who, conscious that the
situation before and after the *Caudillo's* death are different,
choose an intermediate position between immobilism and rupture. Because they know that the political authority of Francisco
Franco, to whom I here and now proclaim my loyalty, to whom
I will never denounce my personal devotion, in whose shadow
I grew up and lived in peace, is impossible to reproduce. Un-
deniably, we have to substitute his authority for another type
of political authority.[41]

Primo ended his opening speech with the phrase, "In the emotional
memory of Franco, and in loyalty to the King, I solicit your
support."

The hard-line opposition was best articulated by Blas Piñar,
who, quoting Franco, made the case for the sacred and immutable nature of the Principles of the National Movement. Piñar complained bitterly that he "would prefer a constituent period to this
stupid masquerade of democratic reform," and his speech drew
considerable applause. Another hard-liner attacked the reform,
claiming it was an attempt to liquidate the regime rather than perfect it: In a fiery passage, de la Vega complained:

All the loose ends were supposedly well secured. Tied with a
permanent knot for the opposition, which walked the roads of
Europe for forty years denouncing the sin of peace and progress
in Spain, feeding the old and immutable anti-Spanish prejudice
with the rotten firewood of franquist tyranny. But all was not
so well secured, because some within the regime, despite their
oaths of loyalty, have simply untied the knot. On July 18, 1936
Spain put itself back on its feet against everything this law
represents.

The legislator in charge of the law's defense rebutted these
amendments, calling on the *procuradores* to support the king: "precisely because we are loyal to the last speech of the *Caudillo*, . . . we
mustn't be an obstacle to the King's consultation with the people."
He claimed to respect the opinions of the hard-liners but urged them
to present their message to the people in the scheduled referendum

campaign. "To vote against this law is not to vote against inorganic democracy, but rather to deny the people the right to choose what type of democracy they want." This statement was met with boos and cries of "no!" and there was a high level of tension in the chamber.

The first session of the Plenum caused considerable unease among members of the government. The warmth with which Piñar and de la Vega had been received, and the open hostility toward defenders of the Law, were worrisome. Amidst an atmosphere of hostility and combativeness, members of the Cortes began to rally around the issue of the electoral law. The crucial moment occurred when a prominent AP leader spoke in favor of a majoritarian electoral system, which he argued should be included as part of the Political Reform Law, so as to prevent the government from any future alterations. AP wanted a system of single-member districts for the lower house, from which it hoped to benefit. While Suárez had expected to negotiate over the issue of the electoral law, he was unprepared to accept the constitutionalization of a single-member district system. He was aware that the opposition would be less willing to accept a system that so clearly favored entrenched franquist elites, especially in rural areas.

The government finally reached a compromise solution with the leadership of AP. Two restrictions regarding elections to the lower house were to be added to the Political Reform Law. First, although the deputies would be elected by proportional representation, "corrective measures" would be added "to avoid the fragmentation of the chamber." Second, the existing provinces would serve as the electoral districts for both houses, and a fixed minimum number of deputies and senators per province would be elected. Before accepting this compromise, Suárez contacted opposition leaders and was assured that they would continue to support his reform plan.[42] The final compromise was presented by AP as an amendment to the Political Reform Law, which was accepted by the government and approved by a vote of 425 in favor, 59 opposed, and 13 abstentions.

The Results

The compromise over the issue of the electoral system seemed to break the dam of opposition to the Law for Political Reform.

When the vote was taken, the law passed by an overwhelming margin, to the surprise of almost everyone. When the outcome was revealed, the chamber erupted in applause. Suárez stood and applauded the *procuradores* in an important symbolic gesture. Observers noted a festive atmosphere among the legislators, as if the *procuradores* truly regarded the reform as their own creation. The measure received 95 more votes than were necessary for approval. Opposition to the Political Reform Law came largely from the enclaves of the regime right in the National Council and the Syndical Organization. Of the 22 syndical representatives opposing the law, over half were representatives of entrepreneurial syndicates. However, hard-liners represented a small minority of the Syndical sector. With the exception of the 40 appointed National Council representatives, Suárez gained the support of the majority of all sectors of the Cortes. Opposition to the law was especially strong within the National Council, especially from the 40 directly appointed councilors.

Suárez's strongest support came from the representatives of local government and from the family sector. This is hardly surprising, given that these *procuradores* tended to be younger and more progressive, and far more in contact with the sociopolitical reality of modern Spain. Suárez's youth, and his background as an ambitious franquist bureaucrat, must have appealed to many of his younger colleagues.

Explaining the Cortes Approval

Almost no attention on the part of social scientists has been paid to the apparent "hara-kiri" of the Cortes. However, a survey administered to a sample of *procuradores* in early 1982 shed some light on this peculiar vote.[43] The findings suggest that the Political Reform Law did not have enough support to pass when it was first introduced to the Cortes. By the time the law was voted on, roughly one-quarter of the *procuradores* had changed their minds and supported it. There was little opposition based on nonnegotiable issues, such as the "inorganic" nature of the new Cortes, or the status of the National Movement. The initial opposition to the law centered on two key issues: the legalization of the Communist Party and the electoral system. The recently reformed Penal Code contained a clause banning "totalitarian" parties or those "subject to international discipline," but aside from Suárez's personal assurances, there was no guarantee that the Communists would be excluded. The electoral system was only vaguely outlined in the Law for Political Reform. The government retained the right to set electoral boundaries and specify the exact rules of the game.

The hard core of supporters for the Suárez reform represented about 27 percent of the *procuradores* and a smaller group of hardliners represented about 10 percent of the total. The remaining *procuradores* could be described as potential supporters of the law, and it was this great mass of legislators that Suárez sought to convince. The fact that the electoral law was so important for so many *procuradores* suggests that many of them expected to participate in future elections, either as candidates or supporters of the right. At the time of the vote, many expected the regime party to be led by well-known franquist politicians, most feasibly as part of AP.

Suárez employed a mixture of suasion and pressure in his campaign to win support from the *procuradores.* Many of them received assurances from the president and his staff concerning the legalization of the PCE, the future of the National Movement, and the electoral law. A great effort was made to identify the Political Reform Law with King Juan Carlos. *Procuradores* ranked the king's support for the reform very highly among the factors influencing their decision to vote for the law.

The *procuradores'* perceptions that the government was willing to compromise also appear to have contributed to the victory of the law. These compromises were far more symbolic than substantial, but the perception that the law was not forced upon the Cortes lock, stock, and barrel mitigated the combativeness of the *procuradores.* A second perception was that the Suárez reform would lead to a conservative democracy. The Communists and regional parties were figured to be excluded. With the proper electoral law, a conservative franquist party appeared to stand a good chance of winning democratic elections. With Franco's hand-picked successor as head of state, and the ex-head of the National Movement as president, few *procuradores* viewed Suárez's reform as the end of the regime. One syndical representative from the cattle-raising sector recalled that

Adolfo Suárez and the Minister of Syndical Relations promised that the Syndical Organization would never be dismantled but would only be reformed. It was unthinkable that Spain would ever become a federal state under Suárez, and the majority of *procuradores* supporting the Law did so thinking that the Fundamental Laws were simply being reformed.[44]

One supporter of the reform claimed that the law gained his vote because "it took place within the very legal system of the regime which had given birth to it."[45] The fairly rigorous adherence to franquist legislative procedure and the acceptance of an unimportant but symbolically visible amendment on the electoral system served to foster this image. For the hard-liners, this "masquerade" was all too transparent. The government went through the motions of listening to the complaints and considering the amendments of the National Council, but by ignoring the National Council's report, Suárez and his government gambled that the silent mass of *procuradores* could be persuaded to support the measure. The final vote was evidence of the successful isolation of the hard-liners.

Winning Popular Approval

In the aftermath of his dramatic victory in the Cortes, President Suárez enjoyed considerable political momentum. His ability to sell the reform to the franquist elite impressed even the most skeptical of observers. The political atmosphere in late 1976 was captured in an editorial on November 19, in the centrist *Informaciones:*

> Step by step, Suárez has been able to erase the doubts surrounding his appointment. This "president by surprise" was rapidly able to eliminate the stupor with which his selection was received. "He is inexperienced and unknown," it was said. But he has gained great respect with his energetic style...Suárez has changed the political style and tone of the country and has carried it to places unknown during the last forty years. He carried out an unprecedented rapprochement with the opposition, to whose benefit his reform program clearly works. Suárez even knew how to gain the backing of the armed forces.[46]

One observer who was originally skeptical about Suárez wrote that "the President has the country starry eyed."[47]

With the Political Reform Law approved, attention rapidly turned toward the PSOE 27th Congress in December, the first tolerated gathering of the Socialists in Spain since the civil war. Would the most important opposition party reject its radically Marxist platform and accept the Suárez reform? The results were not entirely conclusive. On the one hand, the party continued to distance itself from its West European counterparts by defining itself as a "revolutionary and democratic" party. On the other hand, the party began a slow process of moderation that was not completed until September 1979.[48] The top leadership, generally supportive of the Suárez reform, won reelection to the top PSOE posts, and the delegates rejected the term "dictatorship of the proletariat." While the PSOE platform retained much radical rhetoric, the moderates within the PSOE were more visible at the Congress. One such moderate, Enrique Múgica, a member of the Executive Committee and the party's expert on defense matters, commented on December 5:

> In a technologically developed society like Spain, Marxism should respond dialectically to the new social reality and there must be constant ideological renovation. That is why we say that the PSOE is methodologically Marxist as a party, of Marxist inspiration, but one whose members don't have to be Marxists.[49]

PSOE leader Felipe González explicated his own position vis-à-vis the reform during the Congress. He argued that the PSOE had to adopt a very cautious strategy, acknowledging the delicate political realities of the moment. While in theory the Socialists continued to envision a profound transformation of society, the PSOE must mold its tactics to the specific political conjuncture.

Despite this apparent moderation, the PSOE, along with much of the leftist opposition, officially opposed the Political Reform Law Referendum, scheduled for December 15. The leftist opposition felt unable to endorse a political reform conducted by an authoritarian regime, without any participation of or guarantees for the democratic opposition. At the same time, nothing would have hurt the opposition more than a popular rejection of the Suárez reform. Thus, the leftist opposition officially advocated abstention, but only the extreme left actively campaigned for it. Predictably, the referendum split the democratic opposition. The hard-line franquist parties all sought a rejection of the Suárez reform. The moderate franquist parties and most of the moderate democratic opposition were united in their support for the Suárez reform.

Having cleared the major hurdle in the Cortes, Suárez intensified negotiations with opposition leaders. In early December, while the Socialists were celebrating their congress in Madrid, Suárez met with the Christian democratic opposition and agreed on the formation of a delegation of opposition leaders for future negotiations. Despite the insistence of the opposition, Suárez refused to allow Santiago Carrillo of the PCE to join the negotiating team, a move applauded by Spanish conservatives. From the start, the delegation was plagued by internal division. The two socialist parties were distrustful of each other, and the PSOE eventually withdrew. The regional and national party representatives clearly had distinct agendas. By the end of 1976, government-opposition negotiations were being carried out between the president and individual opposition leaders. While the opposition still preached unity, the prospect of democratic elections hindered efforts at opposition cohesiveness.

The referendum on the Political Reform Law made clear the strength of the government's position. As an ex-director of Spanish Television and Radio, Suárez knew how to marshal the state media in order to produce massive approval for the measure. In a country inexperienced with democracy, in which apathy and indifference were the rule, the campaign had to be unsophisticated and easily understood. Using such themes as "take your place in democracy" and "the political reform is change without risk," the government closely imitated the behavior of its franquist predecessors. Like his franquist forefathers, Suárez enjoyed overwhelming success. The Reform Law was approved by 94 percent of those voting. The 77.6 percent turnout rendered the opposition's half-hearted abstention campaign a total failure. With only 2.5 percent of the voters rejecting the law, it appeared that popular support for the hard-line right was minuscule.

If Suárez's victory in the Cortes had gained him political momentum, the referendum results placed him in a virtually unassailable position. The democratic opposition decreased its criticism of the Suárez reform and joined the scramble for votes in the upcoming democratic elections. Although the PSOE had officially opposed the Suárez reform and had counseled abstention in the referendum, it felt comfortable interpreting the government's victory as evidence of the "desire of the immense majority to end franquism once and for all."[50]

Within the franquist regime, Suárez's new political strength enabled him to act with renewed confidence and independence. He began to distance himself from his more cautious and conservative mentor, Torcuato Fernández Miranda, and he even exhibited more autonomy vis-à-vis the king.[51] With elections nearing, the president turned his attention to party politics.

Conclusion

From July to December 1976, Suárez overcame two of the most serious obstacles to democratization in Spain. First, he convinced the franquist regime to approve a constitutional reform that, in effect, ended franquism. Second, he convinced the democratic opposition to play along with his reform from above. The referendum of December 6 endowed the president's strategy with a new democratic legitimacy, weakening the position of regime hardliners and opposition leaders.

Despite these victories, significant obstacles to democratization remained. First, democratic elections entailed significant risks. The victory of either extreme might endanger the delicate balance between the regime and opposition so carefully cultivated by Suárez. The exclusion of Spain's best organized party, the PCE, raised questions about how democratic elections could be. The manipulation of the electoral process by the government, long a practice of the franquist regime, threatened to delegitimate the first elections. Second, democratization opened a veritable Pandora's box of political, social, economic, and cultural demands. The accommodation of competing demands, a problem for all democratic systems, presented more of a dilemma in the Spanish case, given the persistence in power of franquist institutions and elites, especially the military. Thus, leaders of the government and opposition faced many dangers on the eve of the first democratic elections in 40 years.

Notes

1. Samuel D. Eaton, *The Forces of Freedom in Spain, 1974-1979, A Personal Account* (Stanford, Calif.: Hoover Institution Press, 1981), pp. 32-33.

2. For an overview of the franquist political system, see Kenneth Medhurst, *The Government of Spain: The Executive at Work* (Oxford: Pergamon Press, 1973), Chapters 3-9.

3. Joaquín Bardavío, *El dilema* (Madrid: Strips, Editores, 1978), pp. 135-36.

4. Ricardo de la Cierva, *Historia del franquismo: Aislamiento, transformación, agonía (1945-1975)* (Barcelona: Planeta, 1978), pp. 435-36; and Raymond Carr and Juan Fusi, *Spain, Dictatorship to Democracy,* 2d ed. (London: Allen and Unwin, 1981), p. 204.

5. Juan Luis Cebrián, *La España que bosteza: Apuntes para una historia crítica de la transición* (Madrid: Taurus, 1980), p. 38.

6. Enrique Tierno Galván, *Cabos Sueltos* (Barcelona: Bruguera, 1981), p. 567.

7. de la Cierva, p. 435.

8. Alfonso Osorio, *Trayectoria política de un ministro de la corona,* 2d ed. (Barcelona: Planeta, 1980), p. 91.

9. Gregorio Morán, *Adolfo Suárez: Historia de una ambición* (Barcelona: Planeta, 1979), pp. 40-41.

10. See Bardavío's description, p. 179; and Tierno Galván, p. 568.

11. *El País,* July 8, 1976.

12. Morán, p. 306.

13. *Informaciones,* July 8, 1976.

14. Miguel A. Aparicio, *Introducción al sistema político y constitucional español* (Barcelona: Ariel, 1980), p. 20.

15. Osorio, p. 140.

16. For a summary of these arguments, see Guillermo Medina, "Ante un referendum constituyente controlado desde el poder," *Informaciones,* September 4, 1976.

17. An excellent summary of Juan Carlos's statements and activities during his visits to the regions of Spain is found in *Informaciones,* November 22, 1976.

18. Josep Melía, "La estrategia del cambio." *Informaciones Políticas,* July 24, 1976.

19. For coverage of the initial statement, see *El País,* July 17, 1976. Also see Morán, p. 309; and Osorio, p. 155.

20. *YA,* July 27, 1976. For a general survey of reactions to the programmatic statement, see *Informaciones,* July 17, 1976.

21. "Una carrera contra reloj," *El País,* August 3, 1976.

22. Osorio, p. 156.

23. Ibid., p. 169.

24. Ibid., p. 149, gives a fascinating account of this vestige of Spanish traditionalism.

25. Morán, p. 309.

26. Interview on March 9, 1982.

27. Osorio, p. 185.

28. Ibid., pp. 179-80.

29. Tierno Galván, p. 583. Tierno notes that "there was a polemic within the opposition, covered by the press, and it seems to me that the political class and part of the regime understood that there were contradictions in the law, and at the same time, that it was necessary for the document to be ambiguous" (p. 585).

30. *Le Monde,* October 10, 1976.

31. Osorio, p. 145.

32. *Informaciones,* September 1, 1976.

33. *ABC,* November 4, 1976.

34. G. Di Palma, "Derecha, izquierda o centro?: Sobre la legitimación de los partidos en el sur de Europa," *Revista del departamento de Derecho Político,* No. 6, (Spring 1980); and Josep Melía, "La Reforma como reválida del poder," *Informaciones Políticas,* September 11, 1976.

35. Luis Sánchez Agesta, "Las instancias de decisión," *Informaciones Políticas,* October 30, 1976.

36. James Markham in the New York *Times,* November 7, 1976.

37. *ABC,* November 2, 1976.

38. *Cambio 16,* October 9, 1976.

39. Abel Hernández, "La crísis de la reforma," *Informaciones,* October 11, 1976.

40. See Morán, p. 314, and *ABC,* November 3, 1976.

41. This and other accounts of the Plenum were compiled from *ABC, El País, Informaciones,* and the *Diário de Sesiones de las Cortes Españolas.*

42. Osorio, pp. 241-43.

43. The survey and a lengthy analysis are found in Donald Share, "Transition Through Transaction: The Politics of Democratization in Spain, 1975-77" (Ph.D dissertation, Stanford University, 1983), pp. 274-93.

44. Based on written comments collected as part of the survey administered by the author to a sample of *procuradores* in 1982 (Survey number 003). For more details about the survey, see ibid.

45. Survey number 024.

46. *Informaciones,* November 19, 1976.

47. José Jiménez Blanco, *De Franco a las elecciones generales* (Madrid: Tecnos, 1978), p. 174.

48. For a more detailed discussion of the dilemmas and contradictions facing the PSOE, see Chapter 6.

49. *El País Semanal,* December 5, 1976.

50. *Informaciones,* December 16, 1976.

51. Morán, pp. 318 and 320.

5 THE TRANSITION CONSOLIDATED: FOUNDING A NEW DEMOCRACY

It is logical that many people who participated in the regime today proclaim themselves to be democrats. Perhaps the moralists
will be disgusted by this phenomenon, but historians will recognize the "cunning of reason" in the burial of the political system
by the political forces which the system helped to create.[1]

Introduction

This chapter studies the consolidation of transition through
transaction in the two years following the approval of the Political Reform Law by the franquist legislature, and by the overwhelming majority of Spaniards in the referendum of December
1976. The popular acceptance of a democratic constitution in December 1978 marked the formal establishment of a parliamentary
democracy and the end of the transition from authoritarianism.

The Political Reform Law had called for democratic elections,
but serious risks and obstacles remained. The terrorist outbursts
between December 1976 and February 1977 threatened to undermine Suárez's mandate for democratization. The desire to prevent
a leftist victory in the first elections was a source of constant pressure on the president as he planned for elections. The issue of the
Spanish Communist Party also presented some dangers to the Suárez government. The president's ability to overcome both crises ultimately strengthened his political hand and facilitated his own

move toward the center. The elections were a milestone in the democratization process because they established a precedent for elite moderation and civic behavior, and because they produced a centrist government capable of consolidating the transition.

The latter part of the chapter describes the period from July 1977 to December 1978, in which two serious challenges faced political elites. The economic crisis, exacerbated by the uncertainty of the transition and compounded by years of neglect, required immediate attention at a politically sensitive moment. It was also necessary to write a democratic constitution after 40 years of authoritarian rule. The June 1977 elections had produced an ideologically divided parliament, a factor that threatened to prevent the writing of a widely acceptable constitution. The resolution of both crises was possible because of a new spirit of political compromise and moderation on the part of most Spanish political forces.

The Parliamentary Elections of June 1977

Suárez had gained the legal endorsement necessary for the last stages of his reform strategy during the Cortes battle over the Political Reform Law. The December 1976 referendum had given him an unquestionable popular mandate for democratic reform. By January 1977, Suárez had undeniable momentum and popularity and his government clearly held the political initiative. However, elections remained a long way off, and the potential for mistakes, pitfalls, and breakdown should not be underestimated.

Spain's previous democratic experience was undermined by extremism and violence. Party leaders were inevitably implicated in, and partly responsible for, inciting this behavior, and the result was increased political polarization, mutual recrimination, and, eventually, civil war. The widespread awareness of this history and the ability to learn historical lessons from it is a key explanation for the exemplary elite behavior in response to the wave of terrorist violence that shocked Spaniards in late December 1976 and most of January 1977. Had elites acted less prudently, had opposition leaders incited their followers, had the government overreacted by resorting to increased repression, or by slowing down the pace of reforms out of fear or intimidation, transition through transaction could have failed. The events in and around January 1977 reveal an ominous cycle of action and reaction, constituting the type of violence that, at the end of the Second Republic, convinced a previously hesitant armed forces to rebel against the democratic regime.

Right- and left-wing terrorism had increased ever since the appointment of Adolfo Suárez; his program of compromise was anathema to both extremes. Shortly after the president had presented his program to the public, on July 18, a series of bombs exploded throughout Spain. A second wave of explosions followed Suárez's first announcement of a partial amnesty for political prisoners, on July 31, 1976. In September, after Suárez's triumphant meeting with military leaders, terrorists killed a prominent franquist official in the Basque Country. Similar outbursts of violence occurred on the eves of the Cortes vote and referendum. In the latter case, GRAPO, the mysterious terrorist organization (self-proclaimed leftists with alleged ties to the extreme right), kidnapped the president of the Spanish Council of State.

Terrorist activity of a cyclical left-right nature was stepped up after the December 15 referendum in reaction to the obvious success of Suárez's strategy. From the referendum to mid-February, Spain experienced a full-scale destabilization attempt from terrorists of both extremes.

The atmosphere of terror that pervaded Spain during this time reached its peak in late January, leading some to much talk about the *argentinización* of Spanish politics.

> Madrid witnessed a terrorist process almost without precedent, and the capital of the country appeared to be suffocating. Streets were half-empty, mothers would not take their children to school, theatres were empty, and opposition leaders were in hiding. This was a time of extreme tension. . . .[2]

On January 23, during a pro-amnesty rally in downtown Madrid, a rightist terrorist killed a young student, Arturo Ruíz García. A riot ensued in which 12 people were injured. The next day, Lieutenant General Villaescusa, president of the Supreme Council of Military Justice, was kidnapped in downtown Madrid. University violence in reaction to the events of the previous day was widespread, and rightist groups were already reacting to the news of General Villaescusa's sequestor. A huge demonstration in the streets of the capital, in protest over the killing of Ruíz, resulted in several additional injuries and one death, when police fired on the crowd.

Rightist *procuradores* demanded a Cortes plenum to discuss the deterioration of social order. Top government officials met in an urgent session and temporarily outlawed all demonstrations. That evening, nine communist labor lawyers were gunned down in their Madrid offices by right-wing terrorists, killing five of them instantly. The following day, Suárez met with all three military ministers and sent notes to regional commanders and the head of the Guardia Civil, urging calm.[3] The right-wing Fuerza Nueva reacted to the violence in a communiqué stating: "If need be, and if the government is not able to guarantee the public's safety, Fuerza Nueva will resort to legitimate means to fulfill such needs."[4] Later that evening, right-wing thugs terrorized customers in a popular Madrid bar. On January 26 an emergency cabinet meeting was convened and a note was released reassuring that "the State is intact and the Government remains committed to fulfilling its program and continuing down the road that has been freely elected by the Spanish people." A demonstration mourning the deaths of the communist labor lawyers in Madrid, with more than 150,000 attending, transpired without incident, leading the interior minister to applaud "the sensible citizen response and the generalized rejection of violence." The same communiqué announced the arrest of a number of rightist extremists.

On January 29, after yet another day of violence, Suárez appeared on television to make an important speech in defense of the reform and against attempts to intimidate him:

> There can be no capitulation to subversion, no lukewarm response to provocation, no failure to deal with the great problems which could ruin the autonomy of the state. We say yes to a peaceful dialogue and we are open to such an approach. We say yes to opening up the political game in order to normalize political life. We say yes to the recognition of regional differences. We say yes to allowing the various political aspirants to exercise legal power.[5]

Not only had the government acted with prudence and resolve (in the appropriate mixture), but political elites, from across the political spectrum, supported the government's efforts. The opposition parties, especially the PCE and the PSOE, acted with utmost responsibility and caution. A good example of this moderation was their behavior at the height of the destabilization attempt in late January. In order to avoid contributing to political polarization, both parties refused to sign an antiterrorist statement in conjunction with radical parties to their left. The cooperation between the government and the PCE after the murders of the labor lawyers, and the resulting peace that reigned at the funeral activities, greatly impressed all actors involved and initiated a pattern of collaboration that became important in the following weeks and months. Stanley Payne recalled:

> The democratic opposition did not only fail to protest the exceptional decree laws against terrorism, but came to lend its almost unconditional support to the government during the following days of the crisis. They knew, as well as the government, that what was at stake was a successful conclusion of the democratic transition.[6]

The Spanish press was especially important in creating support for the government during this period. On January 29, at the peak of the crisis, Spain's major newspapers united to publish a joint editorial, entitled "For the Unity of All," condemning terrorism and appealing for calm. According to Juan Tomás de Salas, editor of the influential *Cambio 16* and *Diário 16*, this moderation was the result of an unwritten agreement among all major periodicals of the period.[7]

The crisis period ended in early February. However, the evidence suggests that even before these dramatic events, the government, with the cooperation of the political elite in general, had demonstrated the resolve and skill to confront the destabilization attempt.

Concessions to the Right: Preventing a Leftist Victory

The transition to democracy in Spain was controlled at all times by the members of the authoritarian regime. The military and much of the franquist right would never have tolerated the reform were they not confident of such control. A victory by the left in the first democratic elections would have been viewed by the right as a sign that the Suárez government had lost control of the reform, and the possibility of an authoritarian coup would have become greater. At the same time, if the government intervened excessively to prevent a leftist victory, it ran the risk of discrediting the electoral process and discouraging the moderation of the opposition. A further problem confronting Suárez was the equally distasteful prospect of an electoral victory for the franquist right. Such an outcome would imperil the continuation of democratic reform and might lead to a dangerous political polarization. On the one hand, the government, faced with demands by the franquist right, sought to limit the electoral chances of the left by manipulating the electoral system. On the other hand, this strategy promised to play into the hands of the only well-organized rightist political force: the unabashedly franquist Popular Alliance. These dilemmas were not resolved until late in the preelectoral period, when Adolfo Suárez consolidated the political center under his own leadership, ensuring the defeat of the socialist left and the regime right.

The electoral law of March 18, 1977, was written by franquists, approved by the franquist Cortes, and implemented through the remains of the franquist bureaucratic apparatus. Although the Suárez government consulted with members of the democratic opposition on key features of the law, the opposition was clearly at a disadvantage: It had little choice but to participate in the first democratic elections in over 40 years. One of the most important features of the electoral law aimed at cutting into the left's electoral success was the setting of the voting age at 21, in accordance with the still-effective franquist Civil Code. Opinion research showed a marked preference among young Spaniards for parties of the left, when compared with older Spaniards. A 1976 study of Spanish political culture noted that the generational factor was crucial for determining the structure of party identification and political participation on the eve of the first democratic elections. It concluded that "young people are predominantly socialists and old people are predominantly among the forces that compose the National Movement."[8] The electoral law also prohibited most of the nearly 1 million Spanish migrant voters from participating in the first elections, or about 3 percent of the total electorate. By limiting the registration period, emigrant voters were excluded.

A third feature of the electoral system aimed at debilitating the left was the system of counting votes and allocating seats. The Political Reform Law had included, as one of its concessions to the franquist right, the provision that 350 members would be elected to the Cortes as follows: A minimum of two deputies per province were to be elected, plus one additional representative for every 144,500 inhabitants, or remainders of at least 70,000 inhabitants. This system constituted a clear departure from Spanish electoral precedent. The constitutions of 1812, 1836, and 1845 all used the ratio of one deputy per 40,000 inhabitants, and in 1907 the electoral law, which remained in effect through the Second Republic, raised the ratio to one deputy per 50,000 inhabitants. The resulting overrepresentation of Spain's conservative rural provinces was vaguely explained in the preamble to the electoral law as "compensating for [Spain's] irregular demography." While Madrid and Barcelona each had over 125,000 inhabitants per deputy, rural districts such as Soria and Guadalajara had under 45,000 inhabitants per deputy. Of the 18 provinces in which the agricultural sector was predominant, the electoral law provided for overrepresentation in 16 of them.[9] The overrepresentation was all the more serious when considering that the Political Reform Law called for a territorially based Senate, which by its very nature favored conservative and rural regions.

The long period of authoritarian rule had obstructed the emergence of a unified opposition force, and Franco's death, together with Suárez's successful reform, had led to a proliferation of political groups, mostly leftist in ideology. The right, on the other hand, was relatively unified within Fraga Iribarne's AP. It was for this reason that the right demanded mechanisms to limit the electoral fortunes of small and fragmented political forces as a precondition for their approval of the Political Reform Law. For example, the electoral law established a 3 percent threshold for presence in the Cortes. In addition, the *D'hondt* system, a form of vote counting that discriminates against smaller parties and favors larger electoral coalitions, was included in the electoral law. The system has since become widely accepted, and has benefited the left as well as the right, but it was seen originally as a way of minimizing the fears of the franquist right concerning the election of a Cortes dominated by small, leftist, and regionalist parties.

Concessions to the Democratic Opposition: The Holy Week Legalization and the Dismantling of Franquist Political Institutions

There is no greater example of the influence of a single leader on the course of Spanish politics than Adolfo Suárez's surprise legalization of the Spanish Communist Party. This gamble was especially significant because it bolstered the president's credibility among the democratic opposition, and increased the legitimacy accorded to the results of the June 15 elections. Suárez emerged from the PCE legalization with renewed confidence and the momentum necessary for his subsequent "occupation" of the political center.

Interviews conducted during 1982 with Suárez's closest aides revealed that this decision was very much the president's own. Few of his top advisors felt that the PCE should be legalized in April 1977. Among those supporting its eventual legalization, there was a strong feeling that enough had already been reformed in a short period, and that bringing the Communists into the political system before elections would only incite the military. Moreover, Suárez had given his word to the military, the Cortes, and even some of his top aides that democratization would not include the Communists. Even if Suárez was sincere when he made these promises, by spring 1977 he felt relatively unrestrained by past pledges.

Since August 1976 Suárez had maintained indirect contacts with the PCE through several individuals close to the government. These secret contacts revealed that Carrillo was willing to accept the monarchy publicly in exchange for legalization. Publicly, however, up until the surprise legalization Suárez continued to give every impression that the PCE would never be tolerated.

For months, unbeknownst to Suárez, Carrillo had been inside Spain, cautiously moving around incognito. Because his indirect contacts had proved frustrating, Carrillo decided to force the issue of legalization by appearing at Madrid's Barajas Airport for a hastily announced press conference on December 10, 1976. During the appearance, only five days before the referendum on the Political Reform Law, Carrillo demonstrated a mixture of conciliation and aggressiveness.[10] His presence inside Spain wrought a storm of rage that reminded the government of the extent of anticommunist sentiment among Spanish elites. The conservative but normally sensible *ABC* typified the anger with a front-page caption below a photograph of Carrillo: "The old Communist militant doesn't want a democracy: he wants power, all or none. Yesterday, dressed as a bourgeois to lessen the fear of the god-fearing, he appeared in Madrid, made his little speech, lied and left.[11]

The PCE secretary-general, by appearing unannounced, had hoped to force the government to deal with the issue of PCE legalization. Instead, the regime was embarrassed at a delicate moment and was forced to arrest Carrillo. When on December 31 Carrillo was set free on bond, the Spanish right again protested. However, the PCE, though illegal, was mostly tolerated from that point on. Suárez and Carrillo, in an attempt to avoid future embarrassments, intensified their secret negotiations.

Why did Suárez legalize the PCE? By April 9, 1977, when he stunned the country by legalizing the Communist Party, the political environment was much different from that of only six months earlier. First, having survived the most serious challenge to public order since his appointment, Suárez had a clearer idea of where his true enemies and allies were. The left's increasing support for the strategy of transition from above, and its moderation during the January crisis, deeply impressed the young president.[12] His negotiations with the opposition delegation had been much more comfortable than his often tense interaction with the regime right.

Second, Suárez's ability to deliver immediate political change where Arias had twice failed, his firm control of political events during the January crisis, and his "modern" political style had all earned him a popular appeal that should not be underestimated. The referendum had provided an overwhelming popular mandate for his political reform, and the widespread and nonpartisan praise of his subsequent reforms had given him considerable confidence, and a sense of independence.

Third, the secret government-PCE contacts had convinced the president that the Communists could be trusted to help consolidate the new democracy. After rightists murdered five communist labor lawyers in downtown Madrid, the party reacted with admirable serenity. Although 150,000 sympathizers were rallied on short notice, the leadership made every effort to avoid political polarization. Suárez met in secret with Carrillo on February 27, making the president one of the first regime politicians to meet with the PCE leader. The meeting, lasting over six hours, was cordial, and the president was impressed by Carrillo's realistic attitude.[13]

On the same day, the government turned down the PCE's official request for legalization, forwarding the application to the Supreme Court. Suárez reportedly informed Carrillo that he supported PCE legalization but needed to work out legal technicalities. Finally, the president realized that the PSOE would be the major beneficiary if the PCE were excluded; by legalizing the PCE the left's vote would be split, and the PSOE would have to guard against its left flank.

On April 1 the Supreme Court failed to resolve the issue of the PCE's legalization and passed the sensitive issue back to the government, claiming it had no jurisdiction over the matter, but refusing to prohibit the legalization. Suárez then convened his top cabinet officials to explain his decision to legalize the Communists before the elections. The president argued that the PCE's participation would add legitimacy to the first elections, and that it seemed impossible to ban the PCE with recourse to the Penal Code, since the PCE was clearly not a "totalitarian party." He also suggested that the Communists were more of a menace as an illegal force than as a visible actor in the party system. These arguments met fierce resistance within the cabinet.[14] Cortes President Fernández Miranda had become worried by Suárez's political independence, but was especially angered over his decision to legalize the Communists. In May, King Juan Carlos replaced Fernández Miranda, despite the latter's important contribution to the transition.[15]

On April 6, during Holy Week, and while most of Spain's political class had left the capital for the traditional vacation period, the president convened Interior Minister Martín Villa and began to put the PCE legalization in motion. On April 8 Suárez appealed to Carrillo to restrain his party's reaction to the impending announcement, and the PCE consented. On April 9, when the government announced the legalization, most of the government and military elite were caught by surprise. Suárez had opted for a *fait accompli* strategy, anxious to avoid a potentially dangerous debate over the issue. The president took this risk against the advice of his top aides and Spain's most important foreign allies.

The reaction of the hard-liners in the military was immediate. Admiral Pita da Veiga, Navy minister, resigned in protest and other top admirals closed ranks, making it difficult for Suárez to find a replacement. In the Army, Minister Alvarez Arena tried to support the president, but could not prevent the convening of an emergency meeting of the Superior War Council. The Council publicly expressed "disgust" over the legalization, but accepted the *fait accompli* out of the army's "sense of patriotism and discipline." *El Alcázar* noted that "the consequences will be tragic for Spain. This legalization has dynamited the 18th of July."[16] Even Fraga's Popular Alliance called the legalization "a veritable *coup d'état*."[17]

The Communists did the best they could to make Suárez's decision more palatable to the public. On April 14 the PCE Executive Committee publicly delivered on its part of the bargain: It agreed to accept the monarchy and the Spanish flag. The next day, Carrillo held a press conference and stated that, as a realistic party, the PCE would accept the rules of parliamentary democracy.

The legalization of the PCE brought the last major national political force into the democratic reform strategy. Only splinter groups on the extreme left, and some Basque forces, remained excluded. The Communists turned out to be crucial supporters of Spain's young democracy, and their participation in the 1977 elections effectively divided the left. The hostility provoked by the surprise legalization pushed the president closer to the parties of the democratic opposition and helps explain why Suárez began to act more like a populist than a franquist bureaucrat. He had burned his bridges with the military and the regime right, and there could no longer be any turning back.

A second concession to the democratic opposition was the dismantling of franquist institutions. Since in transitions through transaction members of an authoritarian regime control the regime change, these same leaders must dismantle at least some parts of the regime to which they belong. That many leaders would be unwilling or unable to do so, as the case of Arias's presidency so clearly illustrated, seems obvious. Authoritarian institutions may enhance the leadership's ability to control the transition, and are thus surrendered only begrudgingly. Nevertheless, Suárez dismantled some of the most important franquist institutions before the June elections, and this helped to make the break between the authoritarian and democratic regimes less traumatic.

In early January, despite the crisis provoked by political violence, Suárez disbanded the infamous Tribunal of Public Order by decree-law. The tribunal had been established to deal with terrorism, but had effectively prosecuted all forms of opposition. Two other powerful franquist institutions were abolished by the start of the electoral campaign in June 1977: the National Movement and the Syndical Organization. The National Movement was abolished on April 7, when its familiar Falangist standard (the bow and arrows) was removed from its headquarters. Ironically, the fact that the MN was Suárez's own power base made it easier for the president to abolish the vast patronage network. His aides assured many

MN officials that they would find government positions after the elections and that there was no danger of future recrimination. Influential National Movement bureaucrats were instrumental in assuring hesitant MN members that they would be taken care of in the future. By June 2, when Suárez issued a decree law dismantling the powerful Syndical Organization, the Spanish public was already preoccupied with the ongoing electoral campaign. The voices of dissent were drowned out by campaign activity, the likes of which Spaniards had not experienced in over four decades.

The Occupation of the Center

The political "center" was composed mostly of franquist politicians who had taken advantage of the political thaw of the mid-1960s, and who had begun to consider future political options. As intended by its franquist architects, the limited, legal (but only quasi-organized) ideological pluralism that emerged in the twilight of franquism was always contained within the confines of the regime. Nevertheless, the neophyte "associations" and study groups that resulted from this political opening, together with the more progressive sectors of the media, religious organizations, and private sector served to create considerable elite support for the concept of a strong political center after franquism.

However, until 1977 the center was unable to acquire a solid organizational framework. The franquist regime's attempt to deal with the political future realistically, by sowing the seeds for political parties of the center and right, was hopelessly delayed. Creation of political associations in the 1960s might have benefited the subsequent emergence of solid regime parties, but their acceptance only in the last two years of the regime stunted such a development. Instead, protean regime groups and factions remained divided into personalistic cliques led by political "barons."

The uncertainty and ambiguity of the transition split the very elite that could have formed the basis for a political center. Some sought to distance themselves from the regime in which they had earlier participated, believing that franquism had exhausted all possibilities for reform. This group included some prominent conservative franquists, and many in this camp refused to participate in Suárez's first government precisely for this reason. A second group, especially Suárez's allies in the franquist bureaucracy, saw the future political center as an alliance between regime reformists and moderate democratic opposition leaders. For this group, the distinction between regime and opposition would necessarily be obfuscated in a transition controlled from above.

There were long-standing ideological divisions among the various groups claiming to occupy the center. The Christian democrats sought a centrist ground, as did the Center Democrats (CD), a weak coalition of liberals, monarchists, social democrats, Christian democrats, populists, and moderate regional forces. The weakness and internal incoherence of the center encouraged the rightist Popular Alliance (AP), Fraga Iribarne's electoral alliance, to portray itself as centrist, a strategy that proved successful until Suárez intervened only weeks before the election.

Thus by early 1977 it was apparent that the political center was in disarray. The Center Democrats were bogged down in political and personal squabbles, vividly described by the press. The alliance was led by a number of ex-franquist "barons" who were known for their liberalism, and who had distanced themselves from the regime in the twilight of authoritarianism. The incessant infighting within the Center Democrats led most observers to predict electoral disaster for the alliance when facing a unified regime right (Fraga's AP) and a strong socialist left (González's PSOE). A prominent liberal, and a founding member of the alliance, recalled that the Center Democrats "in the months before the election, gradually appeared before the public as a collection of imbeciles."[18]

As early as January 1977, Suárez began to negotiate with Center Democrat officials in an attempt to enter the coalition. Many CD "barons" resented Suárez's interest, fearing that his participation would tarnish their independence, and could be costly at the polls. More importantly, they distrusted Suárez's own motives and suspected that the president sought to use the alliance to launch his own democratic political career. Many centrist leaders resented Suárez's initial appointment and did not want to be eclipsed by him again. This last concern was well founded. A poll conducted in early March 1977 asked a sample of Spaniards to name the candidate they would vote for "if he or she were to run in your province." Suárez was named by 28 percent of respondents, double the percentage of the next closest politician, Felipe González. Only one Center Democratic leader (Areilza, 9 percent) received any recognition.[19]

The last-minute formation of UCD was the creation of Adolfo Suárez and his closest collaborators, and it was motivated by several considerations. First, and foremost, Suárez needed his own political vehicle. He considered the emerging democracy to be largely his own creation, and the young president had no intention of fading away after the first democratic elections. He wanted to win democratic legitimacy and to establish a new career in the new system. In this sense, Suárez represented a whole generation of young franquists who, despite their implication in authoritarian rule, wanted to demonstrate their compatibility with democratic politics. Under his leadership, UCD would encompass "the same politicians acting differently."[20]

Second, Suárez felt his leadership was crucial to the still-unfinished business of consolidating a democratic regime. If democratization from above were to be successfully implemented to its logical end, skillful leadership would be required. Who better knew the possibilities of and limits to Spain's democratic transition? There were few other Spanish politicians who were so well respected by the Spanish left, by many in the center, by the king, and even by many on the right.

Third, Suárez viewed his leadership of the center as essential, and as the only way to defeat a much better organized right and left. The writing of a truly consensual constitution, the ability to arrive at broad social pacts for the resolution of Spain's multiple political and economic crises, the slow but steady democratization of the armed forces, and the devolution of power to Spain's regions would all be more easily achieved by a strong government of the center than by a government of either extreme. Only a powerful and genuinely centrist coalition could displace AP from the center, forcing it into the political space it truly represented. Only a government of the center could push ahead essential reform, while taking note of the continuing constraints and obstacles.

Finally, by ensuring continuity between the authoritarian and democratic periods in the positions of head of state *and* government, the very essence of transition through transaction would be reinforced. Such continuity of top personnel between the two regimes was yet another sign of the absence of any clear *ruptura* between the two periods. This continuity, while frustrating for the Spanish left, and also for a great many individuals in the Spanish center, would constitute a cause for calm among Spain's financial sectors and in the increasingly uneasy Spanish military. For all these reasons, the formation of UCD was encouraged, initially at least, by important financial sectors, by sectors of the church, as well as by Spain's most important allies.

In late February 1977, Suárez and his top aides formed the Independent Social Federation to negotiate with the Center Democrats, and with the competing Christian Democratic Team. In mid-March, Suárez's government issued the electoral law by decree, careful to exclude only ministers, officers, and senior civil servants—but not presidents of the government—from running in the June elections. By late April, some Center Democratic leaders were more interested in having Suárez lead the centrist alliance. After months of squabbling, they had failed to present a coherent image to the public and were seriously worried about an electoral debacle. In addition, Suárez's daring legalization of the PCE had won the president considerable respect among the democratic opposition, so many no longer saw his participation as a liability. By April 25 the president had decided to participate with the Center Democrats, but only on *his* terms. At the end of April, Minister of Public Works Leopoldo Calvo Sotelo resigned in order to dedicate his time to the reorganization of the center under Suárez. The president announced his decision to run on May 3, after a highly successful and widely publicized visit to Washington.

By May 6, the deadline for submitting electoral lists, Suárez's forces had scored a complete victory in their attempt to control the center. Calvo Sotelo had convinced Center Democratic leaders to give the president a virtual *carte blanche* in formulating the lists. To the dismay of Center Democratic leaders, the alliance was rechristened the Union of the Democratic Center (Unión de Centro Democrático, UCD), and Suárez's supporters occupied the highest positions on the lists. Suárez used his political capital skillfully, convincing recalcitrant Center Democratic leaders that his participation was the best guarantee for the center's victory.

Many important centrist leaders refused to participate in the new alliance, angered over Suárez's manipulation of the electoral lists. Even among those who chose to remain in UCD after Suárez's occupation, there was evident surprise over Suárez's tactics.

One prominent Christian democrat admitted that he was shocked by the lists and stated that they were not what he had in mind after negotiating with Suárez's aides. "Had I known the composition of the lists," he noted in retrospect, "I would have thought about UCD more carefully."[21] The Spanish press, normally supportive of the president, reacted to Suárez's decision with hostility. *Cambio 16* entitled its May 22 issue "The Night the Center Died," and *Cuadernos Para el Diálogo* charged that "to dress the reform as 'centrist,' to institutionalize it, to use the hand-picking of candidates to consolidate a parliamentary majority of rightists, is exactly what the present government should not do."[22]

Under Suárez's leadership, UCD enjoyed considerable advantages. The president attempted to foster the image of governmental neutrality in the elections, but Suárez's frequent appearances on the state television network (which blatantly favored the candidacy of its ex-director), and his much-publicized and well-timed trip to the United States, were only two examples of these advantages. In the words of a top staff member, "Spanish radio, television, government press, and provincial governers [were] all at the service of Suárez's candidacy."[23] The president was able to use his position of power to avoid direct confrontation with his adversaries, thus keeping his franquist past off the public agenda. *El País* complained that "a still omnipresent power participates in these elections without giving the rest of the candidates the opportunity to answer the President of the government, who continutes his campaign via the Official State Bulletin."[24] Typically, the government responded that "it is not considered wise for the President, whose position forced him to reject all active dedication to the campaign, to appear in debates."[25]

The controversy over Suárez's candidacy helped turn the general elections into a "new referendum which the government [could] once again win."[26] Even the generally conservative *Informaciones* feared that the "elections run the risk of becoming a 'Suárez Sí, Suárez No' plebiscite."[27] One can hardly fault those critics of UCD who objected to Suárez's participation in the elections. Many, if not most of the observers at the time, still analyzed politics in terms of a strict authoritarianism/democracy dichotomy. Suárez was viewed as a franquist, despite his admirable reformism. There was little comprehension of the fact that transition through transaction blurs the distinction between democrats and authoritarians. UCD welded together the protagonists of the Spanish transition and the centrist opposition. It bridged the division between regime and opposition that the defunct Center Democrats had sought to maintain.

The Electoral Campaign and Elite Moderation

The moderation and caution exercised by political elites during the first democratic electoral contest in over 40 years was an important contribution to the consolidation of transition through transaction. The peacefulness and calm that characterized the electoral campaign, despite the inexperience of the Spanish polity, helped to legitimate Suárez's strategy for reform.

Parties of the left were especially nonconfrontational in their electoral campaigns. The PSOE employed the slogan "Socialism Is Liberty," calling attention away from many of the radical aspects of the party's platform. The party stressed the popular and familial nature of the party. Likewise, Tierno Galván's Popular Socialist Party employed the consensual slogan, "In Changing Times, Responsible Men," focusing on the professorial image of leader. The PCE used the theme "To Vote Communist is to Vote Democracy," and in electoral advertisements the party replaced the traditional red with less conflictual greens, oranges, and browns. Even more than the socialist left, the PCE steered clear of concrete references to policies or goals.

UCD employed a similarly vague message with its slogan, "The Center is Democracy." UCD attempted to portray itself as the only party capable of avoiding a dangerous left-right confrontation, so feared by most Spaniards. In addition, UCD centered its campaign on the person of Suárez by using the slogan "To Vote Center is To Vote Suárez."

UCD's last-minute formation, and Suárez's surprise decision to head the coalition, pushed AP further to the right than had previously been the case. AP did not resort to an openly hostile campaign, but its strategy was to suggest that Suárez had taken the reform too far too fast. AP's original campaign slogan called on Spaniards to "reject the extremes," but after Suárez's entry into the electoral arena, it began to place more emphasis on "Liberty within Order" and "Security and Progress." The latter slogan was well known to Spaniards, since the AP leader had used it in the

1966 referendum to approve Franco's system of organic democracy. For example, one AP advertisement portrayed an elderly couple and stated, "Spain today, with crime and terrorism: let's recover our peace and happiness for the common person." At AP electoral rallies, often well-attended, ex-franquist ministers lashed out at the government's irreverence toward the past, its philocommunism, and its lack of toughness in negotiating with the left. Near the end of the campaign, when opinion polls predicted a disaster for AP, these rallies were often dominated by hard-line franquists and falangists, who attacked not only Suárez but the entire democratic reform.

Suárez's occupation of the center also displaced the Christian democrats grouped into the Christian Democratic Team (Equipo Demócrata Cristiana, EDC). Led by two historic figures within Spanish Christian democracy, the EDC sought to encompass Christian democrats from a wide political spectrum. With the appearance of UCD as a serious contender, EDC found itself without a clear electoral identity. Unable to move left, where the PSOE, PSP, and PCE were firmly entrenched, the EDC was forced into trying to compete for center ground with the president's coalition. This explains why the EDC's campaign was more accusatory than that of parties to its left. The EDC warned voters not to opt for "Continuity Disguised as Opportunistic Change," and accused the government of "promising now what they did not do when they were in power." It branded ex-franquists, and hence Suárez, as "those who were never worried about nationalities and who now pretend to defend autonomy." In one of the most direct attacks on the transition through transaction, the EDC urged voters to reject "those who change faces and shirts." By presenting such an aggressive image to the Spanish public, the Christian democrats undermined one of their chief sources of appeal: their ability to be conciliators. The Catholic Church, a major potential source of support, was unwilling to cast its lot with any one electoral force.

Only the extreme right coalition, the National Alliance (AN) openly campaigned against democracy. Employing such slogans as "Vote for Those Who Did Not Swear Loyalty Falsely," these representatives of the franquist hard-liners aimed their campaign against the center and right. Otherwise, the extreme right emphasized such values as "God, Fatherland, and Liberty." The Spanish press paid scant attention to AN's lackluster campaign, which was poorly funded and organized.

The widespread elite moderation and caution, what became known cynically as the "extreme moderation," created a peculiar atmosphere during the entire campaign. PSP leader Tierno Galván observed that this moderation was largely the result of a conscious effort by political elites.[28] As a result, political parties employed vague electoral messages. This moderation was an attempt to avoid confrontation and to campaign in favor of the Suárez reform, if not always in support of Suárez's government. For most party elites, the establishment of parliamentary democracy took precedence over partisan issues. In addition, this elite effort, echoed in the media, resulted partially from the feeling that the Spanish electorate would not be able to cope with a more politicized campaign after 40 years of franquism. The Spanish public was politically undereducated, and most of the major parties felt it necessary to distribute material instructing voters how to cast ballots and describing the ground rules of democratic politics. Finally, it reflected the need for inexperienced and previously illegal and/or historically suspect parties to gain legitimacy within a democratic context.

The Elections of June 15, 1977

The electoral process transpired with few flaws. Despite evidence of *caciquismo* and *pucherazo* (electoral manipulation and ballot box stuffing), especially in some rural areas, the elections were by and large devoid of tampering. The major political parties were present at most electoral sites to guard against electoral fraud. The extremely high turnout (17.8 million Spaniards voted, or 78.4 percent of the total electorate), the atmosphere of absolute calm, and, finally, the electoral results all helped to consolidate parliamentary democracy.

Table 5 presents a simplified breakdown of the electoral results. While it exceeds the scope of this analysis to discuss the results in depth, several observations are important to make. First, the elections were a vote of confidence for Suárez and his strategy of democratic transition. UCD received the largest percentage of votes and seats, although it failed to win an absolute majority in either house. Suárez was the only logical choice for president, thus ensuring considerable continuity between franquism and the new democracy. The president, whose original mandate derived from a head of state appointed by Franco, now could claim democratic legitimacy.

Table 5. Electoral Results, June 15, 1977

| Party | Number of Votes (millions) | Percent of Voters | Deputies | | Senators | |
			Number of Seats	Percent of Seats	Number of Seats	Percent of Seats
UCD	6.06	34.0	164	46.8	105	42.3
PSOE	5.09	28.5	118	33.7	47	18.9
PCE	1.64	9.2	21	6.0	3	1.2
AP	1.46	8.2	17	4.8	2	0.8
PSP	0.76	4.2	6	1.7	4	1.6
Others	2.89	15.9	24	7.0	46	18.6
Royal appointments					41	16.5
Totals	17.90	100.00	350	100.00	248	100.0

Source: Compiled by the author.

Second, the elections prevented Suárez from imposing a new constitution on parliament. The excellent performance by the two socialist parties (a combined 35.4 percent of the seats in the lower house) meant that the left would need to be consulted and included in the process of writing a new constitution, if the resulting document were to be legitimate.

Third, the poor showing of both the PCE and AP, on the left and right extremes, respectively, in addition to suggesting a popular rejection of "older" politicians, pointed to a genuine moderation of the electorate and support for younger, more modern parties.

Last, despite the admirable showing by regional parties in the Basque Country and Catalonia, the party system was far less fragmented than might have been predicted given the plethora of parties and coalitions on the ballot. Two large center parties, flanked by smaller left and right parties, represented a relatively workable parliamentary scenario. The extreme left and franquist right were convincingly trounced in the elections, further aiding the subsequent compromise over the constitution of 1978.

Establishing the Politics of Consensus

The June elections led to the formation of Spain's first democratic parliament in over four decades. The convening of the Cortes on July 13, 1977, seemed to signal the start of a new political era. The emotion of that inaugural parliamentary session was best symbolized by the first meeting of two newly elected deputies: Dolores Ibarruri, the aging PCE president known as La Pasionaria, recently returned from exile in Moscow, and Adolfo Suárez, only recently head of Spain's National Movement. The two represented opposing ideologies and generations, but both were now sitting in the same parliament. In the summer of 1977, the dissolution of the republican government in exile, and Don Juan's renouncement of his claim to the throne, added unquestionable legitimacy to the monarchy.

Formally, however, Spain retained much of the franquist constitutional edifice. The Political Reform Law opened the door for the writing of a new constitution, but it did not provide for a government responsible to the legislature, nor did it clearly delimit the power of the executive. Only with the approval of a new constitution in December 1978 did Spain formally become a parliamentary democracy. Between the elections of 1977 and the referendum of 1978 two fundamental problems had to be resolved. The most pressing problem concerned the economic crisis, which had been exacerbated by the political uncertainty associated with the transition. A second, but equally important, task was the writing of a new constitution that could be accepted by a wide range of Spanish political forces.

The new legislature facing these problems confronted some serious obstacles. The historic "two Spains" were still in evidence in the electoral results, and the Spanish electorate had divided roughly into halves: The right had won 50.1 percent of the vote (55.8 percent of the seats) to the left's 49.9 percent (44.17 percent of the seats). Unlike the fragmentation of the Second Republic, however, the bipolar composition of the Cortes was not accompanied by party fragmentation. The two major victors, the UCD and PSOE, controlled 80 percent of the seats between them.

Two potential pitfalls faced political elites. First, the traditional left-right cleavage threatened to obstruct any attempt to deal with the short-term economic crisis, politicizing the writing of the constitution. Second, there was the possibility that the two major parties, UCD and PSOE, would band together and exclude regional parties and both extremes. King Juan Carlos, in his July 22 address to the Cortes, noted these dangers. After declaring that democracy had begun, he warned that "the law obliges us to treat each other equally...but the important thing is that nobody feel left out."[29] Spanish elites were tempted by both dangers as they sought to take short-term measures to rescue the economy, and as they wrote the constitution. UCD, the governing party, shifted back and forth between strategies of isolating the PSOE (by allying with the AP and conservative regional parties), and negotiating exclusively with them. The schisms within UCD encouraged this oscillation. The more conservative faction within UCD sought an alliance with the AP in order to obtain a parliamentary majority for a conservative constitution. UCD social democrats advocated a pact with the PSOE, capable of producing a more progressive and widely acceptable constitution. Initially, Suárez rejected both options by attempting to ally with the regional parties and, ironically, the PCE. When this strategy proved unfeasible, UCD moved slowly to the right. As the UCD-AP axis threatened to polarize the Spanish polity, the president moved to negotiate directly with the PSOE, the major party of the opposition. The two parties then reached a consensus that survived the writing of the Spanish constitution.

In the resolution of both problems, political compromise based on elite negotiation was crucial. The ability and willingness of elites to negotiate political compromises was largely the result of the continuing fragility of the transition to democracy: They were unified by their fear of a rightist involution. Elite negotiation and compromise soon became more common and regularized, and has since become a key strength of Spain's young democracy.

Political-Economic Compromise: The Moncloa Pacts

The Spanish transition coincided with a serious economic crisis. In light of the political transition and the delicateness of the Suárez reform, less attention was given to economic problems. Major economic measures were put off until after the election of a new parliament. Economic reforms before such a date might have imperiled the reform from above and the electoral prospects of UCD. The new government and parliament faced a disastrous economic picture by the summer of 1976. Inflation was spiraling out of control, reaching 26.4 percent in 1977, almost double that in other OECD countries.[30] The consumer price index of that year rose by 44.8 percent.[31] By the end of that year almost 1 million Spaniards were unemployed and the balance-of-payments deficit reached an alarming $5 billion. Low rates of profits and productivity as well as a decline in capital investment all spelled serious trouble and threatened the viability of democracy. Compared to the political crisis, the economic crisis would be more of a zero-sum struggle between right and left. Jordi Pujol, a prominent Catalan centrist, stated in mid-June that "until now political liberties have been handed out. Now to distribute a more limited economic pie."[32]

On July 4, Juan Carlos asked Suárez to form his second government, the first time since February 1936 that a government was formed on the basis of electoral results. Ignoring the PCE's call for a government of "national conciliation" (a multiparty transitional coalition), Suárez formed a government composed almost entirely of UCD members. Two important exceptions were the military ministers (who, significantly, remained unchanged) and the vice-president for economic affairs, a nonparty technocrat. While Suárez's aides predominated in the cabinet, the leaders of UCD's constituent parties all received posts. Observers noted the presence of progressives in important positions, but there were a number of UCD conservatives in powerful ministries. Suárez's government signified neither the successful amalgamation of the barons nor the hegemony of a specific ideological line. The internal tensions within UCD were already apparent in July 1977, when the government announced its first set of economic measures. While in many respects a traditional austerity package (the peseta was devalued, prices on gas and electricity were raised, wages were limited, and the money supply restricted), the Spanish right, including influential sectors of UCD, expressed dismay at the "social democratic" bent of other aspects of the reform, especially the extensive fiscal reform.

As the government prepared to submit its Economic Reform Program to the politically divided Cortes, Suárez became more interested in reaching an interparty agreement on economic issues. The initial measures had drawn a hostile response from the right, including sectors of UCD. Mass pressure was increasing and threatening to produce a "hot autumn." In September, a wave of strikes began throughout Spain, protesting the rate of inflation and the high cost of living. These strikes were a source of concern for the left as well, since labor unions were still too weak and divided to successfully aggregate working class demands. On October 8 and 9, leaders of Spain's major political parties met in the Moncloa Palace, the president's official residence, and agreed to share the costs of and responsibility for the economic reform package. The "Moncloa Pacts," which excluded representatives of labor unions or entrepreneurial groups, were a set of traditional austerity measures combined with promises for structural economic reform. On the side of austerity, the parties agreed to a strict limitation on monetary growth (17 percent), a ceiling on wages (20 percent) and prices (22 percent), and a cutback on credit. In return, the parties of the left were promised an increase in unemployment benefits, the creation of new jobs to help offset the expected rise in unemployment, further tax reform, and the convocation of syndical elections. Additional concessions to the left were reforms in the areas of education (room for 700,000 additional students was to be created) and the state media (parliamentary control over it was promised).

There has been considerable debate about the costs and benefits of the Moncloa Pacts for the various signatories. As far as UCD was concerned, the government was able to avoid a coalition government while implicating the opposition in the austerity measures. The Moncloa Pacts guaranteed the passage of key reforms, increased the likelihood that the hot autumn would not persist, and increased the popular acceptance of austerity measures.

From the perspective of the major leftist opposition party, the PSOE, the accord was both necessary and potentially advantageous. It was necessary because party elites felt there was a genuine possibility of a right-wing coup. The Suárez government was subject to charges of being unable to stand up to the left on the issues of tax reform and regional devolution. The socialists wanted to help support these reforms while allowing UCD to expend its political capital in office. Indeed, in November 1977 the Suárez government was able to enact the most profound Spanish tax reform of the twentieth century, eliciting what one observer called "the first great offensive against the democratic reform."[33] The results of the June elections had encouraged the PSOE leadership and created illusions of an electoral victory in the near future, provided the young democracy could survive. In addition, given the weakness of labor unions and party structures, the left was hardly prepared to embark on a combative course of mass mobilization against the government. Moreover, both the PCE and PSOE were able to distance themselves somewhat from the more distasteful concessions resulting from the Moncloa Pacts. Under pressure from their affiliated unions, and faced with continuing labor unrest, the parties began to denounce aspects of the pacts to which they had recently agreed. While the austerity measures were largely successful, the benefits offered to the left in exchange for them were not delivered. For example, inflation in 1978 plummeted to just under 16 percent, exports and tourism boomed, and currency reserves were increased. At the same time, unemployment rose to over 8 percent, and the targeted rate of inflation was greatly exceeded.[34]

The Constitution of Consensus

Elite negotiation and compromise continued in the writing of the Spanish constitution. Even more than with the Moncloa Pacts, the constitution was a product of elite-level negotiation. Moreover, many observers expected the writing of the constitution to bring out the worst in Spanish political parties, and many predicted that consensus politics would not survive the constitutional project.

With the exception of AP, which refused to acknowledge publicly that the elected Cortes was constituent, all parliamentary groups recognized the need to write a new constitution as the most important task at hand. The writing of the constitution was a long and arduous process, characterized by many ups and downs and "mini-crises." The task of writing the document began on August 1, 1977, and was not completed until more than 500 days later. It should be noted that this delay was partially because the Spanish experience differed from other constituent processes in that an elected upper house actively collaborated in the deliberations.

Initially, the government proposed that Justice Minister Lavilla and a team of government lawyers write a draft to be debated by the Cortes. The PCE and the PSOE objected strongly to this proposal, and the left's counterproposal was eventually accepted by the government. A seven-member subcommittee of the Cortes Constitutional Committee was selected. These included three UCD members (Miguel Herrero de Miñon, a conservative Christian democrat; Gabriel Cisneros Laborda and José Pedro Pérez-Llorca, both more progressive deputies); one PSOE member (Gregorio Peces-Barba, a PSOE moderate and a practicing Catholic); one Communist (Jordi Sole Tura); one Catalan centrist (Miguel Roca y Junyent); and one representative of AP (Manuel Fraga). The composition of this important subcommittee was significant, since the PSOE was forced to accept one less position so that there could be a regional representative (Roca). Roca was considered by the Socialists to be a progressive, although he eventually sided with the UCD and AP on most matters. In addition, there was no Basque representative, an omission that initiated a pattern of mutual distrust between the other parties and the Basque petitioners. On the whole, the founding fathers were young professionals: five were university professors, one was a distinguished diplomat, and one was a lawyer and an expert on regional matters.

The subcommittee began its work after agreeing on several ground rules. The work was to take place under a veil of strict secrecy. A joint statement was to be issued after each session, but no detailed public record of the deliberations was to be kept. In addition, despite the numerical superiority of UCD, it was agreed that the chair of the subcommittee would rotate alphabetically. According to subcommittee member Fraga Iribarne, "the sessions took place in an atmosphere of inevitable ideological tension, offset by increasing personal understanding."[35] "We didn't even know each other until several months ago," said the AP leader, "and little by little an enormous mutual respect and comprehension has developed."[36]

The draft developed by the subcommittee, made public on January 5, 1978, was truly the product of an interparty consensus. None of the delegates came into the subcommittee meetings with a preconceived draft approved by their respective parties, although each party had official positions on the various constitutional issues. Judging by the negative public reaction to the constitutional draft, unleashed after a mysterious leak of the draft to the press in late 1977, the subcommittee members had all initially compromised their political positions considerably.[37] The leak brought forth a storm of protest from virtually all political forces, whose members had been kept in the dark during the secret negotiations. Alianza Popular members were angered over the treatment of the regional question, especially the inclusion of the term "nationalities." The UCD Christian democratic sector was irate over the ambiguity surrounding divorce and education. The draft contained no mention of the Catholic Church and did not establish Spain as a confessional state, and there was no provision to protect "freedom of education" (that is, the right to private religious education). The liberal sector of UCD was equally outraged. In a 30-page document circulated among UCD parliamentarians, the liberals attacked the draft on the grounds that it gave too little power to the Senate, too much power to the parliament vis-à-vis the executive, and provided too much room for state intervention in the economy. The document urged UCD leaders to act more in accord with the party's parliamentary strength. It noted that Article 128 provided that "the public powers may intervene, according to law, in the direction, coordination, and exploitation of enterprises, when the general interest demands it." Others charged that the constitution should not recognize the term "nationalities" and should bestow more powers on the monarch. On the left, PSOE members complained about the excessive power granted to the monarchy, the legal age of adulthood (21), and the special and ambiguous treatment of the role of the armed forces. When the period for presentation of amendments to the draft ended in late January, 3,200 recommended modifications had been offered.[38]

As the subcommittee members met at an isolated retreat to discuss the amendments one by one, the consequences of the new public status of the constitutional debate became apparent. The UCD members, under pressure from the party "barons," began to favor some of the more conservative amendments. Leftist members became increasingly frustrated as they lost vote after vote on issues they felt had been previously agreed upon. The situation became critical on March 7, 1978, when the subcommittee, under the rotating chairmanship of Fraga, accepted two amendments that were particularly sensitive for the left. The first limited state control over education, and the second guaranteed the right of employers to stage lockouts. Both amendments passed with the votes of UCD, AP, and the Catalan representative, Roca. In early March Suárez had negotiated a deal with the Catalan minority, aimed at gaining Roca's support for a series of conservative amendments, thus placating UCD's right wing. UCD agreed to accept the term "nationalities" if the Catalans would accept a qualifier regarding the indivisibility of the Spanish nation. UCD even appealed to the Catalan PCE member, Sole Tura, to remain neutral vis-á-vis this pact, helping to isolate the PSOE.

The result of this rightist offensive within UCD, and the effort to isolate the PSOE, was the Socialists' decision to abandon the subcommittee on March 7, 1978. It appeared that the consensus had definitely been broken, and by the time the full Constitutional Committee of the Cortes convened to discuss the draft of the constitution (May 5), the PSOE continued to maintain a hostile attitude. The Socialist Peces-Barba signed the subcommittee draft under protest, but he refused to sit together with his subcommittee colleagues, as a sign of protest.

Even the signature of the PSOE would not have been granted were it not for an important change beginning to take place within UCD. Alarmed over the climate of tension and polarization surrounding the constitution, and concerned about the poor relations between the two major parliamentary parties, Suárez took action to limit the influence of Justice Minister Lavilla and subcommittee member Herrero, both conservatives who had sought to isolate the

PSOE. The president delegated more power to his top aide and confidant Fernando Abril and directed him to unblock the constitutional impasse. Suárez wanted to avoid all potentially dangerous confrontations during the public debates in the full Constitutional Committee of the Cortes, and he felt that Lavilla and Herrero had gone too far in their provocation of the PSOE.

Despite these changes, and although subcommittee members had made an explicit previous agreement to limit rhetoric and decrease levels of tensions, the first public constitutional debates were emotionally charged. UCD's Herrero began with a belligerent speech, and Justice Minister Lavilla provided a surprisingly conservative introduction to the proceedings. The tension increased as UCD, AP, and occasionally the Catalan minority outvoted the left. When the Catalans defected on the issues of the death penalty and the legal age of adulthood, UCD and AP were still able to outvote the remaining committee members. As two journalists noted, "What the government feared most was beginning to take place: The formation of a UCD-AP bloc and the consequent risk that the constitution would be considered rightist."[39] Again on May 15, the PSOE reacted against this isolation by withdrawing from the committee. Subcommittee member Peces-Barba stated that the committee's actions put his party in "a very difficult position vis-à-vis a favorable assessment of the Constitution." Felipe González lamented, "the consensus is broken," and threatened to raise 300 amendments during the plenum of the Cortes. "We will be forced to include constitutional reform as part of our electoral program," said an embittered González. Alfonso Guerra, the PSOE's second in command, charged: "This will be the most reactionary constitution in Europe. It is the work, exclusively, of UCD and AP. There is no longer any consensus."[40]

It was this second withdrawal of the PSOE from the constituent process that finally led Suárez to turn against the right wing of his party and opt for a complete UCD policy shift. Beginning in mid-May, there was a considerable hardening of ideological divisions within UCD, a schism that would later culminate in the ouster of Suárez, the triumph of coalition conservatives, and the disintegration of UCD. In the meantime, however, Suárez moved to bolster the progressive wing of UCD. On May 21, newly appointed UCD party head Arias Salgado stated: "The Executive

Committee of UCD will not do anything which might endanger the consensus in the constitutional debates and will try above all else to maintain it."[41]

As was so often the case during the Spanish transition, face-to-face negotiations by political elites avoided a potentially dangerous polarization of political forces. UCD's attempt to heal the wounds of the consensus took concrete form during a dinner meeting on May 23, 1978, between UCD's number-two leader and three top PSOE officials.[42] The conservative UCD member Herrero refused to attend, sensing correctly that his party was trying to limit his influence. The meeting lasted all night and by the time it was over the two parties had agreed to a renegotiation of articles 25-50 of the Constitution. The PSOE dropped its demands that no mention of capitalist market economy be included in the constitution, and the Socialists accepted a provision limiting civil rights in order to combat terrorism. UCD agreed to the inclusion of a statement concerning the role of public enterprise in the economy, accepted a watered-down version of the right to stage lockouts, and altered its previous stance on educational issues. Recalling the earlier importance of the rapport between Suárez and González, this round of negotiations was carried out by the second in command of each major parliamentary party.

The results of the new PSOE-UCD agreements were spectacular. On the first afternoon of committee activity after the dinner meeting, 25 articles were approved, compared with the ten full days it took to approve the first 24. UCD subcommittee member Pérez Llorca noted: "We have avoided a major bottleneck of the constituent process." PCE member Sole Tura beamed: "We are going to achieve a constitution without winners or losers."[43]

However, not all parliamentary groups were pleased with the new agreements. Although the PCE and the Catalan minority adhered wholeheartedly, AP and the Basque nationalists, uncomfortable bedfellows equally angered over their exclusion, withdrew from the Constitutional Committee, although both later returned. More important was a counterattack by the UCD right, which eventually led to the resignation of the conservative UCD member from the committee. UCD leaders were able to assuage some of the party right by obtaining the support from PSOE negotiators for semantic changes in the articles dealing with education.

With the exception of several "mini-crises," the UCD-PSOE

constitutional consensus survived until the fall of 1980. During this period almost all contentious issues were resolved behind closed doors among a limited set of political leaders. The proceedings in the committee and later in the Cortes plenum became an almost entirely mechanical acting out of previously arranged agreements. At times, the *consenso* had humorous manifestations:

> There were occasions in which poor memory on the part of some deputies of both groups, regarding the role that corresponded to them, almost produced shocking results. More than once the indecision concerning which way one should vote in the "negotiated sense" evoked frantic signaling from deputies of the other group.[44]

As a consequence of the UCD-PSOE consensus, the constitutional project moved swiftly out of committee and through the Cortes plenum. Only the Basques and the AP regularly attacked aspects of the constitution. On June 21, the constitution passed in the lower house, with only the abstentions of AP and the PNV (Partido Nacionalista Vasco, or Basque Nationalist Party), plus two negative votes, detracting from an overwhelming approval. During the Senate deliberations, the UCD-PSOE pact remained intact after several lapses and yet another elite summit (the *reconsenso*) at the end of the summer of 1978. In accordance with the Political Reform Law, a joint committee of both houses ironed out discrepancies between the two drafts by mid-October. On October 31, both houses approved the text of the Spanish constitution, dubbed "the Constitution of Consensus," by a vote of 551 to 11, with 22 abstentions.[45]

Conclusion

As in the case of the economic crisis, elite negotiation was employed to confront the formidable task of writing a constitution that most of the Spanish polity could accept. The result, again like the Moncloa Pacts, was a constitution full of compromises and ambiguities. For example, the issue of church-state relations was resolved in Article 17, which guarantees freedom of religion and explicity rejects a confessional state, but which nevertheless provides that the state will maintain a special relationship "with the Catholic Church and other denominations." The consensus worked especially well in resolving the contentious regional question. The PSOE and UCD were able to fend off attacks from the right and nationalist left, recognizing the "right of autonomy for the nationalities and regions which form part of it." The PSOE was able to include the abolition of the death penalty in the constitution, but only after agreeing to exempt the military justice system from this provision so as not to provoke the military. Article 15 guarantees the right to life "for all," leaving the resolution of the sensitive abortion issue to future governments. The ambiguity of the constitution on this issue was regarded as preferable to raising such an emotionally charged issue. Further inquiry into the issues of the market economy, the right of employers to stage lockouts, the convocation of referenda, and so on, reveals a similar pattern of compromise between the two major Spanish political forces. Time and time again, the UCD and PSOE prevailed against amendments from their right and left.

As was the case with the Political Reform Law and the Moncloa Pacts, most political groups emerged from the constitution-writing process with a sense that they had gained on some issues and had lost on others. Only the extreme right and left, as well as some Basque nationalists, felt alienated from the process of writing and approving Spain's constitution. Transition through transaction had given political elites much experience in negotiation and compromise, and as a result the writing of the constitution was more successful.

On the eve of the constitutional referendum, Suárez appeared on Spanish television to ask for popular approval. Summing up the peculiarity of Spain's transition, the president predicted that with the popular approval of the constitution, "everything will be different, but not everything will have changed."[46]

Notes

1. See the editorial in *El País*, January 8, 1977, p. 2.
2. José Ramon Saíz, *El Presidente: Historia de una transición en la que Adolfo Suárez fue su gran protagonista* (Madrid: Editorial Madrid, 1981), p. 105.

3. Ibid., p. 107.

4. *El Alcázar,* January 26, 1977.

5. Joaquín Bardavío, *El dilema* (Madrid: Strips Editores, 1978), pp. 146-47.

6. Stanley Payne, "The Political Transformation of Spain," *Current History,* No. 431 (1977), p. 116.

7. Interview on January 26, 1982.

8. See Antonio López Pina and E. Aranguren, *La cultura política de la España de Franco* (Madrid: Taurus, 1976), pp. 161-62.

9. Enrique Curiel and J. García Fernández, "La representación teritorial," *Triunfo,* June 4, 1977, p. 42.

10. *YA,* December 11, 1976, has the full text of Carrillo's statements.

11. *ABC,* December 11, 1976.

12. Joaquín Bardavío, *Sábado santo rojo* (Madrid: Ediciones Uve, 1980), p. 176; Juan Pablo Fusi, Sergio Vilar, and Paul Preston, "De la dictadura a la democracia," *Historia 16* (Special Issue), No. 25 (February 1983), pp. 104 and 111.

13. The details of this encounter are discussed by Bardavío, *Sábado santo rojo,* and were confirmed by two off-the-record interviews in January 1982.

14. For Osorio's account of this opposition, as well as his clear rationale, see Alfonso Osorio, *Trayectoria política de un ministro de la Corona,* 2d ed. (Barcelona: Planeta, 1980), pp. 286-89.

15. Fernández Miranda died soon after, deeply disillusioned over the course of the reform, and bitter for having participated in a transition that went further than was his intention. His death represents a serious obstacle for students of the Spanish transition, since no memoirs of this crucial figure were ever published. Three excellent accounts of Fernández Miranda's contribution to the transition and his exit from government are Angel Gómez Escorial, "El día que se fue Fernández Miranda," *Opinión,* No. 36 (June 11-17, 1977), pp. 4-5; "Se fué con el Toisón," *Guadiana,* No. 109 (June 9-15, 1977), pp. 12-13; and José María Esteban, "Fernández Miranda, ahora duque," *La Actualidad Española,* No. 1327 (June 6-12, 1977).

16. Quoted in *El País,* April 14, 1977.

17. Bardavío, *Sábado santo rojo,* p. 192.

18. *Interviu,* May 19, 1977.

19. See the survey appearing in *Cuadernos Para el Diálogo,* May 21, 1977.

20. José Amodia, "The Union of the Democratic Centre," in David S. Bell, ed., *Democratic Politics in Spain* (London: Frances Pinter, 1983), pp. 4-5.

21. *Interviu,* May 29, 1977.

22. *Cuadernos Para el Diálogo,* May 22, 1977.
23. Interview with a top UCD campaign manager, in May 1977.
24. *El País,* Editorial, June 5, 1977.
25. *El País,,* June 7, 1977.
26. *Interviu,* May 19, 1977.
27. *Informaciones,* Editorial, May 14, 1977.
28. Quoted in *El País,* June 12, 1977.
29. José Ramon Saíz, *El Presidente: Historia de una transición en la que Adolfo Suárez fue su gran protagonista* (Madrid: Editorial Madrid, 1981), p. 156.
30. Curro Ferraro, *Economía y explotación en la democracia española* (Bilbao: ZYX, 1978), p. 20.
31. Julio Rodríquez Aramberri, "The Political Transformation in Spain: An Interpretation," in Ralph Miliband and John Saville, eds., *The Socialist Register, 1979* (London: Merlin Press, 1979), p. 190.
32. *El País,* June 21, 1978, p. 1.
33. Saíz, *El Presidente,* p. 160.
34. Ibid, pp. 143-58.
35. Antonio Hernández Gil, *El cambio político español y la constitución* (Barcelona: Planeta, 1982), p. 287.
36. Bonifacio de la Cuadra and Soledad Gallego-Díaz, *Del consenso al desencanto* (Madrid: Saltes, 1981), p. 35. This is an invaluable treatment of the writing of the constitution, from which the present discussion draws heavily. During off-the-record interviews with a number of important political actors involved in the process, it was possible to confirm much of their account. Much of the historical data from the period was drawn from *El País* and *ABC.*
37. For a copy of the leaked draft, as well as the reactions to it, see "PSOE y Alianza Popular son los mayores discrepantes del borrador constitucional," *El País,* November 25, 1977, p. 1.
38. See "Mil propositos de enmiendas," *Cambio 16,* No. 323 (February 12, 1978), pp. 20-21.
39. De la Cuadra and Gallego-Díaz, p. 53.
40. The preceding quotes were compiled in ibid., p. 53.
41. Quoted in ibid., p. 56.
42. Ibid., pp. 56-58.
43. Ibid., p. 63.
44. Ibid., p. 72.
45. Among the deputies there were fourteen abstentions: seven from the Basque Nationalist Party (PNV), three from AP, two from the Mixed Parliamentary Group, one from UCD, and one from the Republican Left of Catalonia. In the Senate there were six negative votes: five by AP

and one by the Basque Euskadiko Ezkerra. In the Senate there were eight abstentions: five from the Basque Group and three from independents. Of the five negative votes, two came from the Basque group and three were from AP.

46. Saíz, *El Presidente,* p. 215.

6 POLITICS IN DEMOCRATIC SPAIN

In the consolidation of transition through transaction in 1977 and 1978, politicians, especially in the UCD and PSOE, maintained an elite-level consensus that facilitated the writing of a widely acceptable constitution, and that fostered compromise over a number of fundamental political economic issues. The overwhelming approval of the Spanish constitution in December 1978 may be viewed as the formal conclusion to the transition process, although important aspects of the constitution remained to be implemented. However, political change rarely conforms to clear-cut chronological categories, and the Spanish transition was no exception. Three interrelated challenges to the nascent democracy remained to be met before it could be fully consolidated.

The first challenge concerned the still-powerful armed forces. The military had reason to feel betrayed by the end result of Suárez's reform. Suárez had won their tacit approval of his Political Reform Law by assuring them of the limits to the democratic transition. As the reform ran its course, he could no longer adhere to these assurances, and important sectors within the military harbored a visceral resentment that was directed at the president.

A second challenge involved the regional question. Spain's constitution contained a hodge-podge of provisions concerning the devolution of powers to the regions, and the "state of autonomies" emerged without any coherent pattern. Suárez's ability to rally important Catalan political actors behind his reform—through a series of "pacts"—was instrumental to the initial success of his project. The Basques were also granted considerable political

154

autonomy, but the negotiations were difficult and the relations between the central government and regional authorities were consistently acrimonious. As other Spanish regions began to clamor for autonomy, successive governments attempted to deal with the regional question globally, and to more clearly delimit the new relationship between center and periphery. This issue proved especially elusive and has plagued every Spanish government since the transition.

A final problem concerned the alternation of power. The alternation of power is not necessarily a test of a regime's democratic credentials. Many democratic systems—postwar West Germany and France, for example—did not experience an alternation of power for many years after their democratic transitions. Nevertheless, in cases of transition through transaction there is reason to believe that the alternation of political power is a more significant sign of the viability of parliamentary democracy. While Spain's transition had already exceeded the limits "imposed" by the right and the armed forces—for example, the legalization of the PCE, the "regionalization" of Spain, the dismantling of franquist institutions—political power had not changed hands. The head of state, although now endowed with a constitutional legitimacy, was an appointee of General Franco. Suárez, the democratically elected president of the government, had impeccable franquist credentials. Many in the military and on the right were deeply embittered over his behavior and this sense of resentment eventually contributed to the demise of UCD. Nevertheless, the Suárez government was seen by many as the guarantor of continuing limits to the transition. Whether the forces within this new democracy would tolerate an electoral victory by the left remained an ominous question, and one that became increasingly relevant as the Spanish center-right disintegrated. As will become clearer below, the leadership of the Socialist opposition did everything possible to ensure the feasibility of an alternation of power.

In addressing the three challenges described above, this chapter is divided chronologically. The first section examines the meteoric rise, and equally dramatic demise, of the UCD from 1979 to 1982. There is a brief treatment of the 1979 elections, the foiled military coup of 1981, and the decline of UCD under Suárez's successors. The second section focuses on Spanish politics since 1982. It begins with a treatment of some of the conditions for party alternation in Spain, and places particular emphasis on the social democratization of the Spanish Socialist Workers Party. It concludes with a general discussion of the achievements and setbacks of the first PSOE government through 1984.

The Rise and Demise of UCD

UCD was born on May 3, 1977, shortly before the June 1977 elections.[1] It was an electoral coalition (it did not become a party until December 1977) of small, elite parties of the center, and its constituent groups ranged from conservative christian democrats, through populists and "centrists" to center-left social democrats.

There can be little doubt that Suárez's "occupation" benefited the squabbling and factious center. UCD's stunning victory in 1977 was largely attributable to the tremendous popularity of its leader, Adolfo Suárez. His youth, good looks, charisma, as well as his proven reputation as an able reformer placed him at a considerable advantage over his opponents. With Suárez at the helm, UCD could count on the still-intact franquist apparatus. The formation of UCD allowed Suárez to kill two birds with a single stone, since it provided him an ideal bureaucracy into which ex-franquist bureaucrats—whose franquist institutions had been dismantled—could be reabsorbed. It therefore allowed him to reintegrate much of the middle-level franquist bureaucracy, of which he was a representative, into the new democracy. Suárez acknowledged this point when stating, at the first UCD Congress in 1978, that "we have built a great party, without questioning people about where they were coming from, but only about where they wanted to go."[2] Thus, as a short-term electoral maneuver, Suárez's occupation of the center was brilliant. As a long-term political formation, UCD was wrought with internal contradictions.

Suárez's occupation of CD, which he rechristened UCD, caused serious dissension and numerous defections. Some resented the heavy handedness with which the president rebuilt the centrist coalition in his own image, and the swiftness with which he placed his own supporters in key party positions. Others, with greater and lesser degrees of naiveté, opposed the presence of bona fide franquists in the ranks of an avowedly democratic party, claiming that Suárez would "taint" its image. Most of all, the original centrists were appalled by the integration into the center of a "rag-bag" of nonideological franquist bureaucrats and technocrats.

UCD emerged from the first democratic elections with 34 percent of the vote, and a near majority in the lower house (46.8 percent of the seats). Suárez's leadership was given a popular mandate and the president was very strong within his own coalition. UCD was successful in creating considerable continuity between pre- and postfranquist politics. For example, 30 percent of UCD ministers in government between 1976 and 1981 were ex-franquists.[3] UCD's chief success was undoubtedly the unique role it played in legitimating the democratic transition. It not only bridged the gap between authoritarianism and democracy, it facilitated the consolidation of the democratic regime and oversaw the implementation of important reforms. However, the very conditions that made UCD an ideal political force for the consolidation of democracy—its heterogeneous political composition, its vague ideological orientation, its connection with the franquist bureaucracy, its identification with the founding of the new regime—worked against the long-term consolidation of UCD as a party.[4]

A number of internal ideological tensions were immediately manifested once negotiations over the constitution began. It is important to note that the strong performance of the left, which together controlled over 40 percent of the seats in the lower house, meant that it would be costly to exclude it from the writing of the constitution. A major bone of contention within the UCD concerned the competing strategies of writing a constitution with the support of the right, and perhaps some minor parties, or negotiating a constitutional compromise with the left. Not surprisingly, this thorny question, concerning an issue so fundamental as the new constitution, agitated the numerous ideological faults within the coalition. UCD's 165 deputies in the lower house were, inauspiciously, fragmented according to its still-intact member parties. Christian democrats had 49 seats; liberals, 22; social democrats, 18; regional groups, 19; and "independents" (supporters of Suárez), 57. As noted in Chapter 5, the tension within UCD between liberals and social democrats, between liberals and Christian democrats, and between centralists and regionalists eventually forced Suárez to take more direct control of the constitutional negotiations, especially after he opted to pursue a compromise with the left. The need to compromise with the left created, as an unintended consequence no doubt, the impression that Suárez was siding with the small minority of UCD social democrats. In addition, the increasingly unilateral decisions being taken by Suárez and his closest aides, over matters of great importance, were deeply resented by his coalition partners.

Within UCD there were essentially two contending strategies for dealing with internal fragmentation.[5] The first solution, what has been called the *authoritarian model*, required Suárez's suppression of internal dissent through the creation of a unified, hierarchically organized party. The second solution, best described as *consociational*, involved accepting, even institutionalizing, the diversity within the party through power sharing and internal compromise.[6] While this tension was never fully resolved in one way or another, the former strategy was pursued between 1977 and February 1981, while the latter was pursued from 1981 until the electoral disaster of 1982.

UCD's clear but narrow victory appeared to create the conditions for internal unification. The myriad of dissenting forces opposing Suárez's domination of the center were now compelled to join it. In an attempt to make peace with the "barons" of UCD, Suárez's first government included representatives of each political force within the coalition. In August 1977, UCD officially registered as a single political party, and in December of that year, UCD's collective leadership organ, the Political Council, agreed that all member parties of the coalition should be disbanded. In a relatively short time, Suárez created a hierarchically organized party, dominated by his supporters. This process of unification culminated with the First Party Congress in October 1978. Unlike most constituent congresses, UCD delegates simply endorsed Suárez's effective domination of the party, and ratified the party's "electoralist" orientation. The effectiveness of this strategy was proven in the 1979 general elections, in which UCD was able to fend off the threat of a PSOE victory. The elections, in turn, allowed Suárez to exclude many of the "barons" from his government, and to increase his personal control over the party.

The 1979 General Elections

After the constitution was approved in the December 1978 referendum, Suárez decided to dissolve parliament and call new elections for March 1979.[7] The president had been in power for only two years of his four-year mandate, and the new constitution did not require him to call new elections. There were several reasons for his surprise decision to dissolve the Cortes. Suárez wanted to hold general elections before the municipal elections, scheduled for April. Despite the protestations of the left, democratic municipal elections had been put off until after the writing of the constitution. However, Suárez was now legally bound to call municipal elections no later than April. The left was expected to perform very well in local elections, and the UCD leadership feared that an opposition victory at the local level could undermine its legitimacy and might sweep the left into power at the national level, after Suárez's term expired. Thus Suárez felt it necessary to gain a new mandate before the local elections took place. In addition, the president hoped for increased strength in the Cortes. The constitution required that he win a new vote of investiture, and he may have feared that minor parties (the Catalan Minority or AP, for example) would exact a heavy price for their support. Finally, by catching the opposition off guard, Suárez hoped to maintain the momentum.

In many ways, the 1979 elections were the first "normal" democratic elections. The number of political parties running had been reduced substantially. The major political options were reduced to five: the rightist Democratic Coalition, led by Fraga's Popular Alliance, but somewhat "democratized" with the inclusion of mutinous centrists; the center-right UCD; the socialists of the PSOE, now including Tierno Galván's PSP; the communist PCE; and myriad of regional parties, most importantly the centrist parties in the Basque Country and Catalonia. The 1977 elections had taken place during the height of the transition, and in many respects they had been converted into a test of Spaniards' willingness and ability to accept democratic rule. Partisan differences were intentionally minimized, and parties presented vague programs in support of democracy. Important social forces, such as the major financial powers and the Catholic Church, refused to intervene actively in the elections.

By 1979 the constitution had been approved after a difficult year and a half of negotiation and compromise. As Alfonso Guerra, the second in command of the PSOE, had promised in October 1978, after the constitution was approved, "the consensus would end and the opposition would begin."[8] Most Spaniards were confident that the delicate period of the transition had concluded and that the political parties could return to "politics as usual." Thus, in the 1979 electoral campaign, some of the traditional political antagonisms, repressed during the first elections, reemerged. For example, in early January, the Catholic Episcopal Conference published a document entitled "The Moral Responsibility of the Vote," urging voters to avoid parties committed to Marxism, the legalization of divorce, abortion, or restrictions on religious education.[9] Likewise, in late February, the Spanish Confederation of Entrepreneurs issued a statement warning against the election of Marxist parties.

UCD also began to campaign in a less cautious fashion, partially because its leaders were aware of the possibility of a PSOE victory. It waged a dual campaign, with positive and negative messages.[10] On the positive side, it emphasized Suárez's charismatic personality and his experience. In addition, UCD presented itself as a party that had delivered on its promises of reform, and had done so responsibly and pragmatically. On the negative side, it launched a fierce attack on its major consensus partner, the PSOE. The PSOE was in the process of an internal political moderation, but it retained some of the ideological baggage of its more radical phase. Despite the PSOE's moderate campaign—there was no emphasis on class struggle or Marxism—UCD efficiently exploited the contradictions between the PSOE's electoral message and the more radical resolutions of its last party congress. Coupled with the warning of the church and the private sector, UCD's attack on the ambiguities of the PSOE was largely successful in raising fear about a socialist victory. It culminated with Suárez's final television address to the nation on the last day of the campaign, in which the president skillfully portrayed the elections as a contest between Christian humanism and Marxist materialism.

The PSOE lost the 1979 general election on two fronts. Its attempt to attract centrist voters from UCD appears to have failed, while its moderate campaign may have cost the party some votes on its left: The PSOE lost three seats in the lower house, while the PCE picked up three. UCD gained a seat, although its overall percentage of the vote fell somewhat. However, the results were most favorable from the perspective of the governing party since UCD's opposition on the right was severely weakened: Fraga's coalition dropped six seats and won just over 6 percent of the vote. The results also confirmed a boost in support for the regional parties, perhaps as a reaction to the perceived failures of the government in the area of regional devolution.

The 1979 electoral results were interpreted as a healthy reaffirmation and consolidation of the 1977 returns (see Table 6) . UCD was reconfirmed as the governing party, but now had an even weaker opposition to its left and right. Given such favorable circumstances, Suárez's attempt to impose a unified party hierarchy on UCD might have been expected to fare well. Curiously, however, after the 1979 elections, the centrifugal internal tendencies of UCD began to reemerge. A number of factors help to explain this paradox. First, the argument that party unity was imperative to protect the transition, or to prevent a socialist victory in general elections, now began to lose its appeal. The PSOE did not improve its position in the 1979 elections, and the transition was viewed by many within UCD—this erroneous view was actually widespread—to be out of danger. Second, the municipal elections of April 1979 were swept by the left. In mid-April the PSOE and PCE reached an agreement allowing for the creation of leftist local governments in most areas of Spain. Almost all of Spain's major cities, including Barcelona and Madrid, were run by leftist mayors. This gave internal opponents to the president renewed confidence to assert themselves. Finally, Suárez's personal appeal had begun to wane after three difficult years in power. He was, in general, favorably viewed as a man of the transition, but enjoyed far less respect as a parliamentary leader. In addition, the PSOE was bitter over the president's last-minute attacks on its democratic credentials. After the 1979 elections, the major opposition intensified its attacks on the government. As Suárez's prestige eroded, many within UCD began to question the desirability of Suárez's domination over the coalition, and the internal ideological tensions stirred up during the writing of the constitution resurfaced.

The Regional Problem

On the eve of the transition the demands of Spain's regions, the Basque Country and Catalonia, presented a severe problem for the government.[11] The franquist regime had fiercely repressed all manifestations of regionalism, and any attempt to "federalize"

Table 6. Electoral Results, March 1, 1979

Party	Number of Votes (millions)	Percent of Votes	Deputies		Senators	
			Number of Seats	Percent of Seats	Number of Seats	Percent of Seats
UCD	6.26	34.9	168	48.0	120	57.6
PSOE	5.46	30.5	121	34.6	69	33.1
PCE	1.93	10.8	23	6.6	0	0.0
CD (AP)	1.03	5.7	9	2.5	3	0.1
Regional	1.88	10.5	28	8.0	14	6.7
Union Nacional	0.37	2.1	1	0.3	0	0.0
Other	1.00	5.5	0	0.0	2	.09
Totals	17.93	100.0	350	100.0	208	100.0

Source: Compiled by the author.

Spain was anathema to the right and the military. At the same time, years of franquist repression had only strengthened and radicalized demands for political autonomy. In the Basque Country, franquist repression rekindled demands for independence, advocated by Basque terrorists, who gained considerable support among the population.

King Juan Carlos, in his inaugural address, called for the recognition by the central government of "regional peculiarities," while stressing the need to protect the "unity" of the kingdom. In so doing he was, typically, walking a tightrope between popular demands and political realities. Nevertheless, his (and his government's) early actions on the regional questions, especially the issuance of decrees protecting regional languages and symbols, appeared to represent a genuine commitment to accommodate regional demands.

The major political parties competing in the June 1977 elections offered a wide gamut of possible solutions to the regional problem. The franquist AP, while accepting the need for some devolution of power to the regions, limited its solution to minimal administrative decentralization. The parties of the left, especially the PSOE and PCE, advocated various forms of federalism, despite their historical and ideological inclination toward centralism. In taking this stance, they were closest to the position held by most nationalist parties, except those on the extreme left. UCD, true to form, adopted an ambiguous, occasionally contradictory approach that one observer has called *laissez faire*. [12] Essentially, it advocated no single solution to the regional problem. Each region would negotiate separately with the central government the terms of its relationship with the state.

During the writing of the constitution, UCD's solution to the question eventually won out, despite strong protests from some nationalist (especially the Basque) forces, and despite some important concessions to nationalist demands. The constitution of 1978 specified two major routes for devolution of power to regions: One form was a direct approach; a second route promised less autonomy to a candidate region and gave the government far more control over the transfer of powers. A third approach, explicated in Article 151.1, provided the only route to full and immediate autonomy for regions not enjoying "nationality" status, but it was extremely complex.

The Suárez government, anxious to avoid a rapid and uncontrollable decentralization of power, favored the first approach only for the "historical" regions of Catalonia, the Basque Country, and Galicia. In these regions, popular sentiment so strongly favored autonomy that any undue delay in the devolution process would be counterproductive. However, the government insisted on the second route for all other regions, since this procedure would slow the devolution process and give the government control over it. Suárez's stubborness on this issue compelled the region of Andalusia to pursue full autonomy via the arcane third route. To make matters worse, in early 1980 the government actively opposed efforts by Andalusia to attain autonomy via this third approach. The government was successful, but just barely, and the near defeat was a serious embarrassment. Eventually, a compromise approach resulted in an Andalusian statute in October 1981, but the insult to Andalusian sensibilities was irreversible, and it led to the resignation of the minister of culture (an Andalusian) and other UCD militants in the region. The government appeared heavy handed and incompetent in its handling of this and other regional issues.

Moreover, the Suárez government's stubbornness on this matter contrasted markedly with its flexibility vis-à-vis Catalan (and to a lesser extent, Basque) demands for autonomy. Critics of UCD alleged that the government, hounded by conservatives within the governing party, had assented too readily to Catalan and Basque demands and was now trying to slow the regionalization process.

Suárez enjoyed his greatest success with the Catalans, although even there the results were mixed. During the Second Republic, Catalonia had enjoyed considerable political autonomy, and by 1977 demands for autonomy reached a crescendo in the region.[13] On September 29, 1977, Suárez responded with a calculated gamble: He had the king unilaterally restore the Generalitat, the region's traditional parliament, and he appointed the elderly and well-respected former premier of Catalonia, Josep Taradellas, as its president. This move horrified the Spanish right, and annoyed some within UCD. Suárez was portrayed by his rightist opponents as "weak" on the regional question. An assembly of Catalan parliamentarians then drafted a statute of autonomy that was approved by the Catalan electorate in October 1979. This rapid achievement of autonomy weakened the nationalist left, and encouraged the formation of a strong Catalan center-right, although it did not appear to help UCD's performance in the region. In the March 1980 regional parliamentary elections, the centrist Convergencia i Unió (CiU) won a plurality of seats, and CiU leader Jordi Pujol became president of the Generalitat with support of UCD and the moderate Catalan nationalists.

Suárez enjoyed far less success in the Basque Country, partly because the political situation there was far more volatile, and partly because relations between the Basques and the central government were far more tense, especially during the writing of the constitution. Basque nationalism was more of a contradictory movement than its Catalan counterpart.[14] It was divided ideologically between conservative Catholic federalists, with roots in nineteenth-century Carlism, and leftist separatists, who since the birth of ETA in 1959 rapidly gained a foothold in the region as the chief opponents to franquist repression. The tension, fostered by persistent Basque terrorism, aimed especially against the military, rendered the problem extremely delicate. The Basques were not included in the subcommittee that drafted the Spanish constitution, an omission that added to a pattern of strained relations between elites of the center and the Basque periphery. Basque representatives were so internally divided on major issues that the region's problems proved especially difficult to resolve. Basque demands that the constitution explicitly recognize historical *fueros* (charters of autonomy) could not be accommodated, despite intense negotiation. The Basques were the only regional group in the Cortes to oppose the constitution. Regional abstention in the December 1978 referendum reached 51.1 percent, and 23.54 percent of the votes were cast in opposition to the constitution.[15] Moreover, unlike the situation in Catalonia, UCD had few political allies in the Basque Country, and its willingness to bargain was consequently diminished.

The bargaining between Basque authorities and the central government was difficult and protracted, and was not completed until July 1979. The protraction of negotiations exacerbated the feeling of distrust between the Basques and the Suárez government. Despite the wide-ranging powers transferred to the Basque Country under the region's statute of autonomy—the region is by far the most autonomous in all of Spain—the Basque nationalist left made important gains among the electorate. In the 1979 general elections, Herri Batasuna (HB), a party with links to ETA, elected three deputies to the Cortes. Abstention rates were high in all Basque provinces. In the 1980 elections to the Basque parliament, three Basque nationalist parties, the moderate PNV and the leftist Euskadi Euskerra and Herri Batasuna, trounced the national parties, winning 42 of 60 seats. In a serious blow to the government, UCD came in dead last and was even defeated by AP!

As the PSOE's experience in power has since demonstrated, Basque terrorism has assumed its own dynamic, somewhat independent from national or even regional politics. The problem has proved elusive to all Spanish governments, whether authoritarian or democratic, left or right.

On the whole, it became evident that the government lacked any clear direction in its attempt to resolve the regional problem. As UCD and the PSOE soon realized, the regionalization process had taken place helter-skelter, and without some legal homogenization it could result in an inefficient and ultimately unworkable set of center-periphery relations. Some of the problems of this *laissez faire* approach became more evident as the government tried to deal with the various regions, some of which were single provinces, that sought autonomy. The Law for the Harmonization of the Autonomy Process was introduced jointly by the UCD and the PSOE, after the coup attempt in 1981. It was an effort on the part of both major parties to correct the damage caused by UCD's *laissez faire* approach to the regional question. Not surprisingly, UCD (and later the PSOE) would be accused of reneging on their commitment to regional devolution.

The government's inability to tackle this multifaceted problem contributed to disastrous electoral setbacks in regional elections in populous Catalonia, the Basque Country, and Andalusia. These setbacks benefited not only the nationalist parties but also UCD's major electoral competitor, the PSOE. Moreover, the regional devolution process helped to make Spaniards weary of politics in general. As described above, the various "routes" to regional autonomy were extremely complex and of excruciating duration. After 40 years of drab authoritarian politics, Spaniards were bombarded by a concatenation of referenda, elections, municipal elections, and regional parliamentary elections. It is hardly surprising that by 1981 many observers detected a profound popular *desencanto* (disenchantment or disillusion) with democracy.[16] Unfortunately for the governing party, UCD was to bear the brunt of this *desencanto*.

The Fall of Adolfo Suárez

The regional disaster gave the multifarious opposition currents within UCD an opportunity to weaken Suárez's leadership. UCD social democrats and liberals clashed openly over economic policy. Christian democrats within the party lobbied publicly over sacrosanct educational matters. Virtually all UCD families took aim at Suárez's unilateral decisionmaking style and his unwillingness to share power with coalition partners. Defections on key parliamentary votes during 1980 were a harbinger of problems to come.

An internal policy shift in March 1980 spelled the end of Suárez's authoritarian rule and initiated a period in which UCD's consociational qualities were again apparent. The creation of the Permanent Commission, the intent of which was to provide representation for all UCD political families in the party leadership, was a sign that Suárez's attempt to control the party from above had failed. The birth of the Permanent Commission marked the reemergence of the UCD "barons," all of whom became members. In September 1980, Suárez was forced to include some of the most powerful "barons" in the government. This attempt at power sharing failed to stem the disintegration of his position within the party, but instead appears to have hastened it. In October 1980 the government's choice for UCD parliamentary leader, a social democrat, was trounced by a deputy from the conservative Christian democratic sector.

The "families" of UCD were also able to force a change in the rules governing the election of delegates to the upcoming UCD Second Congress, scheduled for February 1981. The complex rule changes allowed for the representation of the diverse families among the delegates. During the last three months of 1980, the government was forced to negotiate with UCD deputies over virtually all legislative issues, contributing to the public image of UCD as crisis-stricken.

The intensification of the internal crisis of UCD had severely weakened Suárez's once unassailable position within the party. Even so, few would have predicted his resignation in January 1981 from the posts of president of the government and president of UCD. The exact conditions surrounding the surprise resignation of the transition's most enigmatic character have been the subject of significant debate, and the definitive answer awaits the publication of Suárez's memoirs.[17] It is likely, however, that Suárez found frustrating his steady loss of control over the party. His inability to establish an authoritarian model of party leadership no doubt contributed to his decision to resign. The increasing strength of the conservative Christian democratic sector within the party was anathema to him, and his steady drift toward the UCD social democrats probably made this development even more intolerable. Finally, it seems possible that Suárez felt pressured by conservative forces within the military. The president's betrayal of the armed forces during the transition was never forgotten, and his political behavior since then had done nothing to diminish the military's distrust of him. Suárez's cryptic comment that he was resigning because he "[didn't] want the democratic system to be, once again, a parenthesis in Spain's history," appears to lend some credence to this interpretation.[18]

The Second UCD Congress, held in February in Palma de Mallorca, ratified a provisional solution to the party crisis. The positions of party head and president of the government were separated, and the former remained in the hands of a Suárez supporter, along with a number of key party positions. The presidency of the government went to Leopoldo Calvo Sotelo, once a close supporter and collaborator of Suárez (and a key accomplice in his "occupation" of the center). Calvo Sotelo was more conservative than Suárez, and had better relations with UCD Christian democrats, liberals, and the military. In addition, the Palma Congress democratized the internal structure of the party, allowing for representation of UCD parties in all important governing bodies, and greater control over the composition of electoral lists.

While the important changes implemented after the Palma Congress may have delayed the eventual collapse of UCD, they set the stage for the disintegration that took place over the next 20 months. Once their existence was recognized and their power acknowledged, UCD *familias* proved too ideologically incompatible to permit any salvaging of the coalition. The attempted military coup of February 23, 1981, did nothing to stop the unravelling of the governing party, and may have even fueled a more rapid decay.

The Attempted Military Coup and Its Consequences

The attempted military coup of February did much to remind Spaniards of the peculiarity and precariousness of the transition to democracy. As discussed in Chapter 2, it was a common view that authoritarian rule in the postwar period was an anachronistic aberration. By democratizing, Spain had become homologous with its West European neighbors. Unlike transitions in which the military is defeated by an external force (for example, postwar Italy, Germany, and Japan), or transitions in which the military is overthrown by an internal revolutionary movement or a disgruntled faction of the military (Portugal and Greece in 1974, as examples), Spain's armed forces remained essentially intact throughout the transition. Moreover, while Suárez had bought time from the military in order to carry out the initial stages of transition through transaction, the armed forces soon reemerged as the major actor in opposition to democratization. What the military lacked in popular support was more than compensated for by its sheer coercive force.

The military's (or a sector of the military's) disenchantment with democratization is far less surprising than was Suárez's ability to gain an initial, tacit approval for his project. While the military was far from omnipotent in the franquist regime, it constituted the most powerful component of the authoritarian coalition. The military was thoroughly integrated into the franquist coalition. Franco, and the dictator's heir apparent, Carrero Blanco, were both career members of the armed forces, as were about one-third of all Franco's ministers and about one-fifth of the *procuradores* in the Cortes.

The regime right, centered around the military hard-liners, had successfully torpedoed Arias's reform and had, unwittingly no doubt, contributed to his downfall. The military granted Suárez its "tacit" approval for his controlled transition after being convinced of three limits to the reform. First, the political reform would extend only as far as the socialist left, and would at no time include the much hated communists. Second, the reform would maintain intact a centralized state, while granting only limited administrative autonomy to the regions. Third, Suárez would reform the franquist constitution, not abolish it.

In retrospect, it seems incredible that many in the military and on the franquist right could have had faith in these assurances. However, Suárez was successful, at least in a crucial, initial time period, in assuring important sectors of the regime coalition that these three limitations would be adhered to strictly. To help explain this anomaly, it is useful to keep in mind that the transition was a period of considerable political uncertainty and confusion. In addition, Suárez was able to assure many doubtful regime members of his sincerity, partly because he was regarded as a prominent, successful, and loyal franquist politician who would not betray his own origins. Finally, the constitutional trappings of Suárez's reform may have led many otherwise skeptical franquists to ignore the obvious ambiguities of the Political Reform Law. These ambiguities clearly left the door open for Suárez to betray each of the three assurances.

While an isolated sector of the military was not convinced by Suárez to support his project, the vast majority tolerated the reform enterprise begrudgingly, viewing his proposed reform, with its implicit limitations, as the lesser of evils. In addition, most of the armed forces did not relish a confrontation with Franco's hand-picked successor, King Juan Carlos, nor with Adolfo Suárez, only recently the head of the National Movement. The crucial point is that Suárez gained an initial benefit of the doubt and enjoyed a momentary bit of political space within which to maneuver. From then on, he proved able to divide the military at key points in the transition process.

As we have seen, Suárez's reform exceeded all of the limits expected by the military. By June 1977 the Communist Party had been legalized; Basque and Catalan regional symbols, parties, and mass movements were tolerated; and the major franquist institutions had been dismantled. When the newly elected Cortes began the task of writing a constitution, the sense of deception among sectors of the military was complete.

However, the defection of important military leaders from the reform project, although entirely predictable given the contradictions inherent in it, would not have constituted a sufficient threat to transition through transaction were it not for the problem of Basque terrorism.[19] Terrorism was a significant impediment to transition from above since it consistently incurred the wrath of the most intransigent regime forces. It is imperative to point out that Spanish terrorism during the transition was by and large *Basque* terrorism, and the fact that this terrorism often represented nationalism and Marxism—so abhorrent to the military—meant that the armed forces were all the more intolerant of it. Moreover, terrorists attacks were often directed at members of the military. Basque terrorism dovetailed nicely with the civilian right's campaign to incite the military to intervene in political matters.

Thus, the military bunker and Basque terrorists were locked in a head-to-head struggle that served a common objective: initially, the undermining of the transition to democracy, and subsequently, the destruction of Spanish democracy. For the military bunker, transition through transaction had involved blatant deception. Likewise, for many Basques, transition allowed for the bestowing of "retroactive legitimation" on the franquist regime, by creating a democracy led by franquists.

The sense of deception, coupled with terrorism, explains the increasing hostility of the Spanish military to the democratic regime. In 1983, Pedro Vilanova wrote that "the percentage of officers hostile to democracy . . . is paradoxically greater today than it was in 1975, on the death of Franco, when many soldiers accepted the idea of peaceful, gradual change, and under the King's direction"[20] Suárez's behavior after his September 1976 summit with military leaders had led to a slow but steady hiving off of military support for his leadership in particular, and for the democratic reform in general. On September 21, 1977, First Vice-President Lieutenant General Fernando de Santiago was replaced by the liberal Gutiérrez Mellado. De Santiago had openly opposed any legalization of "those we defeated in the Civil War," referring to the government's deliberations over a proposed syndical reform that would have tolerated socialist and communist trade unions.[21] Many within the military, who understood the "deal" with Suárez as prohibiting any governmental interference in military affairs, were angered at some of the promotions and replacements in key posts in late 1976. Gutiérrez Mellado, who was instrumental in selling the military-government pact within the armed forces, became the target of attacks by the military right. For example, in early January 1979 a funeral for the assassinated military governor of Madrid turned into a raucous military demonstration against the government in general, and Gutiérrez Mellado in particular. Suárez met this offensive with a dual strategy of continuing to replace franquists with democrats, while taking little direct punitive action against antidemocratic sectors. According to two experts on the Spanish military,

> thus began what would become a regular pattern of relations between the government and the military: A combination of adulation of "liberal" and "moderate" generals and praise of the military apparatus in general, along with a timidity when it came

to punishing the increasingly frequent acts of defiance. All this served to encourage the *golpista* sectors and demoralize the isolated democratic nuclei.[22]

The almost unanimous opposition by top military leaders to Suárez's legalization of the PCE in April 1977 created one of the most serious political crises of the transition. Navy Minister Pita da Veiga resigned and there were attempts by other military officials to convince the king to remove Suárez and Guitérrez Mellado.

After the June 1977 elections, Guitérrez Mellado, at the head of the recently consolidated Defense Ministry, began to implement a moderate military reorganization plan that immediately drew hostile reactions from the bunker. In September 1977 a large number of top military leaders met in the province of Valencia to discuss the proposed reform. The meeting produced what was the first serious talk among military elites of a *coup d'état*.[23]

In December 1977 Army Chief of Staff Admiral Carlos Buhigas, resigned in protest over these timid reforms. In May 1978 Lieutenant General Vega Rodríguez followed suit, protesting proposed promotions not based on the sacrosanct seniority system. His resignation reflected a more deep-seated hostility to what was perceived as the military's loss of institutional autonomy. His replacement, Lieutenant General Tomás de Liniers, had reportedly stated during a trip to Argentina, in June 1977, that "Spain and Argentina currently suffer from the most wicked attacks of atheistic materialism. . . . When, faced with this situation, we have tried to employ force, we have been criticized for the use of force, but only history can pass judgement on its use."[24]

In the fall of 1978 a major coup plot was uncovered by the Spanish secret service. *Operación Galaxia*, as the plot was named, was led by Lieutenant Colonel Antonio Tejero (Civil Guard) and Captain Ricardo Saenz de Ynestrillas. The plotters chose a date in September when the king was scheduled to be out of the country, and when top military officials would be outside of Madrid. In a severe embarrassment to the government, military courts meted out prison sentences of under seven months to each of the accused conspirators.

Throughout 1980 there was incessant activity on the part of the military bunker in opposition to the democratic regime. This activity culminated in the aborted coup attempt of February 23, 1981.

The *golpistas*, led by Lieutenant General Tejero, a co-conspirator in *Operación Galaxia*, took the entire Spanish parliament hostage. Spaniards, who were viewing the investiture of Calvo Sotelo as prime minister live on television, watched in horror as the pistol-toting Tejero terrorized Spain's elected representatives. The attempted coup was a serious matter, as evidenced by the presence of tanks in the streets of Valencia, the military takeover of a number of key communications centers, and the initial characterization by the United States of the events as "an internal matter." Poor planning and an unrealistic assessment of the resolve of the top military and political leadership doomed the conspiracy. The *golpistas* were unable to convince a majority of their colleagues to join in the coup, so the plot fizzled and the leaders were arrested. Most importantly, King Juan Carlos, commander in chief of the armed forces, was completely unwilling to consider the demands of the conspirators. His appearance on Spanish television ended any hopes that the young monarch could be persuaded to support the coup, or at least tolerate it through silence.

In the following months, the general political implications of the foiled coup became clearer. It was apparent to everyone that Spain's democracy remained fragile. The attempted coup shocked most Spaniards, although early warning signals had not been lacking, and renewed the sense that the armed forces continued to pose a severe threat to democracy. However, there were encouraging signs amidst the gloom that followed the foiled coup attempt. Most of the Spanish political elite, from right to left, had criticized the attempt unambiguously, a sign that unity among political elites in support of democratic rule constituted the ultimate protection for democracy. Popular support for the new democracy, though suprisingly delayed, was nevertheless effusive.[25] Perhaps most auspicious was the military's internal division regarding the coup. The king commanded loyalty from the majority of the military leadership. Finally, the king's crucial role in foiling the coup attempt again underscored his importance to the continuing survival of Spanish democracy.

The coup attempt seems to have encouraged a rightward shift within the two major political parties, UCD and the PSOE. As will be described below in more detail, after the resignation of Suárez, the governing party gradually moved toward the right, while the PSOE, sobered by the coup attempt, hastened it own moderation.

In the 1982 general elections, most major parties employed non-conflictual campaigns, somewhat in contrast with the 1979 elections.

The Decline of UCD under Calvo Sotelo

For most of UCD's families, Calvo Sotelo's conservatism, and his willingness to work with the diverse currents within UCD, made him a more acceptable party leader than Suárez. However, while he better catered to UCD families, he was far less charismatic than his predecessor. Ultimately he proved equally incapable of shaping a coherent centrist party. Calvo Sotelo's attempts to equalize the internal balance of power away from the dominant *Suaristas* and social democrats and toward liberals and Christian democrats was bitterly fought by the former, who accused the new UCD leadership of seeking a *gran derecha* (a united right), what AP leader Fraga Iribarne euphemistically called the "natural majority."

Whether Calvo Sotelo genuinely hoped for a future alliance with the right, or whether he was simply trying to stem the centrifugal tendencies of his party, UCD was unable to shake its image as a party of feuding barons. In fact, the social democratic, liberal, and Christian democratic currents within UCD became increasingly organized, and now threatened to bolt the party if their concerns went unmet. In the summer of 1981, the UCD right and left again came to blows, this time over the divorce law, a reform of great symbolic importance for social democrats and Christian democrats. In late August, Justice Minister Fernández Ordoñez, chief spokesperson for UCD social democrats, resigned from the government, complaining of the party's rightward drift under Calvo Sotelo.

Two crises in the autumn of 1981 added more fuel to the fire raging within the governing party. In October, elections to the regional parliament in Galicia produced an unmitigated disaster. Galicia is among Spain's most conservative regions, and by all measures should have returned a regional parliament dominated by UCD. A UCD victory, albeit an expected one, might have counteracted the government's trouncing in Catalonia and the Basque Country. Unexpectedly, UCD was defeated by the party to its right, the Popular Alliance, and was able to win only 24 of 71 seats. The defeat in Galicia may be seen as both a consequence of and factor contributing to the disintegration of UCD. Both the left and right wings of the party harvested lessons from the disaster to suit their respective positions. AP's surprise success in conservative Galicia led Christian democrats to claim that UCD, under Suárez and the social democrats, had lost touch with its natural electorate. Social democrats attributed the loss to a lack of coherent leadership, incapable of stemming a rightward drift of the party. Consequently, they argued, most UCD voters failed to perceive a difference between the two parties, and progressive UCD voters had abandoned the party altogether.

A second, extremely elusive issue helped to further erode UCD's strength. In 1981, a major scandal arose over the discovery of tainted cooking oil, which was directly linked to hundreds of deaths. The "toxic oil syndrome" grew to epidemic proportions, and the government searched unsuccessfully (and some alleged inefficiently) for the source and a solution. The frightening issue subjected the government to an emotionally charged attack from the right and the left. The mysterious nature of the "syndrome," and the difficulty locating the cause and cure for it, plagued the government until the October 1982 elections.

Political infighting of the type described above seemed all the more outrageous in light of the epidemic. Simultaneously, as the government became saddled with these problems, and as UCD appeared increasingly to be a sinking ship, dissenting groups had less incentive to stay on board. In November 1981, the UCD experienced defections on its left and right. Fernández Ordoñez, along with a group of social democratic deputies, left the UCD to form the Democratic Action Party (PAD). A group of Christian democrats joined the electoral coalition dominated by AP. The hiving off of UCD deputies, both on the left and right wings of the party, continued up until the 1982 general elections.

In an attempt to prevent the total decomposition of UCD, Calvo Sotelo replaced Rodríguez Sahagún (a *Suarista*) as party leader, thus reinstituting a unified party and government leadership. Calvo Sotelo managed to slow the sinking of UCD in the early months of 1982, but he was unable to stop the centrifuge. Elections to the Andalusian regional parliament in the spring of that year were yet another sign of an upcoming electoral disaster: UCD placed third, behind the victorious PSOE and the renovated AP.

Perhaps the final blow to UCD came with Adolfo Suárez's

abandonment of the party he had created, shortly before the elections. In a rather futile gesture, Suárez formed the Democratic and Social Center (Centro Democrático y Social, CDS). The ex-president had long since failed to benefit UCD, and had operated behind the scenes as a semirecluse. He appears to have hoped that he might be called upon to save the center, as he had in 1977, but by 1982 this scenario was hardly realistic.

On the eve of the 1982 elections, UCD had exhausted all of its options. Calvo Sotelo was assailed by his right for stubbornly rejecting any alliance with the rightist AP. However, he adhered to the view of UCD as a centrist option, and he was undoubtedly aware of the fact—confirmed by the 1982 electoral results—that the electorate was located in the center, and not on the right. Even so, when Calvo Sotelo called for early elections in the autumn of 1982, few could have predicted the calamitous electoral performance of UCD. The governing party experienced an electoral drubbing rare in Western democracies. UCD's 168 deputies and 119 senators were reduced to 13 and 4, respectively (see Table 7). UCD did not win a single constituency, and its percentage of the vote declined from 35 to 7. To add insult to injury, all but two cabinet members lost their parliamentary seats.

The PSOE: From Radical Opposition to Governmental Alternative

As early as 1980, UCD had ceased to be an effective governmental party, but a majority of Spaniards saw no viable alternative. On the right, AP recalled franquist immobilism, and there was little desire to return to the past. On the left, the Spanish Socialist Workers Party appeared to be too radical and inexperienced to be an acceptable replacement for UCD. The Spanish Communist Party was in the process of disintegration that paralleled the decay of the governing party. In short, Spain was desperately in need of party alternation, but the party system was incapable of providing an alternative to UCD.

The remainder of this chapter will examine how the internal evolution of the PSOE eventually permitted party alternation. If it is fair to say that UCD was the most influential political force in the first five years of democracy, it seems likely that the same

Table 7. Electoral Results, October 28, 1982

Party	Number of Votes (millions)	Percent of Votes	Deputies		Senators	
			Number of Seats	Percent of Seats	Number of Seats	Percent of Seats
PSOE	9.83	46.0	202	57.8	138	66.3
CD(AP)	5.41	25.3	106	30.3	54	26.3
UCD	1.54	7.2	12	3.4	0	0.0
PCE	.82	3.8	4	1.1	0	0.0
Regional and other	3.70	17.7	26	7.0	16	7.4
Totals	21.30	100.0	350	100.0	208	100.0

Source: Compiled by the author.

can be said for the PSOE in the second half of the decade. It is interesting to note that as of 1986, while an alternation of power had taken place, there was still only one viable governing party. AP was slowly cultivating its image as a loyal and democratic opposition, but it was not yet able to fill the electoral space vacated by UCD.

The PSOE in Historical Perspective

In order to examine how the PSOE evolved into a governmental alternative, it is necessary to provide an overview of the party's history and its role in the transition to democracy.[26]

Unlike UCD, the PSOE is the oldest of Spain's political parties. Pablo Iglesias founded the party in 1879, and ever since then, it has been divided over social democratic and Marxist ideology and strategy. Despite this internal schism, Iglesias steered the PSOE in an electoralist direction in the first part of the twentieth century. Moderates within the party leadership directed the PSOE toward a gradually expanding parliamentary presence and a slow implementation of welfare legislation. During most of the Primo de Rivera dictatorship, the Socialists collaborated with the regime and derived some benefits from it. Until the emergence of a Communist Party to the PSOE's left in 1920, the maximalist wing of the Socialist Party was in no position to challenge the reformist leadership.

With the advent of the Second Republic in 1931, the PSOE's electoralist orientation was enhanced. The Socialists were among the founding fathers of the republic, and they remained unambiguously committed to parliamentary procedures until at least 1933. However, a convergence of factors soon contributed to a leftward shift within the PSOE. The republic failed to live up to the excessively high expectations placed upon it. The 1933 elections produced a government of the reactionary right, which attempted to reverse even the mild reforms of the first two years. Pressure mounted from the parties to the left of the PSOE, and from the grass-roots constituency of the party itself. Democracy appeared to be under attack worldwide, subverted or perverted by forces of the right. The ill-fated Asturian uprising of 1934, and its brutal suppression by the military (led by General Franco), led many PSOE leaders (like Largo Caballero) and intellectuals (like Arquistaín) to begin to question the value of democratic institutions.[27] By the

1936 election a large the portion of the Socialist leadership had rejected the parliamentary road to socialism and had come to support armed struggle.

General Franco's victory prohibited a resolution of this internal conflict and forced the PSOE to struggle for its survival in an extremely inhospitable environment. Franco's forces quickly smashed most of the PSOE's organizational structure. By 1948, six consecutive PSOE Executive Committees had been arrested, and their members were executed or imprisoned. The PSOE had been a mass electoral party and, unlike the PCE, it was hardly suited to conditions of clandestine existence. For this reason, the party virtually ceased to exist within Spain until the late 1960s and survived mainly as a party in exile. Even in exile, the PSOE failed to have any real impact on Spanish politics. Its leaders clung to the increasingly naive hope that Western democracies would asphyxiate franquism, and when the Cold War eliminated such a possibility, the PSOE waited for the franquist regime to be overthrown from within. Moreover, the PSOE leadership in exile adopted an exclusivist coalition strategy, refusing to ally with the only political force with any influence inside Spain: the Spanish Communist Party.

In the 1960s, during a period of rapid economic growth, and after the period of harshest repression had ended, the PSOE began to reemerge within Spain. Its leaders were mostly students and young middle-class professionals, and they were centered largely in the Basque Country and Andalusia. This younger generation differed significantly from the old guard in exile. Their youth inclined them toward a more radical politics, or at least more radical rhetoric. Their daily encounter with the political realities of franquist Spain convinced them of the need for flexibility in the choice of coalition partners in the common struggle against authoritarian rule. Not surprisingly, this young guard also demanded more control over the PSOE by militants within Spain. By 1972, the interior faction had wrested control of the PSOE from the old guard, forcing much of the more conservative leadership in exile to bolt the party and form a social democratic rival.[28] The exit of the most conservative sector of the PSOE, and the rejuvenation of the leadership, led to a temporary radicalization of the party. At the PSOE 27th Congress in December 1976—the first tolerated PSOE Congress in Spain for over 40 years—the Socialists adopted an extremely radical party platform.[29] The fact that the PSOE was still semiclandestine no doubt added to the revolutionary emphasis of the platform, but the shift leftward was also prompted by the rapid influx of young, inexperienced, and ideologically oriented members.

The PSOE in the Transition

Suárez's transition through transaction presented an uncomfortable dilemma for the democratic opposition. Officially, the PSOE called for a *ruptura democrática* (a democratic break) and the formation of a provisional government composed of all opposition parties. As long as Arias proved unable to implement a controlled transition to democracy, the PSOE's call for a *ruptura* appeared reasonable. However, as Suárez successfully implemented his strategy, the PSOE's insistence on a democratic break appeared more contradictory. On the one hand, it was increasingly unlikely that a democratic break would take place. Suárez was able to maintain the regime's control over the democratization process, and there was virtually no possibility of a provisional government. Moreover, the *end* pursued by Suárez's reform, a parliamentary democracy, was entirely acceptable to the PSOE, and the party leadership had to be careful not to contribute to the failure of transition through transaction. As most PSOE leaders were aware, Suárez's failure would almost certainly lead to an authoritarian involution, and such an outcome was contrary to Socialist goals.

On the other hand, the *means* employed by Suárez to achieve democracy were especially hard to swallow for the democratic opposition. On a theoretical level, it appeared counterintuitive that an authoritarian regime could oversee a transition to democracy without the participation of the democratic opposition. On a more practical level, there were few, if any, such cases in history to inspire such a form of democratic change. More concretely, Arias had already failed miserably to democratize from above, so PSOE leaders were most skeptical. It would be especially traumatic for a political party like the PSOE, which advocated socialist revolution and a democratic break, to publicly support a transition to democracy led by the ex-secretary-general of the franquist National Movement!

As long as there was some possibility of a *ruptura*, there was

little incentive to abandon the maximalist rhetoric of the 27th PSOE
Congress. It would be premature to abandon this platform before
party leaders could be convinced of the scope and possibilities for
success of the president's reform plan. Four factors convinced the
PSOE leadership to pursue a more moderate and conciliatory
strategy, and to gamble on the Suárez reform. First, in the early
months of 1977, the Suárez reform program remained on course,
despite a wave of terrorist violence that shook the country in January and February. Suárez's own calm, and his refusal to be intimi-
dated into slowing down the reform, reassured a still-skeptical opposition. Second, and more importantly, was the impending
electoral campaign. PSOE elites were aware that maximalist rhetoric, as well as a continued insistence on *ruptura*, would not appeal to the Spanish electorate. A third factor was Suárez's unexpected legalization of the PCE in April. Suddenly, the PSOE was
faced with a serious challenge to its left, and from Spain's best organized political party. Moreover, the PCE, in exchange for its
legalization, had agreed to accept the monarchy and the rules of
transition through transaction, thus adding to the pressure on the
PSOE to do likewise. Finally, Suárez's dismantling of the National
Movement and the Syndical Organization in May added to the impression that the president was serious in his goal of democratization.

The PSOE electoral campaign for the June 1977 elections
reflected a continuing ambivalence vis-à-vis the emerging
democracy. For the most part it attempted to moderate its image,
playing down the revolutionary aspects of its program, while emphasizing the personal appeal of Felipe González and the party's
desire for democracy. There were no attempts to attack Suárez's
strategy, and there was no mention of a provisional government.
However, the PSOE continued to portray itself as a party of the
workers, and it stressed the fact that "for almost one hundred years
[the PSOE] has defended the interests of the working class."[30] The
PSOE's ambivalence was reflected in its 34-year-old secretary-
general Felipe González. González, a Sevillian labor lawyer, had
gained his early political experience within the Catholic working-
class movement. In 1962 he joined the Socialist Party Youth, and
became an active PSOE militant in 1964. His election as PSOE
general secretary only ten years later made him somewhat of an
enigma. González had a reputation as a skilled, radical, and often

fiery orator, but he was also seen as a pragmatist who did not carry the ideological and emotional baggage of those who had lived the civil war.

The PSOE's excellent performance in the first elections led to the intensification of a long-standing internal debate over strategy and ideology. The rejuvenation of the leadership, the swelling of party ranks, and clandestine struggle against franquism had all endowed the party with a revolutionary socialist program. After the first elections, the question became whether or not to shed this radical program. Some, Felipe González included, felt that the PSOE could now take its place in a competitive democracy as the major progressive opposition party. Its parliamentary strength could give it influence over the new constitution, and a further moderation of its image could eventually allow the PSOE to take power. Based on these assumptions, the party leadership performed as a loyal opposition in the period following the elections. When the PSOE reached a consensus with UCD over a new constitution, and in the Moncloa Pacts, some within the party, the so-called *sector crítico* (critical sector), attacked this strategy of moderation. They noted that these elite-level interparty agreements were prejudicial to the PSOE's working-class constituency, and feared that this compromise would strengthen Suárez's hand and needlessly delay an alternation of power. The *críticos* abhorred the electoralist drift of the party leadership, which they feared would culminate in the PSOE's social democratization.

After the 1977 elections, the *críticos* were increasingly in the minority within the PSOE. Socialist leaders were encouraged by the influence they had in the writing of a progressive constitution. As they lived the reality of parliamentary democracy, they placed greater value on the democratic freedoms so long denied than on ideological commitments. Moreover, the threats to democracy, from sectors of the military, from terrorists, and from the economic crisis, convinced Socialist leaders of the need for moderation. Javier Solana, a PSOE Executive Committee member, articulated this feeling quite directly:

> Democracy and its consolidation come first, before our political programs. These might take twenty or thirty years to put into practice. Why this order of priorities? Because the Spanish right has shown that it can live very well under both authoritarian and democratic regimes, while the left can only survive within

the democratic framework. We have a lot of pain and suffering, and many years behind bars to prove that.[31]

Thus, PSOE leaders and intellectuals began to distance themselves from Marxist ideas, and encouraged the PSOE to abandon a strictly working-class definition of the party. However, this shift in strategy could not be implemented overnight. Instead, it required a redistribution of power within the PSOE, and a marginalization of the *sector crítico*.

The Defeat of the PSOE Left

Although the Socialists failed to win the 1977 elections, its leaders had high hopes for the next elections. With the integration of Tierno Galván's PSP, the PSOE became the only socialist party, and it hoped to increase its percentage of the vote considerably. The PSOE expected to pave the way for a national victory with a strong showing in the municipal elections, scheduled for April 1979. However, as noted earlier, Suárez outmaneuvered the opposition by calling for early general elections. Moreover, he launched a bitter attack on the PSOE, exploiting the ambiguities between the radical program of the 27th Congress and the more moderate image of its leadership. UCD emphasized the contradictory statements emanating from different sectors of the party. The church and the private sector added to the fears raised by the governing party. The PSOE was bitter over these scare tactics, and the 1979 electoral returns added to the frustration: The PSOE failed to make any significant gains and actually lost ground to the PCE. The Socialists were hurt by a very high abstention rate in areas of PSOE strength, and this was interpreted by the *críticos* as the party constituency's punishment for overly consensual behavior. In contrast, the leadership concluded from the PSOE's disappointing performance that the party must broaden its appeal, clearly explicate its ideology, and adjust the party platform accordingly. González, for example, argued that "there can be no democratic social transformation without a majority. And in order to obtain a majority it is essential to represent a much wider spectrum than originally planned."[32]

The opposing analyses for the causes of the PSOE's performance clashed head on at the party's 28th Congress, held in May 1979. They were manifest in three concrete issues that had long divided the leadership from the *críticos*.[33] First, and most crucial, was the ideological question. Ever since May 1978, when González announced his intention to remove the term "Marxist" from the party's constitution, the Marxism/non-Marxism polemic had gained steam. A second, organizational issue concerned the critical sector's demand for a system of proportional representation for selecting representatives for party congresses and all other governing bodies of the PSOE, thus ensuring representation for critical viewpoints and continued influence over party strategy. The party leadership feared that this would prevent it from articulating a coherent and moderate image to the electorate. The third bone of contention involved alliance strategy, with the *críticos* favoring a leftist front with the PCE, along the lines of the successful PSOE-PCE alliance at the municipal level. While this alliance had proved fruitful at the local level, the leadership wanted to avoid anything reminiscent of the Popular Front. The PSOE had enough problems demonstrating its commitment to democracy without allying with the widely distrusted PCE.

The results of the 28th Congress were unexpected. While the PSOE leadership was successful in defeating the *críticos* on organizational and alliance issues, it was dealt a sound defeat on the Marxist/non-Marxist question. González's proposal to define the PSOE as a "social bloc" lost to an explicitly Marxist definition. The executive's choice for president, the moderate Gregorio Peces-Barba (a practicing Catholic), was defeated by a more radical candidate, a vote interpreted as an attack on the leadership's moderate policies and electoral strategy. In response, González refused to stand for reelection, in a clear attempt to force the membership to choose sides. When explaining his resignation, González argued that "the country cannot wait ten years for the Party to mature."[34]

González's challenge to the PSOE membership eventually proved successful. The *críticos* were not prepared for a full-scale assault on the leadership, and had not intended to unseat the popular and charismatic González. They sought only to gain some representation and influence with the party apparatus. Moreover, the losses suffered by the *críticos* on the organizational question, especially the changes in procedure for delegate selection to future congresses, put them at a serious disadvantage. These changes included a majoritarian electoral system for delegate selection and party posts, and a bloc-voting provision during congresses. All of these revisions enhanced the power of the executive in the future.

The weakness of the *crítico's* position was made evident at an Extraordinary Congress, convened in September 1979 in order to break the impasse of the 28th Congress. The more moderate delegates overwhelmingly endorsed the party leadership.[35] The ideological question was resolved by acknowledging the importance of Marxism as "a critical, non-dogmatic theoretical tool," while vowing to "include a variety of contributors, Marxist and non-Marxist, who have helped make socialism the great liberating alternative of our time."

The Extraordinary Congress marked the defeat of the critical sector, which continued its existence within the party as a study group named Izquierda Socialista (Socialist Left). It has made somewhat of a resurgence in support of specific issues (most recently, to protest the leadership's position on NATO), but it poses little real threat to the unity of the PSOE. After the Extraordinary Congress, González's attempt to move the PSOE rightward progressed unimpeded. The scare created by the 1981 coup attempt only served to emphasize the importance of a cautious and conciliatory strategy. The dangers entailed by the self-destruction of UCD also augured well for such a moderation. The defection of UCD social democrats encouraged the PSOE strategists to seek votes from the center-left electorate.

The October 1981 29th PSOE Congress attempted to convince the electorate that the Socialists were a serious, unified, and moderate party. Compared with the turbulent 28th Congress, the unanimity went to such an extreme—the leadership was reelected with 99.6 percent of the vote—that one observer remarked wryly that "everything is working so well that this seems like a West German Congress."[36] Members of Izquierda Socialista boycotted the Congress, and the press questioned whether the "homogenization" of the party hadn't gone too far, but the leadership was largely successful in presenting an image of internal unity and ideological moderation. This turn to the right was instrumental in allowing the PSOE to increase its share of the vote from 30.5 percent (in the 1979 elections) to 46 percent (in the October 1982 elections).

The Logic of a Social Democratic Left

The PSOE has become Spain's social democratic left. In just under five years, the PSOE has changed from being one of Europe's most radical socialist parties into one of its most conservative. Such a rapid change is unusual, and it required single-minded and occasionally authoritarian leadership. In retrospect, the PSOE's radicalization was an aberration and its moderation appears more logical.

To begin with, the PSOE was always poorly equipped to pursue a confrontational strategy. Compared with the PCE, and even compared with other European socialist or social democratic parties, the PSOE is a very small, intellectually oriented party, with a very weak organizational base. In 1981 the PSOE had the smallest percentage of members per voters of any European socialist or social democratic party (1.8 percent).[37] Its current membership is considerably inferior to its counterparts in even the much smaller West European countries. In addition, the new social democratic orientation of the party is much more in line with the social composition of its membership. PSOE members and leaders are highly educated, upwardly mobile, and professionally employed. At the top level, those with working-class backgrounds are virtually absent. Even at party congresses, manual workers represent a tiny minority, and professionals and technocrats predominate.[38]

These characteristics of the PSOE supported the moderation of the party, but the peculiar circumstances of the transition were equally influential. It is difficult to envision any feasible alternative to the strategy pursued by the party leadership. Initially, failure to participate in the Suárez reform might have endangered democratization and would likely have diminished the party's mark on the new political system. In addition, the PSOE might have been eclipsed by competing forces of the left, such as the PCE (which was more than willing to accept transition through transaction). After the first elections, failure to abandon its radical ideological baggage would have worked against the Socialists. It would have left the Spanish party system dangerously polarized after the disappearance of UCD, and it might have threatened the democratic system itself. Furthermore, even had the PSOE retained its commitment to radical change, the constraints imposed by the transition—for example, the hostility of the still-powerful military—would have prevented the implementation of its programs.

Thus, the rightward drift of the PSOE has contributed to the stability of Spanish democracy. It endowed the new party system with a viable governmental alternative on the center left. With the disintegration of UCD, the presence of such an alternative was especially important. It is still uncertain whether AP will be able to replace UCD as the party of the moderate right, but as of 1985 the signs are encouraging.

The PSOE in Power

Since taking power in December 1982, the Socialists have continued their drift toward the center. By 1984, only two years into González's term as president, one scholar was already questioning whether the PSOE had become Spain's new center party.[39] Despite the fear surrounding a socialist victory, and compared with the social democratic policies pursued by socialist counterparts in Europe, the PSOE's moderation has exceeded all predictions. Like UCD under Suárez, the PSOE has not governed according to strict ideological tenets. Instead, González has focused his government's energy on completing the project begun by his predecessors. He has sought to achieve a more complete consolidation of transition through transaction, and has attempted to make democracy perform better.

In many respects, the 1982 elections were historic. They produced the first socialist parliamentary majority and the first single-party government of the left in Spanish history. More importantly, they marked the first instance of democratic party alternation in government since 1936. The PSOE's sweep of the general elections was followed by a similar performance in the municipal elections of May 1983, thus creating the best conditions for single-party government since the transition. Finally, the opposition's weakness placed the Socialists in a virtually unassailable position. UCD was unable to survive its electoral debacle, and the party officially disbanded in early 1983. AP made a spectacular comeback, but it still won only one-quarter of the vote and held only 28 percent of the seats in the lower house. As of 1986, AP still had along way to go in its attempt to present a unified, moderate, and democratic image to the electorate.

For the PSOE leadership, these elections also presented an historic opportunity to consolidate democracy, to gain the electorate's confidence in the moderation, skill, and diligence of the PSOE leadership, and to implement some long-overdue reforms. Even before the elections, the PSOE approached these goals with extreme caution. The Socialists called for change, but ruled out nationalization of industry, radical reform of the military, significant redistribution of income, or major social reform. Nevertheless, just before the elections, Spain's anticoup brigade foiled plans for a coup, scheduled for the eve of the expected PSOE victory. The *Operación Cervantes* involved several high-ranking military officers and suggested significant complicity from other sectors within the armed forces. The aborted coup was another factor counseling the PSOE toward caution and patience.

González's first government was tailor-made for moderation. Social democrats were in a large majority, and occupied most of the crucial ministries. For example, the powerful Ministry of Economic Affairs—known as a "superministry" for its jurisdiction over a wide range of financial, trade, and economic matters—went to Miguel Boyer, who had been a social democratic member of the original Center Democrats, and later joined forces with Fernández Ordoñez. Carlos Solchaga, a social democrat, and an MIT graduate with ties to Spain's banking elite, was appointed minister of industry. Narcís Serra, previously the mayor of Barcelona, and well respected within the military, became minister of defense. Only two cabinet posts, the Ministry of Foreign Affaris and the Ministry of Labor, went to less moderate Socialists. Moreover, one of the few influential leaders of the PSOE left, Ciriaco de Vicente (slated for the Health Ministry), was passed over in the formation of the cabinet. In addition to its moderate composition, the new government had two important characteristics. First, its members were extremely young, with the average age about 41. Second, it was composed of a large number of party members with roots in the progressive Catholic opposition during franquism.

The new government's early actions were aimed at presenting an image of moderation. In what was widely seen as a gesture toward the church, Gregorio Peces-Barba, a founding father of the constitution and a representative of the Catholic wing of the PSOE, became speaker of the lower house. In an effort to make peace with the business sector, the PSOE initiated meetings with the Spanish Confederation of Entrepreneurial Organizations (Confederación Española de Organizaciónes Empresariales, CEOE), and both parties stated a willingness to reach tripartite agreements on major economic issues.

While the Socialists advocated moderate policies, and the pace of change was slow, the PSOE managed to make progress in a number of important areas during its first years in power.[40] Surprisingly perhaps, the Socialists were most successful in the area of military reform. In the immediate aftermath of the election, the PSOE did not try to tackle this sensitive issue head on. Instead, it courted the military hierarchy by pushing a huge increase in military spending, and taking a hard line on Basque terrorism. In October 1983, a full year after the elections, Defense Minister Narcís Serra announced the government's plans for military reform. These included a drastic reduction in the size of the military, including a 25 percent reduction in the inflated officer corps, a reorientation of the military toward national defense and away from internal surveillance, a weakening of the power of military tribunals, a consolidation of the military hierarchy, and a more complete subordination of the military to the civilian government. On the other hand, plans to demilitarize the Civil Guard were shelved indefinitely.

The government has made slow but steady progress in all these areas. The military reforms gained momentum in January 1984, with the appointment of Spain's first military chief of staff directly responsible to the defense minister. The government also replaced the heads of all three military branches with supporters of the constitution. However, the democratization of armed forces appears to have exacted a price. The government has committed itself to a political and military modernization of the Spanish armed forces, and this has required increasing budgetary commitments in a time of economic crisis. In addition, those in the more democratic wing of the armed forces are strong supporters of Spain's membership in NATO.[41]

In this light, it is easier to explain the PSOE's radical about-face on the NATO issue. When Calvo Sotelo's government approved Spain's entry into NATO in 1982, the Socialist opposition called for a nationwide referendum to approve such a commitment. The polls indicated that the majority of the population opposed NATO entry, and the PSOE leadership followed suit, advocating a withdrawal from the alliance. Even at that time, however, the PSOE's position contained serious contradictions. González opposed NATO membership, but favored the continuing presence of U.S. military bases in Spain. After the elections, the PSOE government began to waffle on the issue. First, it put off discussion of a referendum, and subsequently promised a referendum by early 1986. The party leadership then began to manifest serious internal divisions over the NATO question. In October 1984 González publicly advocated a political (as opposed to military) integration, but now called for a moderate reduction in the number of U.S. bases! the PSOE's ambiguity on this question subjected it to a steady stream of criticism in the media during 1983 and 1984, but the government did an admirable job of pulling off such a drastic policy reversal. The issue was finally resolved at the PSOE's 30th Congress in December 1984.[42] Just as González had purged his party of its Marxist ideological baggage in 1981, the president now convinced a majority of party delegates that NATO membership was necessary for "external and internal stability."[43] This development is particularly surprising, given the fact that opinion polls continued to show a majority of Spaniards opposed to NATO membership.[44]

The PSOE's record on economic issues was similarly unanticipated. While its electoral platform had indicated its desire to make capitalism work better and more fairly, and had eschewed any plans for massive state intervention in the economy, few predicted the vigor with which the government subsequently pursued its austerity policy. Following an essentially neoconservative analysis, Minister of Economic Affairs Miguel Boyer took early action to lower inflation, hoping that a concomitant reactivation of the economy would produce more jobs. Despite previous assurances to the contrary, Boyer announced an 8 percent devaluation of the peseta on December 5, 1982, and by 1984 the government had let the currency slide 32 percent relative to the dollar. In order to limit inflation and cut spending, the government negotiated the National Employment Agreement between the CEOE and the trade unions, continuing the precedent established by the 1977 Moncloa Pacts. In October 1984, trade unions and the CEOE agreed to a two-year pact that held wages equal to the forecast inflation rate in the private sector, and below predicted inflation in the public sector.[45] The government pledged to reduce state-sector jobs 10 percent by 1986, and especially targeted the gigantic bureaucracy, which ballooned during Suárez's presidency. Finally, the government tried to reduce state expenditures for pensions through a mixture of privatization and modification of existing contribution schemes.

These political economic policies led to a moderate reduction in the inflation rate, and a rise in the rate of economic growth (over 2 percent). Export growth boomed while imports expanded more slowly, thus alleviating the balance-of-payments deficit. However, the government's most serious failure was in the area traditionally of greatest concern for a government of the left: employment. Despite Felipe González's campaign pledge to create 200,000 new jobs annually, unemployment has risen steadily. The government's attempt to "streamline" Spain's outdated and inefficient industrial structure was, in the short term, contradictory to its concern about employment. As part of the government's industrial conversion plan, Labor Minister Joaquín Alumnia, one of the two cabinet members considered to be furthest to the left, introduced legislation to undermine the franquist job security system. After tense negotiations with angry trade unions, the government was able to facilitate the hiring of part-time workers and the layoff of redundant employees. Nevertheless, the PSOE's economic analysts have deemed such a reindustrialization effort to be paramount to Spain's integration into the EEC. While Boyer's austere economic policies won the PSOE support from financial sectors, they strained relations between the trade unions (even the PSOE affiliate, the General Union of Workers) and the government: The incidence of strikes rose over 30 percent in 1984.[46] As with the NATO issue, González successfully consolidated party support for his government's political economic policies. The 30th Congress approved some vague assurances regarding insurance schemes for workers and the timetable for industrial conversion plans, but the delegates did not substantially alter González's policies.

The government's economic policies exacerbated the already tense relationship between center and periphery. Layoffs in the steel, iron, and shipbuilding industries increased labor militancy in the Basque Country and Catalonia. The government's desire to continue with the implementation of the Law for the Harmonization of the Autonomy Process led many in these regions to view the PSOE as yet another centralist party. Thus, in its first two years the PSOE suffered setbacks in the Basque Country and Catalonia, not unlike those experienced by UCD. In order to deal with the continuing menace of Basque terrorism, and to calm the military, the PSOE introduced a strict antiterrorist law. The alarming success of the Basque nationalist left, with ties to ETA, the schism within the governing Basque Nationalist Party and its rocky relations with Madrid, and the continuing tension created by terrorism of the left and right have all obstructed any political solution to the crisis. The level of frustration on the part of all involved was demonstrated by the increasing talk of a "Lebanization" of the Basque Country.

In Catalonia, center-periphery relations worsened in comparison to the situation under UCD governments. In April 1984 the PSOE was dealt a surprising blow in the Catalan regional elections. Jordi Pujol's CiU retained power and defeated the PSOE. Three weeks later, the government indicted Pujol in relation to an alleged bank scandal.

In addition to the clearly mixed results in all of the above areas, PSOE took action that antagonized important interests. On February 23, 1983, the government announced the nationalization of RUMASA, Spain's largest private holding company. The move shocked large sectors of Spanish private enterprise, although the government's rationale for the nationalization—it charged that RUMASA had become so fraudulently overextended that it posed a threat to the Spanish economy—and its determination to denationalize the company at the earliest possible date eventually defused most opposition. In 1983, the Socialists successfully passed legislation allowing for abortion in extremely limited circumstances, although the Constitutional Court subsequently overturned the legislation. In the spring of 1984, Education Minister Maravall introduced legislation to give the state increased control over the vast system of private (mostly religious) schools that very many Spanish students attend. The church, together with AP, was able to mobilize .5 million people for an antigovernment rally in November of that year. In September 1983 the Penal Code was revised to allow possession of many drugs, a move that angered not only the church but also sectors of the police and the army.

With all these changes in its first two years in power, one might have predicted a serious erosion of González's position within the PSOE, and a dramatic decline in the party's popular support. Nevertheless, by 1985, González and the party moderates appeared to be in a strong position within the party. The president emerged from the 30th Congress stronger than ever. Even among the population, polls showed the PSOE to be more than twice as popular as its nearest rival.[47] How can this paradox be explained?

First, some of the government's failures have come in areas that also proved elusive for the UCD. Terrorism, labor unrest, relations with Spain's regions, and unemployment are seen as problems beyond the control of any one government. Even within the PSOE, trade union leaders have criticized only some aspects of the government's political economic policies. The overall strategy of streamlining the Spanish economy has been widely accepted, even if the costs have fallen mostly on the working classes.

Second, Felipe González remains immensely popular as a politician. While he has lost some of his boyish charm, and even some of his aura of honesty and integrity, he remains the most popular Spanish politician. Within the PSOE, serious divisions on important issues, like NATO membership, have often been resolved in favor of the party moderates due to the overwhelming prestige accorded to González.

Finally, as late as 1985, the PSOE continued to lack a credible opposition. On the left, the PCE proved unable to carry out an internal renovation, despite the replacement in November 1982 of Santiago Carrillo with the younger, less dogmatic Gerardo Iglesias. In early 1984 the PCE split into pro- and antieurocommunist factions. Due to this internal chaos, the PCE had surprisingly little success exploiting the many contradictions in PSOE policy, although it strongly opposed NATO membership and the socialist political economic policy. In the future, the PCE is likely to exercise most influence through its affiliated trade union, the Workers Commissions (CCOO). Even so, given the weakness and fragmentation of Spanish trade unions—itself a partial explanation for the PSOE's survival—this influence will be limited.[48]

The Popular Alliance has tried to replace UCD as the party of the center right, but by 1985 it was only partially successful. Its leader, Fraga Iribarne, had a difficult time establishing his democratic credentials, and his domination of AP has created internal divisions. Ideologically, AP inherited some of the problems of UCD, and its internal divisions mounted as it became a more powerful parliamentary force. AP's opposition to the PSOE on such issues as educational and Penal Code reform, abortion, and the emergency nationalization of RUMASA often allied it with forces of the extreme right. The presence of important figures from the franquist regime will be an additional liability.

The apparent limits to AP's potential led to a number of efforts among the remnants of UCD to create a new centrist party. The most important effort has been stewarded by Miguel Roca, a prominent Catalan centrist and a founding father of the Spanish constitution, but it will be especially hard for an upstart centrist party to avoid the pitfalls experienced by UCD, and to compete with the more established PSOE and AP.

Thus the Spanish party system continues its search for a coherent conservative political party, capable of combining the disparate forces of the moderate right. The presence of a responsible and moderate socialist left has rendered this deficiency less serious. However, as the PSOE inevitably expends its political capital in office, and as it contends with some of Spain's historically intractable problems, the need for a viable political alternative will again be paramount.

Notes

1. Of the many works on the UCD, see José Amodia, "The Union of the Democratic Centre", in David S. Bell, ed., *Democratic Politics in Spain: Spanish Politics after Franco* (New York: St. Martins Press, 1983); Carlos Huneuus, "La Unión de Centro Democrático, Un partido consociacional" *Revista de Política Comparada,* No. 1 (Winter 1980-81); Luis García San Miguel, "The Ideology of Unión de Centro Democrático," *European Journal of Political Research,* No. 9 (1981).

2. Quoted in García San Miguel, p. 442.

3. Amodia, p. 17.

4. This argument is advanced persuasively by Richard Gunther in his "Democratization and Party Building: Contradictions and Conflicts Facing Party Elites in the Spanish Transition to Democracy," presented at the Annual Meeting of the American Political Science Association, New Orleans, August 29-September 1, 1985.

5. This distinction is made in Jorge de Esteban and Luis López Guerra, *Los partidos políticos en la España actual* (Barcelona: Planeta, 1982), pp. 83-112.

6. For a full description of this concept, see Huneuus.

7. On the 1979 general elections, see Pedro J. Ramírez, *Así se ganaron las elecciones de 1979* (Madrid: Editorial Prensa Española, 1979); Jorge de Esteban and Luis López Guerra, eds., *Las elecciones legislativas del 1 de Marzo, 1979* (Madrid: CIS, 1979).

8. Quoted in de Esteban and López Guerra, *Los partidos* p. 658.

9. On the role of the church in the 1979 electoral campaign, see Eusebio Mujal-León, "The Left and the Catholic Question in Spain," *West*

European Politics 5, No. 2, (April 1982): 50; and Richard Gunther, Giacomo Sani, and Goldie Shabad, "Spain After Franco: The Making of a Competitive Party System." Unpublished manuscript, 1985, p. 5.

10. An excellent discussion of UCD's strategy is Richard Gunther, "Strategy and Tactics and the New Spanish Party System," presented at the International Symposium, Spain and the United States (Gainesville, Center for Latin American Studies, University of Florida, December 1979), pp. 36-38.

11. A useful treatment of the regional problem is Mike Newton, "The Peoples and Regions of Spain," in David Bell, ed., Democratic Politics in Spain: Spanish Politics After Franco (New York: St. Martin's Press, 1983).

12. Ibid., p. 123.

13. On Catalan nationalism, see N. L. Jones, "The Catalan Question Since the Civil War," in Paul Preston, ed., Spain in Crisis (New York: Harper and Row, 1978); and Salvador Giner, The Social Structure of Catalonia (University of Sheffield: Anglo-Catalan Society, Occasional Papers No. 1, 1984).

14. On Basque nationalism, see Robert P. Clark, "Language and Politics in Spain's Basque Provinces," West European Politics, No. 1 (January 1981); and Stanley Payne, Basque Nationalism (Reno: University of Nevada Press, 1975).

15. On the Spanish constitutional referendum, see Paul Preston, "The Spanish Constitutional Referendum of 6 December 1978," West European Politics, No. 2 (May 1979).

16. Among the many writings on the desencanto, see Juan Luis Cebrián, La España que bosteza: Apuntes para una historia crítica de la transición (Madrid: Taurus, 1981); and Juan Pablo Fusi, "Spain: The Fragile Democracy," in West European Politics, No. 3 (July 1982), pp. 229-33.

17. For an excellent and provocative treatment, see José Oneto, Los últimos días de un presidente (Barcelona: Planeta, 1981).

18. From Suárez's resignation speech of January 29, 1981.

19. On Basque terrorism, see Stanley Payne, "Terrorism and Democratic Stability in Spain," Contemporary History, No. 451 (November 1979); Fusi, pp. 223-26; Julio Busquets, Pronunciamientos y golpes de estado en España (Barcelona: Planeta, 1982), pp. 158-60.

20. Pedro Vilanova, "Spain, The Army and the Transition," in David Bell, ed., Democratic Politics in Spain: Spanish Politics After Franco (New York: St. Martins Press, 1983), p. 162.

21. José Luis Morales and Juan Celada, La alternativa militar: El golpismo después de Franco (Madrid: Editorial Revolución, 1981), p. 32.

22. Ibid., p. 34.

23. Ibid., p. 38.

24. See *El País,* July 19, 1978, for a fascinating account of his statements.

25. Victor Alba, *La soledad del Rey* (Barcelona: Planeta, 1981).

26. This section draws heavily on my "Two Transitions: Democratisation and the Evolution of the Spanish Socialist Left," *West European Politics* 1 (January 1985).

27. Paul Preston, "La lucha contra el fascismo en España: Leviatán y las contradicciones de la izquierda socialista, 1934-1936," *Sistema,* No. 34 (January 1980); Santos Juliá, *La izquierda del PSOE, 1935-1936* (Madrid: Siglo XXI, 1977). In addition, see Juan Linz, "From Great Hopes to Civil War: The Breakdown of Democracy in Spain," in Juan J. Linz, ed., *The Breakdown of Democratic Regimes: Europe* (Baltimore: Johns Hopkins University Press, 1978).

28. This faction, led by former Secretary General Llopis, broke away in 1974, forming the PSOE "histórico." The PSOE(h) became an openly social democratic party, which ran in the 1977 elections as part of a social democratic slate.

29. For a record of the radicalized 1976 congress, see *XXVII Congreso Del Partido Socialista Obrero Español* (Barcelona: Avance, 1977).

30. See the PSOE's "Manifiesto Electoral 1977" (Electoral Document, Madrid, 1977).

31. Interview with Javier Solana, January 1982.

32. Quoted in Enrique Gomáriz, "La sociología de Felipe González," *Zona Abierta* 20 (1979): 62.

33. A good overview of these contentious issues is found in de Esteban and López Guerra, *Los Partidos,* p. 121.

34. Statements made in an interview with Fernando Claudín, in *Zona Abierta,* No. 20 (May-August 1979), p. 8.

35. The moderate slate received 85.9 percent of the votes, compared with only 6.9 percent for the *críticos* and 7.2 percent abstentions. For a summary of the results of the Extraordinary Congress, see Fernando Ollero Butler, "El Congreso Extraordinario del PSOE," *Revista Del Departamento de Derecho Político,* No. 6 (Spring 1980), pp. 205-15.

36. *Diario 16,* October 22, 1981, p. 4. For other criticisms of the PSOE Congress, see editorial entitled "Un Congreso Lamentable," *Diario 16,* October 27, 1981, p. 2.

37. José Manuel Arija, "Cómo son los Socialistas," *Cambio 16,* No. 498 (June 15, 1981), pp. 29-31.

38. De Esteban and López Guerra, *Los partidos,* p. 128, estimate the PSOE's membership figures as follows: 1933, 80,000; 1974, 4,000; 1976, 8,000; 1977, 50,000; 1979, 100,000; 1982, 99,000. On this point, see also Fernando Barciela, *La otra historia del PSOE* (Madrid: Emiliano Escolar, 1981), pp. 97-98. On the sociological composition of delegates at PSOE

congresses, see José Félix Tezanos, "Estructura y dinámica de la afiliación socialista en España," *Revista de Estudios Políticos*, No. 23 (September-October 1981), pp. 117-52; and his "Radiografía de dos congresos. Una aportación al estudio sociológico de cuadros del socialismo español," *Sistema 35*, March 1980, pp. 79-99.

39. For an overview of the PSOE in power, see Maier Serfaty, "Spain's Socialists: A New Center Party?" *Current History* 83, No. 492 (April 1984).

40. For an overview, see "The Quiet Changes Sweeping González's Spain," *The Economist, December 3, 1983.*

41. For example, in January 1985, Chief of Staff Angel Liberal argued that Spain could not afford to be "neutral," a clear support for NATO membership. See his statements in *El País*, January 7, 1985.

42. On the PSOE 30th Congress, see *El País*, December 17, 1984.

43. Quoted in *The Economist*, December 22, 1984.

44. See *The Economist*, November 10, 1984.

45. See the New York *Times* October 9, 1984. In the article, the author concludes that "the pact tends to favor business interests."

46. *The Economist*, October 27, 1984.

47. The results of the poll appeared in *El País*, October 29, 1984.

48. On Spanish unions, see Gary Prevost, "Change and Continuity in the Spanish Labour Movement," *West European Politics*, No. 1 January 1984.

7 TRANSITION THROUGH TRANSACTION RECONSIDERED

Given a regime in which the opponents of the government cannot openly and legally organize into political parties in order to oppose the government in free and fair elections, what conditions favor or impede a transformation into a regime in which they can?[1]

This chapter provides a brief summary and recapitulation of the material presented in the preceding chapters and exacts some general conclusions concerning the conditions for transition through transaction in Spain.

Democratization in Spain: A Recapitulation

Chapter 1 surveyed the inauspicious historical legacy of Spanish politics, and it revealed very little democratic tradition upon which to construct a democracy after Franco's death. Chapter 2 more closely examined the context within which democratization took place. In its twilight, the franquist regime was faced with *environmental* challenges from all fronts: the increasingly politicized and militant working class, a democratic student movement, the rejuvenated political opposition, a hostile and partially radicalized church, an inhospitable international environment, and the efficient and visible specter of terrorism. However, these challenges were not successful, per se, in toppling the franquist regime. While they did reflect the eroding popular legitimacy of authoritarian rule, they never constituted a serious threat to the continuation of franquism.

Nevertheless, in the context of a crisis of leadership succession, these factors were important. While the regime never lacked the ability or resolve to meet such environmental challenges with coercion, their very existence added to the overall uncertainty and apprehension surrounding the evolution of Spanish politics after Franco.

Chapter 3 argued that the chief component of this crisis was located *within* the authoritarian coalition itself. The struggle among regime *familias* to control the transition intensified as Franco's death became imminent, and it exploded after the dictator died and Juan Carlos assumed power. Arias Navarro, who remained as Juan Carlos's first president, failed to build a political coalition that could either preserve the status quo or establish a new political system.

Arias was unsuccessful for four interrelated reasons. First, he failed to propose a genuinely democratic reform plan. He thus lost the support of the most reformist sectors within the franquist regime, and he could not obtain the cooperation of the moderate democratic opposition. Ironically, the Arias reform was democratic enough to incur the wrath of the franquist right, but Arias lacked a political coalition or a clear political strategy that might have enabled him to respond to this resistance. Second, Arias was not even capable of maintaining intact his own government. The reformists within his government soon became frustrated with the president's rigidity, and they vented their frustration with ambiguous and often contradictory statements and actions. A government so internally divided was easy prey for opponents to its right and left. Third, the incompetence of the Arias government generated the very conditions for the failure of its reform project. The reform's lack of success was reflected at the mass level by an increase in civil disorder and an intensification of the environmental pressures. This, in turn, exacerbated the fears and intransigence of the regime right, and, ironically, led hard-liners to torpedo a project whose interests the Arias reform sought to protect. Finally, Arias lacked the skill and will to impose his limited democratic reform over the objections of his opponents. Chapter 3 described the personal vacillations and reticence of Arias. He was no match for the regime right (to which he still felt attached) or the reformists of the regime and opposition (which he feared and suspected.)

It is intriguing to ponder whether a more skilled and convinced reformist, perhaps even Suárez, could have imposed a reform plan similar to Arias's. On the one hand, it seems likely that a more dynamic and less ambivalent leader would have had more success rallying regime reformists and neutralizing the regime right. After all, Arias was able to gain the initial benefit of the doubt from regime reformists during the first few months of his tenure. In addition, more skilled leaders might have been able to persuade some hard-liners to support a limited democratic reform as the "lesser of evils." Suasion plus a willingness to use the loopholes of the franquist system to overcome hard-line opposition might have led to success. It is important to remember that Suárez, under essentially similar political conditions, was able to impose a more genuinely democratic reform, by employing exactly such a combination of the carrot and the stick.

On the other hand, Arias probably failed, at least in part, because his reform was simply too limited to be acceptable to regime reformists. Suárez had a tough time gaining the allegiance of regime and opposition democrats for a far more ambitious project. While some moderate opposition groups might have been rallied to the defense of a more limited reform, important political actors, such as the socialist left, would have been excluded. In other words, Suárez's success was partly attributable to his willingness to steadily increase the scope of the reform far beyond the boundaries originally established. The Political Reform Law allowed him the leeway to do so, but the Arias reform would have been too restrictive.

Arias's failure had important implications for the future course of events. First, Juan Carlos was compelled to intervene more directly in the political process, at considerable risk to the still-nascent institution of the monarchy, by sacking Arias and gambling on Suárez. The protracted regime crisis was a potential threat to the institution of the monarchy. To the extent that Juan Carlos was unable to oversee a transition to democratic rule, the monarchy would increasingly be identified with its franquist origins. Both a democratic *ruptura* (which could have abolished the monarchy) and an authoritarian coup (which would limit the life of the monarchy to the life of the resulting authoritarian regime) would have threatened the institution of the monarchy. The king's intervention placed him on the side of reform, and thus weakened the regime right's resolve to obstruct the reform process. Few regime forces, the mililtary included, relished a head-to-head confrontation with the new monarch, who was Franco's hand-picked successor and a figure of increasing popularity since his coronation.

Second, Arias's failure discredited the limited reform approach among many regime elites, and this factor may have convinced many franquists to support a more ambitious reform under Suárez. Ironically, the perceived exhaustion of the limited reform approach initially alienated many franquist reformers from the Suárez plan. As Chapter 4 documented, many (understandably) underestimated the resolve and skill of the young president, and they viewed his appointment with skepticism.

Third, Arias's failure had an identical influence on the democratic opposition, which now became even more skeptical about the regime's ability to democratize from within. Suárez was thus forced to start with a serious handicap, but one that may have served a purpose. The new president made a concerted and early effort to negotiate with the democratic opposition, and to deliver visible signs of his genuine resolve.

Fourth, Arias's failure emphasized the need for a new coalition of forces. The regime right's sinking of the Arias reform, limited as the plan was, helped demonstrate to regime elites that this intransigent sector could not be counted on to support democratic change. Suárez was ultimately successful in constructing a new coalition that marginalized the regime right, and that included (eventually) the leftist opposition.

Fifth, Arias's failure heightened the sense of crisis looming large over the politics of the post-Franco period. It raised the specter of open confrontation between the regime and the opposition. Given the inauspicious legacy of Spanish politics, such a possibility was especially undesirable. The events in neighboring Portugal were instructive and counseled caution for both the regime right and the democratic opposition. Thus, while the Arias government had demonstrated it could control the streets, it had also raised fears of rising repression and increasing uncertainty. For this reason, many in the regime and opposition viewed the Suárez reform as a last chance to avoid such a scenario, although few thought it would be successful.

Chapter 5 described how Adolfo Suárez, aided by the king, Fernández Miranda, and a small circle of collaborators, implemented a democratic reform within the legal confines of the regime. Transition through transaction involved a mixture of strategy and improvisation, calculated risk and good fortune, and persuasion, coercion, and negotiation. Its leaders were motivated by a mixture of personal ambition, political realism, and ideological conviction.

Suárez began his enterprise by rejecting the limited democratic reform of his predecessor. Arias's failure had much to do with his unconvincing reform proposals, especially when compared to Suárez's youth, his weaker commitment to authoritarian rule, and his openness to democratic politics. Suárez was far more in touch with the changing environment of Spanish politics, which were surveyed in Chapter 2. Early on, he was able to envision himself as a successful actor within a democratic political system. Unlike Arias, he was not haunted by the ghosts of his franquist past. Suárez had more to fear from the extreme right than from the democratic opposition, and many of the latter belonged to the same generation.

Suárez was convinced of the need to pursue democratic reform through the franquist institutional framework. His familiarity with the regime convinced him that there were limits to immediate and far-reaching democratic reform. He had a vested interest in avoiding a *ruptura*, from which he might be excluded, and which the military would surely oppose. He sensed that an alliance could be built within the regime in support of genuine democratic change. Following this conviction, Suárez crafted an entirely ambiguous Political Reform Law. The law left the door open for a new constitution, but did not necessarily advocate one. The fact that Suárez submitted it as a constitutional reform, all within the arcane legal framework of franquist authoritarianism, created the impression of a limited democratic reform, not unlike that of Arias.

Moreover, Suárez was willing to go beyond the legal confines of the Political Reform Law. In addition to submitting a constitutional amendment to the Cortes, Suárez embarked on an ambitious plan of negotiation and coalition building. In this respect he radically departed from the behavior of his predecessor. He negotiated with virtually all political forces and actively communicated with the opposition of the left, and center, persuading them to give his reform a chance. He convinced the military to maintain a bystander posture, by ensuring them of the limits to his reform. Suárez encouraged Spain's allies of his democratic convictions, and he excelled in the far less tangible area of politics involving persuasion, compromise, communication, deception, and intimidation.

Suárez's ability to construct a coalition in support of democratic reform was also crucial to the consolidation of transition through transaction, discussed in Chapter 5. As the president's dismantling of authoritarianism alienated powerful sectors of the franquist regime, Suárez broadened the coalition supporting democratic rule to include the socialists, and, finally, the communist left. The widespread political backing created an important momentum for the transition and helped to sustain it despite threats from terrorism of the extreme left and right, and despite a serious economic crisis.

The role of the opposition in helping to sustain the momentum of democratization must not be underestimated. This book has demonstrated how difficult it was for the opposition to accept transition through transaction. There were no guarantees that the reform would be carried out, and there was no direct representation in the process for opposition leaders. For the opposition, the transition involved large doses of faith: faith that Suárez was sincere about democratization, faith that he had the skill to implement the reform, and faith that he had the courage and power to confront the regime right. The fact that political parties were extremely weak enabled party elites to insulate themselves from their constituencies somewhat. This, in turn, facilitated their ability to gamble on transition through transaction. Nevertheless, for both major parties of the left, the PSOE and the PCE, acceptance of the Suárez reform entailed considerable, even drastic, contradictions between ideology and praxis. Leaders of both parties were forced to walk the political tightrope created by such contradictions, and this required formidable skill.

In the early stages of the transition the opposition compromised in order to assure a transition to democratic rule. After the 1977 elections, elites in the regime and opposition shared a single overriding objective: the consolidation of parliamentary democracy. UCD, with a plurality of seats, the PSOE, with a surprisingly strong second place showing, and even the PCE, with almost 10 percent of the vote, now had an overwhelming incentive to arrive at a consensus over the new rules of the game. The environment surrounding the inauguration of the new regime was hardly auspicious: The economic situation had deteriorated, terrorism was rampant, the pent-up desire for regional autonomy was threatening to explode, and the military was increasingly restless about the transition.

As Chapter 5 makes clear, party elites worked together to face these serious challenges. In the broad areas of the constitution and the political economic crisis, the major parties, with few and sporadic exceptions, reached a consensus. In so doing, two inter-related changes were encouraged. On the one hand, party elites became accustomed to the politics of dialogue, negotiation, and compromise. They tended to shun public confrontation, and in parliament they seldom operated according to the arithmetic of the majority. On the other hand, the parties themselves moved toward the political center. UCD under Suárez and the PSOE under Fe-lipe González both attempted to occupy center ground, and they reformed their party platforms and electoral campaigns accord-ingly. As Chapter 6 argues, Suárez and the UCD social democrats were ultimately unsuccessful in moving the governing party toward the center of the political spectrum. They were met with opposi-tion from conservatives and liberals within the party, who even-tually forced Suárez from the party leadership. One consequence of this failure was the disintegration of UCD. González, in contrast, successfully moved the PSOE toward the center. Like Suárez, he briefly resigned from his post as party leader to protest the inter-nal resistance to this change.

In contrast, González not only survived this resistance, he vir-tually extinguished it and in so doing consolidated his uncontested control over the Socialist Party. This allowed the PSOE leader to complete the social democratization of the party, in preparation for the 1982 elections. As a consequence, President González has ex-perienced much less internal party dissent than his UCD predeces-sors, and this has facilitated a surprisingly profound rightward drift of the governing party.

The PCE and the AP have faced a dilemma similar to that of the two major parties. They have been compelled to seek votes to-ward the center, and this has entailed a modification of their "ex-tremist" image. The PCE performed surprisingly well in the first two democratic elections, and its municipal-level alliance with the PSOE promised to enhance its respectability. However, as with UCD, internal squabbling undermined the party's public image. Carrillo's unwillingness to extend the democratic emphasis of Eu-rocommunism to the PCE's internal politics led to the defection of many of the most well respected communist leaders in 1982. Car-rillo's resignation represented a long-overdue rejuvenation of the

PCE leadership, but not until after the communists were decimated in the 1982 general elections. Under new leadership, the PCE's prospects have continued to decline. Continuing internal disputes, and a popular socialist government, have threatened to erode the party's popular support even further.

If AP's experience is any indication, the PCE should consider itself down, but not out. AP performed dismally in the first two democratic elections, plagued by the constantly shifting organizational structure, and by its inability to shed its franquist image. Its leader, Fraga Iribarne, proved to be both a liability and an asset to his party. His impetuousness was often embarrassing, but he established a reputation as a diehard, and as an underdog capable of spectacular comebacks. Since the 1977 elections, AP has attempted several alliances with liberal and Christian democratic parties to its left. Fortunately for AP, UCD's disintegration was well timed: It coincided with regional elections in Galicia and Andalusia, where AP defeated the government party, thus giving Fraga's party new hope and credibility. UCD's disaster in October 1982 allowed AP to add to its renaissance, and the electoral returns placed it in an ideal position from which to establish a reputation as the responsible and loyal opposition. Whether AP elites can grasp this opportunity remains an open question.

The Conditions for Transition
through Transaction in Spain[2]

Until recently, more scholarly interest was directed toward conditions maintaining stable democracy than on the question of the genesis of democratic regimes.[3] This emphasis partially reflects the biases of scholarship conducted in advanced democratic countries, in which democracy resulted from a long and incremental historical evolution. Democratic political systems were, erroneously, seen to be the *norm* from which authoritarian regimes deviated.[4] This *deviation* was seen to result from the absence of the same conditions contributing to stable democracy; there was a widespread tendency to equate the conditions for *democratization* with the conditions for stable democracy. Finally, many academics in the 1970s turned their attention to the *structural* conditions for democracy and democratic breakdown. In explaining the breakdown of democracy, or its failure to emerge, throughout the Third World, these scholars pointed to underlying structural distortions in the international political economic system.

A new wave of democratization began in the mid-1970s with the return to democracy in Portugal, Greece, and Spain. This trend continued through the mid-1980s in countries such as Peru, Turkey, Argentina, Brazil, and Uruguay. Recently, scholarly interest has again focused on the important question of the conditions facilitating the democratization of authoritarian regimes.[5] Along with this renewed interest in the genesis of democracy has come a heightened awareness of the role played by political elites. Of course, the study of leadership in political change enjoys a long tradition in political science, but it was notably underemphasized in the 1960s and 1970s.[6]

This study has emphasized the role of elite strategy and skill in Spain's democratization. Following Dos Santos, it suggests that in the contemporary world "the nonauthoritarian organization of power results, and should result, not from a natural evolution of the political and social process, but rather from deliberate intervention with the objective of implementing a stable institutional order."[7] Chapter 1 painted a portrait of Spanish political history in which a mixture of hostile environmental conditions and poor leadership obstructed the emergence of democratic rule. Chapter 2 contended that environmental conditions were insufficient per se to destroy franquism, and Chapters 3 and 4 suggested that transition through transaction emerged from the internal political struggle waged among franquist elites. Chapters 4 through 6 argued that the behavior of the regime and opposition elites was crucial to the implementation and consolidation of transition through transaction.

The discussion below specifies some of the conditions for the success of transition through transaction after Franco's death. While this study places strong emphasis on elite strategy and skill, it is important to acknowledge the important, often crucial, role played by environmental factors (for example, the international environment, mass pressure, economic crisis) in obstructing or facilitating democratic transition.

For the sake of clarity, it will be useful to divide the treatment of these conditions into three stages: first, the conditions that facilitated the *initiation* of transition through transaction in the summer of 1976; second, the conditions that encouraged the *implementation* of Suárez's reform strategy in the fall of 1976 and the winter of 1977; third, the conditions that contributed to the *consolidation* of democracy after the spring of 1977.[8]

The Initiation of Transition through Transaction

Why did the franquist regime initiate a democratic transition in Spain? Chapter 2 argued that franquist leaders were not compelled to democratize by pressure from below, the international environment, or the economic crisis. These factors clearly made democratization a more desirable political outcome for some, but the regime could have sustained itself far longer than it did. While there are many cases of authoritarian regimes leaving power when faced with economic crisis, international pressure, or pressure from below, the Spanish case does not fall in this category.

There were three major conditions facilitating the initiation of transition through transaction in Spain. First, the franquist regime experienced a *succession crisis* in the years immediately before and after Franco's death. Leadership succession almost always presents problems for authoritarian regimes. As was the case in Spain, the delicate balance of regime *familias* was upset by the prospect of Franco's absence. The franquist coalition had become dependent on the unusual longevity of its leader, and his disappearance made the succession crisis appear all the more problematic. While Franco had hoped to leave things *atado y bien atado* (very well secured) with the designation of Juan Carlos, the new monarch was young and inexperienced, and his political views, whether undeveloped or concealed, were not widely known until after the dictator's death.

Virtually all components of the franquist coalition agreed to some degree of adaptation to the new leadership situation. The struggle took place over the *pace* and *extensiveness* of the reform. The so-called *inmovilistas* of the bunker sought no real change of the franquist system. The *aperturistas*, of which Arias was a representative, envisioned a considerable democratization of the franquist regime, stopping short of a full-fledged parliamentary democracy. Moreover, most of them desired the change to be cautious and gradual.

In the years surrounding Franco's death, most franquist elites, including Adolfo Suárez, were *aperturistas*, even though there was disagreement over the timing and extensiveness of the reform. As Chapters 3 and 4 argue, it was the failure of President Arias to democratize the franquist regime rapidly and substantially, both before and after Franco's death, that convinced the king and many franquist elites to favor a more extensive reform. Even then, the exact end point of transition through transaction was not known by its leaders.

Adolfo Suárez, supported by the king and aided by powerful allies within the regime, initiated a more genuine democratic reform, largely because he was convinced that the more limited approach was exhausted. Thus, a second condition for the initiation of transition through transaction was *the absence of feasible and desirable alternatives*. There was no reason, such as a military defeat or an inability to maintain order, obliging the franquist regime to vacate power. A continuation of the regime's power, within a system reformed to accommodate the new monarch, was no longer feasible after Arias's repeated failures.

In explaining Suárez's initiation of the ambitious democratization project, it is important to discuss a third condition, *the generational factor*. [9] In this regard, Suárez had several advantages over Arias. First, his youth meant he had no attachment to the foundation of franquism. He had experienced neither the Spanish Republic nor the civil war. He thus did not harbor the type of personal reticence about democratic politics found in Arias. Suárez represented a new generation of Spaniards, more aware of Spain's democratic neighbors, more open to contrasting opinions, and more tolerant of social change. His generational peer, Juan Carlos, was similarly less bound to franquism than suggested by his personal attachment to Franco.

The Implementation of Transition through Transaction

As the failure of the Arias reform illustrated, the desire to enact democratic change does not ensure success. Leaders of an authoritarian regime face numerous obstacles when attempting to implement transition through transaction.

Three conditions were met that help to explain how Suárez disproved predictions of failure. First, *a degree of support or toleration for political reform was mustered from the most powerful members of the authoritarian coalition*. A coalition of regime forces favoring (or at least tolerating) change must be cultivated. In Spain, this meant that the military hierarchy, as well as the most powerful political leaders within the franquist system, had to be convinced to support democratic change.

Suárez worked methodically and diligently to satisfy this condition. Immediately after his appointment, he initiated an extensive series of contacts with virtually all representatives of regime factions and opposition groups. Within the regime, Suárez reassured the military of limits to the reform, and convinced important regime elites to support his project as the best solution possible to the succession crisis. By respecting the legal framework of franquism, and by adhering to institutional rules of authoritarianism, Suárez and the king were able to win the initial support of most of the franquist elite.

It is imperative to note that the presence of King Juan Carlos was paramount to Suárez's ability to gain support within the regime. For regime supporters, the king embodied the legitimacy of the franquist system. Even the most hard-line franquists were hesitant to oppose Franco's hand-picked successor, since opposition to the monarch would be tantamount to an admission that the caudillo had erred. In fact, many hard-liners eventually argued that the appointment of Juan Carlos *had* been a mistake, but only after Suárez's reform had reached an advanced stage. Like Suárez, the monarch played his role to perfection by continually reassuring the regime right that he would continue to act as the guardian of franquism. His strict participation in franquist ritual, his deferential treatment of the franquist elite, and his incessant assurances that there would be no attempt to wipe the slate clean contributed immensely to Suárez's success. While the presence of such an exceptional head of state is not necessary for successful transitions through transaction, there can be no question that these transitions are far more difficult without such well-respected and talented leaders.

Second, *the democratic opposition, or at least sectors of it, had to be convinced to participate in the resulting system.* Opposition leaders had to be assured that they would have a role to play in the future system, and that they would enjoy increasing freedom to operate. In the Spanish case, this requirement entailed winning the confidence of the disparate opposition groups, some of which were highly radicalized and hostile toward regime leaders. Moreover, this confidence had to be obtained while the entire franquist apparatus, including the security forces, remained intact. In fact, the independent and often irresponsible behavior of the security forces was a constant source of tension between the regime and opposition.[10]

Nevertheless, Suárez quickly won the opposition's admiration and respect for his willingness to dialogue and for his flexibility. The comparison between Arias and Suárez was completely evident to opposition leaders, and they soon indicated their satisfaction with the improvement. Suárez's ability to push his Political Reform Law through the franquist system encouraged them to weaken their opposition to the principle of transition through transaction. By the end of 1976, many opposition leaders had come to accept the Suárez reform as the only possible route to democracy. As we have seen, this change in the opposition's posture was neither easy nor complete, but the thawing of regime-opposition relations gave Suárez the momentum necessary for the completion of the reform.

A more intractable and less prudent opposition might have undermined Suárez's effort. For example, Carrillo's attempt to force the PCE's legalization, by appearing suddenly in Madrid, almost had disastrous consequences for the entire reform project. A more confrontational attitude by the opposition, in reaction to the massacre of the labor lawyers in February 1977, could have had similar consequences. Refusal on the part of the PSOE to participate in the first democratic elections could have imperiled the transition. A hostile campaign against the monarchy, or against Suárez himself, would surely have alarmed the franquist right and sectors of the military.

The ability of opposition elites, regardless of ideological persuasion, to act responsibly in a difficult environment had several explanations.

1. Opposition elites were well aware of the dangers entailed by the failure of the Suárez reform. After all, many of them had suffered under authoritarian rule. The opposition was aware that a popular insurrection to topple the regime was extremely unlikely. While on the eve of Franco's death much of the opposition adhered to the notion of a *ruptura democrática*, many opposition leaders acknowledged the need for an alliance with reformist sectors of the regime. Even so, opposition leaders were constantly challenged by the fear that they might be outflanked by radical groups who could successfully accuse them of *collaborationism*, using such accusations in their attempts to gain support among newly politicized sectors.

2. Many opposition leaders were cognizant of historical lessons learned from the breakdown of democracy during the Second Republic, as well as from the more recent collapse of democracy in such countries as Brazil and Chile. These lessons warned them of the dangers of excessive rhetoric and premature mass mobilization.

3. The moderation of the opposition was facilitated by the generally low levels of political mobilization of Spanish society and the organizational weakness of the left. Where mass pressures were strongest (in the universities, the Basque Country, and Catalonia) national parties and trade unions were unable to aggregate demands or harness dissent within organizational structures. The very weakness and fragmentation of the opposition provided an incentive for its leadership to participate in a transition through transaction. Since these leaders lacked legitimacy based on organizational power, elite-level negotiation provided a means to enhance their prestige and visibility. In this state of weakness, the leaders of the democratic opposition stood little to gain from a policy of mass mobilization, political polarization, and confrontation with the authoritarian regime. At the same time, a negotiated transition to democracy, culminating with democratic elections, offered the opposition time to strengthen their organizations, augment their visibility, and to seek legitimacy in the electorate at large.

Third, and directly related to the first two conditions, *regime leaders had to maintain enough control over the political situation to allow for an incremental and orderly transition.* The Spanish leadership had to be able to resist pressure from the regime right for an authoritarian involution and calls from the left opposition for a democratic break. This required a delicate equilibrium between an adherence to the basic rules of the authoritarian regime and a well-planned and incrementally implemented set of democratic reforms. In discussing the dilemmas facing leaders of transitions through transaction, O'Donnell provides an almost exact description of Suárez's difficult situation during the transition:

> In these circumstances, it is evident that the demands on the quality of political leadership are extraordinarily severe. There is not only the problem of deciding at critical junctures which are the fundamental issues and adversaries, but also of being able to convince followers and opponents that the leaders' tactical flexibility is only an instrument which is guided by a firm sense of direction toward democratization.[11]

Between July 1976 and June 1977, Suárez implemented key aspects of his reform plan. While not every facet of the reform was foreseen ahead of time, and although Suárez appears to have improvised a great deal, the reforms were surprisingly well staggered and timed. A simple chronology of the major highlights of the reform demonstrates that Suárez avoided cumulative reforms where possible. The reform began with the limited amnesties in the summer of 1976, and continued through the constitutional reform of November, the referendum in December, the legalization of most political parties in early 1977, the legalization of the PCE in April, and the dismantling of important franquist institutions in May. The latter reforms provoked open hostility from sectors of the military and the right that had previously tolerated Suárez's plan. However, by that time, Suárez had gained important popular support and a crucial vote of confidence from the opposition.

Conditions for the Consolidation of Transition through Transaction

Even when leaders of authoritarian regimes have convinced important sectors of the regime and opposition to support the transition, democratization remains a fragile enterprise, and it can easily fail. Unlike other forms of democratization, in transition through transaction the military remains intact and constitutes a constant threat. In Spain, the continuing specter of a military involution was the most serious problem confronting the consolidation of a new democracy. A severe economic crisis, the persistence of terrorism, and the need to deal with potentially divisive issues all threatened to undermine the new regime.

However, by 1986 it appeared that Spain was well on its way to consolidating its democratic system. Several interrelated factors appear to have facilitated the consolidation of transition through transaction. First, *the leaders of the transition were able to form a centrist political coalition to oversee the transfer of power between the authoritarian and democratic periods.* As argued in Chapters 5 and 6, Suárez's successful occupation of UCD and UCD's successful domination of politics in the early years of Spanish democracy, contributed to the consolidation of the new democracy. As a coalition of franquist reformists and moderate opposition leaders, UCD was a perfect bridge between authoritarian and democratic rule. The presence of important franquist leaders in UCD guaranteed that the new regime would not retroactively harass those responsible for abuses during authoritarian rule, thus lessening the right's hostility to democratic rule. Suárez's presence at the helm of UCD salvaged the prospects of the center and prohibited a victory of either extreme, or an unworkable fragmentation of the nascent party system. Finally, it helped to ensure that a reasonable agenda was associated with the inauguration of the new regime. New democracies that are inaugurated by political forces seeking primarily to attack the symbols and officials of the preceding regime may needlessly antagonize otherwise democratic constituencies.[12] While Suárez pledged to implement important reforms, UCD's victory prevented the formation of an initial political agenda that could have needlessly antagonized ex-franquists, the church, the military, or the private sector.

A second factor contributing to the consolidation of transition through transaction in Spain was *the ability of party elites to reach a consensus on the most important issues confronting the early years of democratic rule*. On the level of public political discourse, the moderation and calm on the part of elites, and the refusal to fall victim to the use of irresponsible rhetoric have deintensified Spanish political conflict in a mostly encouraging fashion. Most party elites have consistently opted to hammer out contentious issues behind closed doors rather than risk popular mobilization. In the early years of the new regime, there were few attempts to attack past complicity in the franquist regime, nor was the behavior of politicians during authoritarianism raised as an issue. With some rare exceptions, Spanish political discourse was unusually consensual. Electoral campaigns have been composed almost entirely of positive images and shy away from appeals based on criticism of political adversaries. Within the major political parties, those individuals accustomed to making rash, conflictual statements have been marginalized.

The interparty consensus also was evident on the level of concrete political decisions. The best examples, discussed in Chapter 5, were the writing of the Spanish constitution and the tripartite agreements on major political economic issues. In both cases, the major political parties, but especially UCD and PSOE, compromised their ideological inclinations considerably. Both major parties, fearful of an authoritarian involution, saw elite-level consensus as preferable to political polarization or public discord. At the same time, both parties found it difficult, and often costly, to reach a consensus with their major political adversaries. For the Socialists, the constitutional and political economic pacts of the first years of democracy implicated the PSOE in a government over which it had little influence, and from which it could expect little gain. By eschewing mass mobilization, by encouraging labor acquiescence in agreements that were prejudicial to workers, and by often refusing to embarrass the government when it had the opportunity, the Socialists sowed the seeds of internal discontent. The social democratization of the PSOE described in Chapter 6, by weakening internal critics, allowed the party to continue the politics of consensus.

Ultimately, the UCD paid a much higher price for its desire to compromise with the left. In a very real sense, UCD was a disposable party: In order to further the consolidation of democracy, its leaders (especially Suárez) often acted in a fashion contrary to the interests of the party membership.[13] For example, Suárez's insistence on reaching a consensus with the PSOE on constitutional issues, and with the Catalans in the sphere of regional autonomy, angered and alienated the powerful UCD conservative sector. The tension between Suárez's vision of how democracy should be consolidated and the partisan views held by many of his UCD colleagues only added velocity to the party's centrifugal dynamic.

While the maintenance of a consensus on both levels clearly contributed to the consolidation of democracy, there was a widely noted side effect. Political observers became worried about an increasing popular alienation from the new democratic system. This phenomenon was measured by some in terms of the declining voter turnout in the first years of the new regime.[14] As mentioned elsewhere, this decline was at least partly the result of the popular fatigue with the many electoral contests held at the local, regional, and national levels. The dose of politics may have been excessive for a population not accustomed to political mobilization and participation. However, the turnout in the 1982 general elections was encouraging, and may portend a certain normalization of levels of electoral participation.[15]

Another manifestation of this alienation was captured by the term *desencanto* (disenchantment), employed by political elites and the media to describe the sense that democracy was incapable of resolving Spain's most critical problems. Many Spaniards had high expectations associated with democracy. For example, it was widely assumed that Spain's EEC membership would be approved once democracy was consolidated, an assumption that in retrospect

proved extremely naive. Other problems, such as terrorism, inflation, crime, and bureaucratic inefficiency, did not disappear, and
in some cases they were perceived to have worsened. While the
politics of consensus did much to resolve contentious issues divid-
ing the Spanish polity, dependence on elite-level politics was often perceived as constituting a continuation of authoritarian forms
of leadership. When combined with the incessant feuding within
some of the major parties (notably UCD and PCE), the elitism of
Spanish politics contributed to the view that political decisions continued to come *desde arriba* (from above).

Less impressionistic studies have corroborated this view of
Spanish politics. Survey data have revealed that Spaniards are
among the least politically interested in Western Europe, and point
to a "fragility of the conventional signs of political institutionalization."[16] One sample, conducted during the early years of Spanish democracy, revealed that only 13 percent belonged to two or
more organizations of any kind, and only 23 percent to one organization, and membership in political organizations was low in comparative perspective.[17] The Spanish polity is deficient in terms of
forms of conventional political participation, and a surprisingly
large percentage of the population are "non participants" in
politics.

Consistent with this image of Spanish politics is the fact that
Spanish political organizations remain weak. Spanish parties and
trade unions stand out for the paucity of their membership.[18] In
1981, for example, the largest Spanish party, the PCE, had an estimated 170,000 members, followed by the UCD (140,000) and the
PSOE (110,000).

A third condition for the consolidation of democratic rule in
Spain has yet to be fully met. The consolidation of transition
through transaction requires *the establishment of a reasonably stable party system, with the potential for political alternation.* As long
as UCD held power, the link between the authoritarian and
democratic regime remained unsevered. It remained to be seen
whether a transfer of power—from the heirs of franquism to those
once persecuted by the regime—was possible. The moderation of
Spain's socialists was crucial in facilitating the feasibility of such
a transfer. The moderate and prudent behavior of the Socialists in
power will no doubt put an end to fears about the new democracy's
ability to tolerate party alternation.

However, UCD's disintegration posed a new problem for the new democracy. There are serious doubts about the ability of the Popular Alliance to act as a conservative loyal opposition. It is unlikely that UCD's disappearance represents a serious threat to democracy. Its heterogeneous composition always obviated its long-term viability, and it could be argued that UCD's painful self-destruction did much to harm the early years of Spanish democracy. The emergence of a more coherent and unified party of the right might augur well for the future of democracy. It is undoubtedly true, however, that the yet uncertain ability of AP to fill the void created by the demise of UCD will be one of the crucial questions 1980s.

By Way of Conclusion

Transition through transaction is a delicate and complex form of democratization. The conditions facilitating such transitions are demanding. In Spain, the presence of a succession crisis in a stable and well-entrenched authoritarian regime, the exhaustion of limited reform, and the emergence of a younger generation of leaders all facilitated the initiation of transition through transaction. The implementation of democratization was successful because its leaders were able to gain initial support from within the regime, to convince a skeptical opposition, and to maintain a balance between control and reform. The consolidation of transition through transaction occurred because franquist elites were able to establish a successful centrist party that bridged the two historical periods, and that mitigated political conflict. Consolidation was also facilitated by the elite, interparty consensus in the early years of democracy. Both factors have led to the foundation of a democracy based on a political compromise, and which consequently is acceptable to a wide range of political forces.

The Spanish case demonstrates that transition through transaction is possible, and it raises hopes about the potential for this type of democratization elsewhere. However, future cases of transition through transaction will not conform to the Spanish model exactly, or even closely. The conditions for it may not contribute similarly in other countries and in different environments. Likewise, other cases of transition through transaction may not require the conditions present in the Spanish case.

The classical route of gradual democratization over centuries, experiened by the United Kingdom and some Scandinavian countries, appears to be historically closed. Military intervention, an historically important path to democracy, is hardly a feasible form of democratization in the modern world. Given the coercive power of contemporary authoritarian regimes, transition from below, via revolution, is always costly and its outcomes are not always democratic. Regimes and oppositions in authoritarian political systems will thus be encouraged by the success of the Spanish transition to democracy, although the extreme difficulty with which transition through transaction was achieved in Spain should warn against excessive optimism. Nevertheless, those who value the peaceful reestablishment of democracy will view the Spanish experience as evidence that it is at least possible to square the circle of transition through transaction.

Notes

1. Robert A. Dahl, *Polyarchy* (New Haven Conn.: Yale University Press, 1971), p. 1.

2. A more extensive treatment of the conditions for transition through transaction, and one that benefits from a comparative perspective, is Donald Share and Scott Mainwaring, "Transitions Through Transaction: Democratization in Brazil and Spain," in Wayne A. Selcher, ed., *Political Liberalization in Brazil: Dynamics, Dilemmas, and Future* (Boulder: Westview, 1986).

3. Dankwart A. Rustow, "Transitions to Democracy: Toward a Dynamic Model," *Comparative Politics*, No. 2 (April 1970), p. 339.

4. Wanderley Guilherme Dos Santos, Poder e Política (Rio de Janeiro: Forense Universitaria, 1978), pp. 146-47.

5. For the most important examples of this recent scholarship, see Guillermo O'Donnell, Philippe Schmitter, and Laurence Whitehead, eds., *Transitions from Authoritarian Rule in Southern Europe and Latin America* (forthcoming); John Herz, ed., *From Dictatorship to Democracy: Coping with the Legacies of Authoritarianism and Totalitarianism* (Westport, Conn.: Greenwood Press, 1983); and Samuel Huntington, "Will More Countries Become Democratic?" *Political Science Quarterly*, No. 99 (Summer 1984).

6. For an introduction to the study of political leadership, see Glenn D. Paige, *The Scientific Study of Political Leadership* (New York: Free Press,

1977); and the introduction to Dankwart A. Rustow, *Philosophers and Kings* (New York: Brazilier, 1970). For a discussion of the role of political leadership in political change, see Robert A. Packenham, *Liberal America and the Third World* (Princeton, N.J.: Princeton University Press, 1973).

7. Dos Santos, p. 151.

8. This analytic division was inspired by the framework employed in Gabriel A. Almond et al., *Crisis, Choice and Change* (Boston: Little Brown, 1973). Rustow, in his "Transitions to Democracy," uses a similar framework.

9. See Max Gallo, *Spain Under Franco* (New York: E. P. Dutton, 1974), p. 195. On the political relevance of the generational factor, see Paul H. Lewis, "The Spanish Ministerial Elite, 1938-1969," *Comparative Politics* No. 1 (October 1972). In addition, see Juan J. Linz, "Opposition in and Under an Authoritarian Regime: The Case of Spain," in Robert A. Dahl, ed., *Regimes and Oppositions* (New Haven, Conn.: Yale University Press, 1973); and Juan J. Linz, ed., *Informe sociológico sobre el cambio político en España. 1975-1981* (Madrid: Euramérica, 1981). Raymond Carr and Juan Pablo Fusi, *Spain, Dictatorship to Democracy*, 2d ed. (London: Allen and Unwin, 1981), pp. 194-95; and Ricardo de la Cierva, *Historia del franquismo: Aislamiento, transformación, agonía (1945-75)* (Barcelona: Planeta, 1978), p. 322.

10. This tension did not disappear after the first elections, as demonstrated by the roughing up of Socialist deputy Jaime Blanco in the summer of 1977 demonstrated. See Paul Preston, "Spain's Road to Freedom," *New Society*, May 19, 1977, p. 327.

11. Guillermo O'Donnell, "Notes for the Study of Processes of Democratization from the Bureaucratic Authoritarian State," presented at a workshop on "Prospects for Democracy: Transitions from Authoritarian Rule in Latin America and Latin Europe" (Washington, D.C.: Woodrow Wilson International Center for Scholars, 1980), p. 30.

12. An excellent discussion is in Juan Linz, *The Breakdown of Democratic Regimes: Crisis, Breakdown and Reequilibration* (Baltimore: Johns Hopkins University Press, 1978), p. 42.

13. On this general point, see Richard Gunther, "Democratization and Party Building: Contradictions and Conflicts Facing Party Elites in the Spanish Transition to Democracy," delivered at the Annual Meeting of the American Political Science Association, New Orleans, August 1985).

14. On the declining voter turnout between 1976 and 1980, see Rafael López Pintor, *La opinión pública española: Del franquismo a la democracia* (Madrid: Centro de Investigaciones Sociológicas, 1982), p. 107.

15. In 1982, voter turnout was 79.6 percent, up from 68.1 percent in 1979, and more than the 77.9 percent in 1977.

16. Peter McDonough, Antonio López Pina, and Samuel H. Barnes, "The Spanish Public in Political Transition," *British Journal of Political Science*, 2 (January 1981), p. 77, footnote 48.

17. Samuel H. Barnes and Antonio López Pina, "Political Mobilization in Old and New Democracies," delivered at the Annual Meeting of the American Political Science Association, Denver, September 1982.

18. Jorge de Esteban and Luis López Guerra, *Los partidos políticos en la España actual* (Barcelona: Planeta, 1982), p. 227.

SELECTED BIBLIOGRAPHY

Aguirre, José Antonio. *La política económica de la transición española: 1975-1980*. Madrid: Unión Editorial, 1981.

Alba, Victor. *Transition in Spain: From Franco to Democracy*. New Brunswick, N.J. Transaction, 1978.

——. *La soledad del Rey*. Barcelona: Planeta, 1981.

Amodia, José. *Franco's Political Legacy: From Dictatorship to Façade Democracy*. London: Allen Lane, 1977.

Aramberri, Julio Rodríguez. "The Political Transformation in Spain: An Interpretation." In *The Socialist Register, 1979*, edited by Ralph Miliband and John Saville. London: Merlin Press, 1979.

Arango, E. Ramón. *The Spanish Political System: Franco's Legacy*. Boulder, Colo.: Westview Press, 1978.

——. *Spain: From Repression to Renewal*. Boulder, Colo: Westview Press, 1985.

Areilza, José María de. *Diário de un ministro de la monarquía*. Barcelona: Planeta, 1977.

Armario, Diego. *El Triángulo: El PSOE durante la transición*. Valencia: Fernando Torres, 1981.

Bardavío, Joaquín. *El dilema*. Madrid: Strips Editores, 1978.

——. *Los silencios del Rey*. Madrid: Strips Editores, 1979.

——. *Sábado santo rojo*. Madrid: Ediciones Uve, 1980.

Barnes, Samuel H. et al. "The Development of Partisanship in New Democracies: The Case of Spain." *American Journal of Political Science* 29 (1985).

Bell, David, ed. *Democratic Politics in Spain: Spanish Politics After Franco*. New York: St. Martin's Press, 1983.

Biescas, José Antonio, and Manuel Tuñón de Lara. *España bajo la dictadura franquista (1969-1975)*. Barcelona: Labor, 1980.

Blaye, Edouard de. *Franco and the Politics of Spain*. New York: Penguin, 1976.

Caciagli, Mario, "Spain: Parties and the Party System in the Transition." *West European Politics* 2 (1984).

Carcassone, Guy, and Pierre Subra de Biuesses. *L'espagne ou la democratie retrouvée*. Paris: ENAJ, 1978.

Carr, Raymond. *Spain, 1805-1975*. 2d ed. Oxford: Clarendon Press, 1982.

———, and Juan Pablo Fusi. *Spain, Dictatorship to Democracy*. 2d ed. London: Allen and Unwin, 1981.

Cebrián, Juan Luis. *La España que bosteza: Apuntes para una historia crítica de la transición*. Madrid: Taurus, 1980.

——— et al. *España 1975-1980: Conflictos y logros de la democracia*. Madrid: José Porrúa Turanzas, 1982.

Cierva, Ricardo de la. *Historia del franquismo: Aislamiento, transformación, agonía (1945-1975)*. Barcelona: Planeta, 1978.

Cloverdale, John F. *The Political Transformation of Spain After Franco*. New York: Praeger, 1979.

Cuadra, Bonifacio de la, and Soledad Gallego-Díaz. *Del consenso al desencanto*. Madrid: Saltes, 1981.

Del Campo, Salustiano et al. "La élite política española y la transición a la democracia." *Sistema* 48 (1982).

Di Palma, Giuseppe. "Founding Coalitions in Southern Europe: Legitimacy and Hegemony." *Government and Opposition* 2 (1980).

Eaton, Samuel D. *The Forces of Freedom in Spain, 1974-1979: A Personal Account*. Stanford, Calif.: Hoover Institution Press, 1981.

Esteban, Jorge de, and Luis López Guerra. *La crísis del estado franquista*. Barcelona: Labor, 1977.

———. De la dictadura a la democracia: Diário político de un período constituyente. Madrid: Universidad Complutense, Facultdad de Derecho, Sección de Publicaciones, 1979.

———. *Los partidos políticos en la España actual*. Barcelona: Planeta, 1982.

Fernández de Castro, Ignacio. *De las Cortes de Cádiz al posfranquismo, 1957-1980*. Vol. 2. Barcelona: El Viejo Topo, 1981.

García San Miguel, Luis. *Teoría de la transición: Un análisis del modelo español, 1973-1978*. Madrid: Editorial Nacional, 1981.

González Ledesma, Francisco. *Las elecciones del cambio*. Barcelona: Plaza and Janes, 1977.

González Navarro, Franciso. *La nueva Ley Fundamental Para La Reforma Política*. Madrid: Presidencia del Gobierno, Servicio Central de Publicaciones, 1977.

Graham, Robert. *Spain: Change of a Nation*. London: Michael Joseph, 1984.

Gunther, Richard et al. *Spain After Franco: The Making of A Competitive Party System*. Berkeley: University of California Press, 1986.

Hermet, Guy. "Spain Under Franco: The Changing Nature of an Authoritarian Regime." *European Journal of Political Research* 4 (1976).

Hernández Gil, Antonio. *El cambio político español y la constitución*. Barcelona: Planeta, 1982.

Herz, John H., ed. *From Dictatorship to Democracy: Coping With the Legacies of Authoritarianism and Totalitarianism*. Westport, Conn.: Greenwood Press, 1983.

Huneuus, Carlos. "La transición a la democracia en España: Experiencias para América Latina." In *Transición a la democracia en América Latina*, edited by Francisco Orrego Vicuña. Buenos Aires: Grupo Editor Latinoamericano, 1985.

Kohler, Beate. *Political Forces in Spain, Greece and Portugal*. London: Butterworths, 1982.

Krasikov, Anatoly. *From Dictatorship to Democracy: Spanish Reportage*. Oxford: Pergamon Press, 1984.

Lancaster, Thomas D., and Gary Prevost, eds. *Politics and Change in Spain*. New York: Praeger Publishers, 1985.

Lieberman, Sima. *The Contemporary Spanish Economy: An Historical Perspective*. London: Allen and Unwin, 1982.

Linz, Juan J. "Opposition in and Under an Authoritarian Regime: The Case of Spain." In *Regimes and Oppositions*, edited by Robert A. Dahl. New Haven, Conn.: Yale University Press, 1973.

——, ed. *Informe sociológico sobre el cambio político en España, 1975-1981*. Madrid: Euramérica, 1981.

Lizcano, Pablo. *La generación del 56: La universidad contra Franco*. Barcelona: Grijalbo, 1981.

López Pina, Antonio, and E. Aranguren. *La cultura política de la España de Franco*. Madrid: Taurus, 1976.

López Pintor, Rafael. *La opinión pública española: Del franquismo a la democracia*. Madrid: Centro de Investigaciones Sociológicas, 1982.

López Rodó, Laureano. *La larga marcha hacia la monarquía*. 7th ed. Barcelona: Plaza and Janes, 1979.

Maravall, José María. *Dictadura y disentimiento político: Obreros y estudiantes bajo el franquismo*. Madrid: Alfaguara, 1978.

——. *La política de la transición, 1975-1980*. Madrid: Taurus, 1981.

——. *Transition to Democracy in Spain*. London: Croom Helm, 1982.

McDonough, Peter et al. "The Spanish Public in Political Transition." *British Journal of Political Science* 2 (1981).

Medhurst, Kenneth. *The Government of Spain: The Executive at Work*. Oxford: Pergamon Press, 1973.

——. "The Prospects of Federalism: The Regional Problem After Franco." *Government and Opposition* 2 (1976).

——. "The Military and Prospects for Spanish Democracy." *West European Politics* 1 (1978).

——. "Spain's Evolutionary Pathway From Dictatorship to Democracy." *West European Politics* 2 (1984).

Morales, José Luis, and Juan Celada. *La alternativa militar: El golpismo después de Franco*. Madrid: Editorial Revolución, 1981.

Morán, Gregorio. *Adolfo Suárez; Historia de una ambición*. 3d ed. Barcelona: Planeta, 1979.

Morodó, Raul. *La transición política*. Madrid: Editorial Tecnos, 1984.

Osorio, Alfonso. *Trayectoria política de un ministro de la corona*. 2d ed. Barcelona: Planeta, 1980.

Payne, Stanley. *A History of Spain and Portugal*. 2 vols. Madison: University of Wisconsin Press, 1973.

Preston, Paul, ed. *Spain in Crisis*. New York: Harper and Row, 1978.

Pridham, Geoffrey. "Comparative Perspectives on the New Mediterranean Democracies: A Model of Regime Transitions?" *West European Politics* 2 (1984).

Ramírez, Pedro J. *Así se ganaron las elecciones*. Barcelona: Planeta, 1977.

——. *Así se ganaron las elecciones de 1979*. Madrid: Editorial Prensa Española, 1979.

Rodríguez Osuna, Jacinto. *La reforma política: la ideología política de los españoles*. Madrid: Centro de Investigaciones Sociológicas, 1977.

Rubottom, R. Richard, and J. Carter Murphy. *Spain and the United States Since World War II*. New York: Praeger, 1984.

Rustow, Dankwart A. "Transitions to Democracy: Toward a Dynamic Model." *Comparative Politics* 2 (1970).

Saíz, José R. *El presidente: Historia de una transición en la que Adolfo Suárez fue su gran protagonista*. Madrid: Editorial Madrid, 1981.

Schwartz, Pedro. "Politics First—The Economy After Franco." *Government and Opposition* 1 (1976).

Share, Donald. "Two Transitions: Democratisation and the Evolution of the Spanish Socialist Left." *West European Politics* 1 (1985).

————, and Scott Mainwaring. "Transitions Through Transaction: Democratization in Brazil and Spain." In *Political Liberalization in Brazil: Dynamics, Dilemmas, and Future*, edited by Wayne A. Selcher. Boulder, Colo.: Westview Press, 1986.

Suárez González, Adolfo. *Un nuevo horizonte para España: Discursos del Presidente, 1976-1978*. Madrid: Servicio de Publicaciones, Presidencia del Gobierno, 1978.

Tusell, Xavier. *La oposición democrática al franquismo*. Barcelona: Planeta, 1976.

Ysart, Federico. *¿Quién hizo el cambio?* Barcelona: Argos Vergara, 1984.

INDEX

ABOUT THE AUTHOR

DONALD SHARE received his B.A. degree from the University of Michigan, and his M.A. and Ph.D. degrees in political science from Stanford University. He is currently assistant professor of politics and government at the University of Puget Sound, in Tacoma, Washington. Dr. Share's published research on Spanish politics and comparative democratization includes "Two Transitions: Democratisation and the Evolution of the Spanish Socialist Left," *West European Politics*, January 1985.